India Studies in Business and Economics

India is one of the fastest growing economies of the world, with the country being an important G20 member. It is a significant player in the global market with a notable demographic advantage, and an important geo-political and geo-trade position. Additionally, due to its position of being not only the most populous country in the world, but also the world's largest youth population, India has a pivotal role to play in meeting global SDG goals. This makes research from the country to be of immense interest to the global community.

With this backdrop, this series aims to bring forth the latest studies and research specific to India from all areas of economics, finance, business, trade, and management science, often with strong social science and political economy linkages. The titles featured in this series present rigorous research, both empirical and non-empirical in nature, usually accompanied by policy recommendations. They evoke and evaluate various aspects of the economical and/or the business and management landscape in India, with a special focus on India's relationship with the world. The series also tracks research on India's position on social issues, on health, on politics, on agriculture, on rights, and many such topics which directly or indirectly affect sustainable growth of the country.

The series welcomes contributions from scholars or practitioners belonging to the academic community, corporates, think tanks and/or non-governmental organizations, and also policymakers to publish their work in the form of authored monographs, edited volumes or collection of case studies. Each proposal undergoes at least two double blind peer review where a detailed concept note along with extended chapter abstracts and/or a sample chapter is peer reviewed by experienced academics. The reviews may be more detailed if recommended by reviewers. The series follows the Ethics Statement as per Springer Nature's standard guidelines.

Balwant Singh Mehta · Ravi Srivastava ·
Siddharth Dhote

Predicting Inequality of Opportunity and Poverty in India Using Machine Learning

INSTITUTE FOR HUMAN DEVELOPMENT

Springer

Balwant Singh Mehta
Institute for Human Development
New Delhi, Delhi, India

Ravi Srivastava
Institute for Human Development
New Delhi, Delhi, India

Siddharth Dhote
Institute for Human Development
New Delhi, Delhi, India

ISSN 2198-0012 ISSN 2198-0020 (electronic)
India Studies in Business and Economics
ISBN 978-981-96-2543-7 ISBN 978-981-96-2544-4 (eBook)
https://doi.org/10.1007/978-981-96-2544-4

This work was supported by Institute for Human Development.

This Springer imprint is published by the registered company Springer Nature Singapore Pte Ltd.
The registered company address is: 152 Beach Road, #21-01/04 Gateway East, Singapore 189721, Singapore

Foreword

It is my great pleasure to write the foreword for the important and timely book *Inequality of Opportunity and Poverty in India: A Machine Learning Approach*. This book addresses some of today's most pressing global issues—inequality of opportunity (IOp) and poverty. By combining traditional economic analysis with cutting-edge machine learning techniques, the authors offer a fresh and innovative perspective on these critical topics. In a world where socio-economic disparities are increasingly evident, this book's approach is both relevant and necessary.

The authors have conducted significant research that delves into the dimensions of IOp and poverty in India, examining these issues through the lenses of three fundamental aspects of human well-being: income, education, and health. This approach illuminates how these factors intersect and impact people's lives.

Poverty, as discussed in this book, extends beyond a lack of financial resources; it encompasses the inability to meet basic needs and fully participate in society. Inequality of opportunity, on the other hand, refers to the extent to which an individual's outcomes are influenced by factors beyond their control, such as place of birth or parental education and occupation. Building on the work of scholars like Roemer, who distinguish between inequalities due to individual effort and those arising from circumstances beyond one's control, this book emphasizes that while individuals should be accountable for their efforts, they also deserve compensation or support for factors beyond their control.

Moreover, the book expands the concept of poverty by introducing innovative methods for its measurement, incorporating non-conventional sources such as geospatial data, including nightlight intensity and points of interest. By integrating data from traditional surveys with these unconventional sources, the book presents innovative approaches to predict poverty with greater accuracy, timeliness, and granularity. This is particularly valuable in a developing country like India, where conducting regular surveys can be costly and time-consuming.

Some unique features of the book include: *Interdisciplinary Approach:* The book integrates theories and methodologies from sociology, economics, geography, anthropology, and computer science to provide a comprehensive analysis of IOp and poverty in income, health, and education. *Cutting-Edge Techniques:* The use of advanced machine learning techniques is a significant feature. The book extracts and integrates data from unconventional sources, such as satellite images, and combines them with traditional data to offer a richer analysis. *Cross-Regional Analysis:* The book explores poverty and IOp across different regions (e.g. states and groupings of states) and within states (e.g. districts) in India. This detailed regional analysis is crucial because, despite economic growth leading to reductions in income poverty in many regions, inequality has often remained stagnant or even increased.

In light of ongoing debates about the measurement of poverty and inequality in India, the innovative methods presented in this book advance our understanding of these challenges. They also provide practical insights that can help policymakers develop more effective strategies to reduce inequality and alleviate poverty.

This book is an important outcome of the multi-country project, *Inequalitrees—A Novel Look at Socio-Economic Inequalities using Machine Learning Techniques and Integrated Data Sources,* funded by Volkswagen. Apart from the Institute for Human Development (IHD), researchers from Bolivia, Italy, and Germany were also involved. I congratulate the authors on their rigorous research and the timely publication of this significant work. The book stands as an excellent example of the power of interdisciplinary collaboration and the potential of new data sources to enhance our understanding of socio-economic issues. I am confident that this book will be a valuable resource for researchers in their future work and will be helpful for policymakers and other stakeholders in devising effective strategies to combat poverty and inequality of opportunity.

Alakh N. Sharma
Director and Professor
Institute for Human Development
(IHD)
New Delhi

Preface

This book, *Inequality of Opportunity and Poverty in India: A Machine Learning Approach*, addresses two most current critical global issues—inequality of opportunity and poverty—with a specific focus on India. It is an outcome of a collaborative, multi-country research project, *INEQUALITREES*, supported by Volkswagen, Germany. The analysis presented in this book is multidimensional, focusing on three fundamental aspects of human well-being: income, education, and health, with a particular emphasis on understanding regional disparities within India and highlighting the distinct challenges faced by different parts of the country.

A key feature of this book is its use of machine learning techniques to integrate and analyse large-scale, diverse datasets from various sources. This innovative approach addresses common limitations in previous studies, such as small sample sizes and limited geographical coverage. By combining data from traditional national surveys with non-conventional sources like geospatial data including satellite imagery, this book provides a more detailed and comprehensive understanding of the factors driving socio-economic disparities across different regions of India.

The book is structured into seven chapters, addressing different facets of inequality and poverty. Some of the initial chapters were initially presented at various seminars and workshops held in India, UK, and Germany. The feedback and insights received at these events were instrumental in refining and shaping the final manuscript.

We extend our heartfelt gratitude to everyone who contributed to this project. Special thanks go to our colleagues—Sandip Sarkar, Bhim Reddy, Swati Dutta, and Prashant Arya—and to the reviewers, and members of the *INEQUALITREES* study team: S. Madeshwaran from the Institute for Social and Economic Change, Bengaluru; Arup Maitra from South Asian University, Delhi; Oliver Rix, Policy Analyst at the House of Lords Select Committee for Environment and Climate Change; Morris Triventi from University of Milan, Pedro Salas Rojo and Paolo Brunori from the London School of Economics; Lykke Andersen from the Sustainable Development Solutions Network, Bolivia; Andreas Peichl, Hannes Taubenboeck, Julia Baarck, Oana Garbasevschi, and Paul Schüle from the ifo Institute, Munich, Germany. Their invaluable support and insights at various stages of the study have significantly enriched this work.

We also extend our sincere thanks to the participants of the Indian Society of Labour Economics (ISLE) annual conferences at the Indian Institute of Technology, Roorkee, and Rajiv Gandhi University, Itanagar; the Indian Association of Social Science Institutions (IASSI) annual conference at the Indira Gandhi Institute for Development Research, Mumbai; the international conference on 'Advancing Human Development in the Global South' at India International Centre, Delhi; the *INEQUALITREES* project conference at ifo Institute, Munich, Germany; and the project workshops at the London School of Economics, UK. Their contributions and engagement have been pivotal in shaping and refining this work.

Special thanks are also due to Alakh N. Sharma, Director, Institute for Human Development, for his unwavering support and encouragement throughout this project. We acknowledge the valuable assistance provided by the IHD administrative team, Priyanka Tyagi and Jyoti Girish, whose support has been essential throughout our journey. We are thankful to the Springer team, especially Noopur Singh and Suresh, for their prompt assistance in bringing this book to publication.

By offering insights and innovative approaches to measurement, we aim to contribute to the development of more effective and informed strategies for improving socio-economic conditions and fostering greater equity in society. We hope that this book serves as a useful resource for policymakers, researchers, and anyone interested in understanding, and addressing the challenges of inequality and poverty.

New Delhi, India

Balwant Singh Mehta
Ravi Srivastava
Siddharth Dhote

Contents

About the Authors

Balwant Singh Mehta is Professor at the Institute for Human Development (IHD), New Delhi, India. He holds a Ph.D. from Jamia Millia Islamia, New Delhi, and postdoctoral in Economics from ICSSR, New Delhi. He has authored 10 books and published over 75 articles, in national and international journals. His primary research area includes employment and labour, poverty, inequality, child well-being, education and technology. In recognition of his scholarly contributions, he was selected as 'Amy Mahan International Fellow' by the UPF, Spain (2010–11); awarded a 'Research Fellowship' by SIRCA, Singapore (2009–10); and selected as an 'Emerging Researcher' by the International Development Research Centre (IDRC), Canada (2009). He has also received alumni status from the International Training Centre of the ILO. Prof. Mehta serves as Associate Editor of *The Indian Journal of Labour Economics* (Springer) and regularly contributes opinion pieces and editorials to national dailies.

Ravi Srivastava is Director of the Centre for Employment Studies, at Institute for Human Development, New Delhi, India. He was earlier Professor of Economics, and Chairperson, Centre for the Study of Regional Development, Jawaharlal Nehru University, India. He holds a Ph.D. from the University of Cambridge, UK. His main areas of research and publication include labour and employment, migration, social protection, rural poverty and development, and the informal sector. Prof. Srivastava has published six books, five monographs, more than one hundred and ten papers, and has carried out nearly forty major research projects sponsored by agencies such as UNICEF, ILO, The World Bank, ESRC (UK), UNFPA, University Grants Commission, Indian Council for Social Science Research, Shastri Indo-Canadian Foundation and others.

Siddharth Dhote is Senior Research Associate at Institute for Human Development, New Delhi, India. He has completed his masters in Development Studies from the International Institute for Social Studies in The Hague. His main research interests focus on social justice, poverty, inequality, employment, and labour market.

Abbreviations

ADB	Asian Development Bank
Cforest	Conditional Inference Forest
Ctree	Conditional Inference Tree
D-Index	Dissimilarity Index
EC	East and Central
EUS	Employment and Unemployment Survey
GDP	Gross Domestic Product
GLS	Generalized Least Squares
HOI	Human Opportunity Index
IHD	Institute for Human Development
IHDS	Indian Human Development Survey
IIPS	International Institute for Population Sciences
ILO	International Labour Organization
IOp	Inequality of Opportunity
KNN	K-Nearest Neighbours
LMIC	Low Middle-Income Countries
LST	Land Surface Temperature
ML	Machine Learning
MLD	Mean Log Deviation
MMR	Maternal Mortality Ratio
MPCE	Monthly Per Capita Expenditure
MPCI	Monthly Per Capita Income
MPI	Multidimensional Poverty Index
NCAER	National Council of Applied Economic Research
NDVI	Normalized Difference Vegetation Index
NFHS	National Family and Health Surveys
NN	Neural Networks
NNESW	North, North East, South, and West
NSO	National Statistical Office
OBC	Other Backward Classes
OECD	Organisation for Economic Co-operation and Development

OLS	Ordinary Least Squares
OPHI	Oxford Poverty and Human Development Initiative
PLFS	Periodic Labour Force Survey
POI	Point of Interest
PPP	Purchasing Power Parity
RF	Random Forest
RMSE	Root Mean Squared Error
SC	Scheduled Castes
SDG	Sustainable Development Goals
SNPP	Suomi National Polar-orbiting Partnership
ST	Scheduled Tribes
TrT	Transformation Tree
UNICEF	United Nations Children's Fund
VIIRS	Visible Infrared Imaging Radiometer Suite
WHO	World Health Organization
WIR	World Inequality Report

List of Figures

List of Tables

List of Maps

Chapter 1
Introduction

1.1 Background

Inequality and poverty are pressing global issues affecting millions of people worldwide. Addressing these issues is essential for creating a fair and just society. These two concepts are deeply intertwined, creating a vicious cycle that is difficult to break, impacting individuals, households, regions, and countries globally. Understanding and addressing these issues requires a multifaceted approach, involving both theoretical and empirical perspectives. Poverty, as defined by Sen's capability approach (1999), refers to the condition where people or households lack the resources necessary for full social participation and to meet their basic needs, such as food, shelter, and health care. Poverty can be absolute, where individuals cannot afford the minimum standard of living, or relative, which considers individuals' standard of living compared to the broader society they reside in (Sen, 1999). Poverty is often measured by a poverty line, which defines the minimum income level required to meet basic needs. On the other hand, inequality refers to the uneven distribution of resources and opportunities among different groups of people. It can take many forms, including economic inequality, which focuses on differences in income and wealth, and social inequality, which includes disparities in education, health, and access to basic services (Atkinson, 2015).

High levels of inequality can exacerbate poverty, as resources and opportunities are concentrated in the hands of a few, leaving many without access to what they need to escape poverty. In this context, distributive justice in society, which addresses various outcomes of fair (justifiable) and unfair (unjustifiable) inequality, has been widely discussed by scholars such as Rawls (1971), Dworkin (1981), Arneson (1989), Cohen (1989), and Sen (1980, 1985, 1992). This concept is concerned with ensuring that everyone in society has access to what they need to live a decent life, regardless of their background or circumstances. It advocates policies that promote a more equitable distribution of resources (Rawls, 1971). Further, Roemer (1993, 1998,

B. S. Mehta et al., *Predicting Inequality of Opportunity and Poverty in India Using Machine Learning*, India Studies in Business and Economics,
https://doi.org/10.1007/978-981-96-2544-4_1

2006) formalized this concept as 'Inequality of Opportunity' (IOp), which distinguishes between outcomes influenced by personal effort and those determined by circumstances. Roemer's theory posits that inequalities arising from circumstances are unjust and should be addressed through compensatory measures (Hufe et al., 2018; Roemer & Trannoy, 2015). Circumstances refer to differences in life outcomes that are beyond an individual's control, such as family background, place of birth, and other inherited characteristics.

Poverty and Inequality Trends: Over the past decades, substantial progress has been made in reducing poverty globally. The percentage of the world's population living in extreme poverty declined from 29% in 2000 to about 9% in 2019 (World Bank, 2020). In particular, extreme poverty decreased much faster in South Asia, from 43% to around 10% in the same period. Despite substantial economic growth resulting in notable poverty reduction, challenges of inequality persist. The Gini coefficient, which measures income inequality, rose from 0.32 in 2000 to 0.35 in 2019 (Chancel et al., 2022). Similarly, India saw a decline in poverty from 37% to around 10% in the same period (World Bank, 2020), but inequality also increased from 0.32 to 0.35 (World Bank, 2020). However, these figures have lately changed somewhat. Recent data reflect that extreme poverty in India fell below 3% in 2022–23, with multidimensional poverty also declining sharply from 29.2% in 2005–06 to 11.3% in 2019–21 (NITI Aayog, 2024).

Challenges of Addressing IOp and Poverty: In developing countries such as India, where access to quality education, healthcare, and job opportunities is often unevenly distributed, IOp plays a significant role in perpetuating income inequality (Ferreira & Peragine, 2016). In India, IOp is a major driver of overall inequality, with factors such as social groups (caste), gender, and parental background significantly influencing individuals' access to education, employment, and income opportunities. Studies suggest that IOp ranges from 30% to 50% in India (Azam & Bhatt, 2015; Kundu, 2020; Mehta et al., 2023; Motiram, 2018; Singh, 2012). In particular, the measurement of IOp has gained popularity among government policymakers, academics, and other stakeholders in recent years. However, traditional data sources have many limitations, lacking timely and granular level estimates. To address these challenges, innovative approaches are being explored. One such approach involves the application of machine learning (ML) techniques to integrate conventional sample survey or census data with non-conventional data sources such as administrative records and geospatial data, including satellite images or nightlight data, which are regularly updated and readily available.

In this context, the book aims to delve into the complexities of Inequality of Opportunity (IOp) and poverty, with a particular focus on India. It examines the underlying factors contributing to these issues and proposes innovative solutions to address them. By providing insights into these dynamics, the book seeks to assist policymakers and stakeholders in crafting more effective strategies for equitable resource distribution and ensuring access to essential opportunities for all individuals. Ultimately, this approach aspires to disrupt the cycle of poverty and inequality, fostering a more just and equitable society over the long term.

1.2 Relevance

The relevance of the topic lies in several critical aspects:

Meeting Sustainable Development Goals (SDGs 2030): The United Nations' SDG 1 aims to end poverty in all its forms, while SDG 10 focuses on reducing inequality within and among countries. Addressing inequality of opportunity (IOp) is crucial to achieving these goals, as it ensures that everyone, regardless of their background, has a fair chance to succeed.

Promoting Social Justice: Reducing inequality of opportunity is essential for building a just and equitable society. Equal access to opportunities fosters social cohesion and reduces social tensions, creating a more harmonious and stable social fabric.

Economic Growth: An equal society where everyone has the opportunity to succeed can lead to sustainable economic growth. When people have equal access to education and employment, they can contribute more effectively to the economy, enhancing overall economic productivity and innovation.

Human Capital Development: Investing in people's education, health, and skills development enhances the overall human capital of a country. This boosts productivity and innovation, participation in decent and productive work, and leading to a more competitive and resilient economy.

Innovative Methodologies: Utilizing innovative data sources and methodologies can significantly improve the analysis of IOp and poverty. By integrating diverse datasets, including survey data and geospatial information, and applying advanced data analytics, such as machine learning (ML) techniques, this approach offers a more timely and comprehensive understanding of these complex issues.

1.3 Key Questions

This book addresses several critical questions to understand the interrelated issues of poverty and IOp, with a focus on India:

- What are the current levels of poverty and IOp in education, income, and health outcomes in India?
- What are the most important circumstances affecting individual outcomes in these areas?
- Which intersections of circumstances characterize the most disadvantaged groups?
- What is the spatial distribution of IOp and poverty across different regions?
- Are geographical areas with unequal opportunities also those with high poverty rates?
- What key areas need urgent attention to improve poverty and IOp in India and across its regions?

By exploring these questions, the book aims to provide a comprehensive understanding of the mechanisms driving poverty and IOp in India. It seeks to offer insights into effective interventions and policies that can foster a more equitable society. The findings are intended to guide policymakers in crafting targeted strategies to reduce both poverty and inequality, ensuring that all citizens have the opportunity to achieve their full potential.

1.4 Value Addition and Contribution

The book contributes to the field of IOp and poverty through several innovative approaches and methodologies. Some of the key value additions and contributions are discussed below:

Use of Innovative Approaches: Traditional measures of inequality and poverty often focus solely on outcomes, such as income and wealth, without considering the opportunities available to individuals. This approach is limited because it overlooks the underlying factors that create disparities. Traditional methods are also frequently costly and time-consuming, which can delay data availability. This book addresses these gaps by emphasizing the importance of understanding distributive justice and advocating the use of innovative data sources to predict IOp and poverty more effectively. By incorporating a broader perspective on opportunities, the book provides a more nuanced view of how disparities arise and persist.

Application of Advanced Data Analytics: A key innovation in this book is the application of advance data analytics, particularly machine learning (ML) techniques to analyse large and diverse datasets. ML algorithms can handle intricate patterns and provide granular insights that traditional methods often miss (Jean et al., 2016). This book uses ML to improve the understanding of IOp and poverty within country settings. Unsupervised learning algorithms are employed to identify latent groups and patterns, while supervised learning techniques determine key factors affecting IOp and poverty. This analytical approach improves accuracy of predictions, helps uncover hidden relationships, and offers fresh perspectives on socio-economic patterns (Donaldson & Storeygard, 2016; Wurm & Taubenböck, 2018).

Utilization of Unconventional Sources: The book also demonstrates the benefits of utilizing unconventional data sources, such as geospatial data including satellite images and night-time light data, to uncover socio-economic patterns and environmental conditions across different geographies. With advances in satellite technology, high-resolution images and ML algorithms can extract valuable socio-economic information, including data on nightlight emissions, the built environment, and pollution patterns. Utilizing free datasets, such as those from the Sentinel fleet of the European Copernicus program or night-time lights data from the SNPP-VIIRS[1] sensor, allows for extensive geographic coverage and enhances the accuracy

[1] Suomi National Polar-orbiting Partnership (SNPP) Visible Infrared Imaging Radiometer Suite (VIIRS).

of socio-economic condition assessments. This approach fosters a more detailed understanding of socio-economic disparities across regions.

Integration of Conventional and Non-Conventional Data: The book integrates traditional survey data with unconventional sources, including administrative data and geospatial information. Recent research has shown that integrating diverse data sources can improve the reliability of inequality and poverty statistics and reveal new patterns (Alderman et al., 2002; Bricker et al., 2016; Dämmrich & Triventi, 2018). By combining conventional data with innovative sources, this book uncovers hidden patterns of IOp and poverty, and contributes to the understanding of 'Resource Distribution and Inheritance' and 'Socio-Ecological Processes of Inequality'. This novel approach provides a standard operating procedure for applying ML to analyse socio-economic inequality across different regions, which is especially valuable for countries like India, where comprehensive and granular data is often lacking.

Multidisciplinary Approach: Incorporating insights from various disciplines—such as computer science, economics, geography, and philosophy—enriches the analysis of IOp and poverty. Computer science contributes through innovative data processing and modelling techniques, economics offers frameworks for understanding resource distribution and socio-economic behaviour, geography provides context on spatial disparities, and philosophy contributes ethical perspectives on justice and fairness. This interdisciplinary approach ensures a well-rounded and robust analysis.

Practical Insights for Policymakers: The practical insights derived from these methodologies are invaluable for policymakers and stakeholders. By providing timely and detailed information on the factors influencing IOp and poverty, this approach enables more informed decision-making. Policymakers can develop targeted interventions that address the root causes of disparities, improve resource allocation, and promote a more equitable society. The ability to act on precise, data-driven insights enhances the effectiveness of policy measures and fosters more equitable social outcomes.

1.5 Study Framework and Methodology

The following details the study framework, methodology, data sources, and analytical tools and techniques employed in the book to address the key questions discussed above.

Study Framework and Methodology: This book employs a robust analytical framework integrating the theoretical concepts of IOp and poverty as articulated by leading scholars such as John Roemer and Amartya Sen. Roemer's theory distinguishes between outcomes resulting from personal efforts and those influenced by external circumstances, positing that individual outcomes should be analysed in light of both personal agency and external conditions (Roemer, 1998). Sen's capabilities approach, on the other hand, focuses on what individuals are able to do and be, focusing on the role of personal capabilities in achieving well-being (Sen, 1999).

To measure income-related outcomes, the analysis uses data on household consumption and labour earnings. For education outcome, the primary indicator used is the number of years of schooling. Health outcomes are assessed by looking at access to maternal and child health services, including vaccinations, institutional delivery, antenatal care, prenatal care, and care by trained staff. These five factors are combined into a single indicator called "adequate care" to assess health outcomes. Poverty is measured using two main approaches: the international poverty line, set by the World Bank at $2.15 per day (2022 update) in purchasing power parity (PPP) terms, and the Multidimensional Poverty Index (MPI). The MPI, developed using the Oxford Poverty and Human Development Initiative (OPHI) methodology, evaluates poverty through three dimensions beyond income: education, health, and living standards. In-depth discussions of these methodologies are also provided in the relevant chapters of the book, elucidating how these frameworks contribute to a comprehensive understanding of poverty and IOp.

National Level Traditional Survey Data Sources: The Employment and Unemployment Surveys (EUS) were conducted roughly in every five years interval up to 2011–12, thereafter Periodic Labour Force Surveys (PLFS) were conducted annually from 2017 to 2018 by National Statistics Office (NSO), India. These surveys provide key data on demographic information of households, employment, and income (earnings and consumption). Household Consumption Surveys, also conducted by NSO, offer data on household consumption expenditure as a proxy of income and poverty measurement. National Family and Health Surveys (NFHS) conducted by International Institute for Population Studies, Mumbai, India. This survey provides data on demography, health, education, and living standards, and was last conducted in 2015–16 and 2019–21. In addition, the census of India, is conducted by the office of registrar general and census commissioner of India in every 10 years. The most recent census was conducted in 2011.

Non-Conventional Geospatial Satellite Data: The high-resolution satellite images, sourced from European Copernicus program and the SNPP-VIIRS sensor, provide data on nightlight emissions, built environment morphology, and pollution patterns. These images are utilized to infer geo-information about electricity access and living conditions. Recent advancements in remote sensing demonstrate that built environment characteristics can also serve as proxies for urban poverty (Taubenböck et al., 2018; Wurm & Taubenböck, 2018).

Cross-Country Data on Poverty, Inequality, and IOp: The comparative cross-country data on inequality is sourced from the World Inequality Database, while the poverty data is obtained from the World Bank, which is complemented by reports from the OECD, ADB, ILO, and other institutions. This cross-country data enables comparative analysis to identify how different socio-economic structures and cultural values impact IOp and poverty.

India-Focused and Comparative Analysis: Apart from country level analysis for India, regional comparative analysis has been done across state and district level to identify local level differences and craft targeted policy interventions. In addition, India's situation in relation to other nations has also been compared wherever necessary to understand the influence of various factors on IOp and poverty, offering insights into potential solutions.

Temporal and Trend Analysis: To assess both the present conditions and long-term trends in poverty, and IOp. This approach helps in understanding the impact of economic growth and policy initiatives on these issues, identifying ongoing challenges, and suggesting short- and long-term solutions.

Machine Learning Algorithms: The advanced ML algorithms such as linear and logistic regression, decision trees, ensemble methods (e.g. random forest, gradient boosting), and confusion matrices have been used for the analysis. These techniques are implemented using R and Python software to analyse complex datasets and derive actionable insights.

Geospatial Analysis: The geemap library in python was used to extract geospatial data from google earth engine at the district and state level and the Q-GIS software has been used to create detailed maps at the state and district levels in India. This visualization of spatial data related to poverty and IOp, facilitate more nuanced regional analyses.

1.6 Chapterization

This book is divided into seven chapters providing an in-depth analysis of inequality of opportunity (IOp) and poverty in India. It explores various aspects of these issues using data from national surveys and unique sources like night-time satellite images and location data of points of interest. The book combines traditional econometric methods with newer machine learning techniques, such as regression trees and random forests, to analyse the data. It aims to offer practical insights for policy-makers and researchers who want to address social and economic inequalities in India.

This introductory chapter sets the stage by outlining the importance of studying inequality of opportunity and poverty in India. It discusses the limitations of traditional measures of inequality, which often focus solely on outcomes rather than opportunities, and highlights the significance of distributive justice. The chapter emphasizes the potential of innovative approaches, such as using geospatial data and machine learning techniques, to analyse complex data and derive timely, granular insights.

The second chapter 'Concept and Measurement' explores the theoretical underpinnings of inequality of opportunity and poverty. It discusses the philosophical concept of distributive justice and its relation to IOp. The chapter provides an empirical framework for measuring IOp and poverty in India, using data from National Statistical Office (NSO) surveys and geospatial data, such as nightlights and points of interest. The analysis reveals that unequal circumstances, such as parental education and occupation, significantly contribute to income inequalities. It also highlights the critical role of gender and regional factors in shaping economic opportunities and poverty.

Chapter 3 'Decomposition of Inequality of Opportunity' introduces innovative measures to decompose inequality of opportunity in India. It utilizes machine learning algorithms like conditional inference trees to distinguish between the effects of circumstances and effort on income inequality. The findings indicate that a significant portion of income inequality stems from circumstances beyond an individual's control, such as parental occupation and regional disparities. The chapter emphasizes the need for targeted policies to address these structural inequalities and promote a more equitable society.

Chapter 4, 'Predicting Poverty with Geospatial Data and Machine Learning', explores the application of machine learning techniques to predict both income-based (consumption) poverty and multidimensional poverty in India. The chapter integrates consumption-based poverty data from the Periodic Labour Force Surveys with Multidimensional Poverty Index (MPI) data from the National Family Health Survey and geospatial sources such as satellite imagery to generate district-level poverty statistics. Various machine learning techniques are employed to estimate poverty levels, with tree-based methods demonstrating superior performance. The analysis identifies nightlights and the density of points of interest as key predictors of poverty. The spatial analysis reveals significant regional disparities, particularly high poverty levels in the eastern and central regions of India. The findings suggest that new data sources and advanced analytical techniques can improve the accuracy of poverty measurements and support more effective policy interventions. Additionally, the chapter advocates for the use of geospatial data as a cost-effective and timely method for predicting poverty at a granular level.

Chapter 5 'Inequality of Opportunity in Education' explores the factors contributing to educational inequality in India. It uses large-scale data from the Periodic Labour Force Survey to predict years of formal education using machine learning techniques. The analysis reveals that parental educational levels and type of occupation they engaged in are the primary determinants of educational IOp. The chapter highlights the persistent educational disparities across different regions and social groups contributing inequality in education in the country.

Chapter 6, 'Inequality of Opportunity in Health' examines how unequal the opportunities are for accessing maternal and child health services. The study uses the Human Opportunity Index (HOI) and the Dissimilarity Index to analyse this inequality. It also employs hierarchical clustering, an unsupervised machine learning method, to identify regional patterns of access to these services at the district level across India. The analysis shows significant inequality in access to health services, with over three-fourths of the population lacking adequate or proper access, especially to prenatal care, immunization, and at least four antenatal visits. The main factors contributing to health inequality are geographical regions, wealth, parental education (particularly the mother's education), and social groups.

Chapter 7, the concluding chapter, summarizes the key findings and challenges discussed in various chapters of the book. It also provides policy recommendations and suggests areas for future research. It emphasizes the importance of addressing inequality of opportunity and poverty through targeted interventions that consider regional and social disparities. The chapter also outlines potential future research directions and the need for innovative data sources and analytical techniques to enhance our understanding of social and economic inequalities.

References

Alderman, H., Behrman, J. R., & Hoddinott, J. (2002). *Antenatal care and maternal health* (World Bank Policy Research Working Paper No. 2821).

Arneson, R. J. (1989). Equality and equality of opportunity. *Philosophy & Public Affairs, 18*(2), 159–185.

Atkinson, A. B. (2015). *Inequality: What can be done?* Harvard University Press.

Azam, M., & Bhatt, N. (2015). Inequality of opportunity and poverty in India: Evidence from National Sample Surveys. *Journal of Development Studies, 51*(10), 1372–1386.

Bricker, J., Dettling, L. J., & Hsu, J. W. (2016). Measuring wealth inequality in the U.S. *Brookings Papers on Economic Activity, 47*(2), 289–356.

Chancel, L., Piketty, T., Saez, E., & Zucman, G. (2022). *World inequality report 2022*. UNDP, World Inequality Lab.

Cohen, G. A. (1989). On the currency of egalitarian justice. *Ethics, 99*(4), 906–944.

Dämmrich, J., & Triventi, M. (2018). The role of data integration in measuring inequality and poverty. *Social Indicators Research, 135*(2), 655–672.

Donaldson, D., & Storeygard, A. (2016). The view from above: Applications of satellite data in economics. *Annual Review of Economics, 8*, 1–28.

Dworkin, R. (1981). What is equality? Part 1: Equality of welfare. *Philosophy & Public Affairs, 10*(3), 185–246.

Ferreira, F. H., & Peragine, V. (2016). *Inequality of opportunity: Theory and evidence* (World Bank Policy Research Working Paper No. 7878).

Hufe, P., Weick, S., & Otsuka, K. (2018). *Measuring inequality of opportunity in developing countries* (World Bank Policy Research Working Paper No. 8447).

Jean, N., Burke, M., & Lobell, D. B. (2016). Combining satellite imagery and machine learning to predict poverty. *Science, 353*(6301), 790–794.

Kundu, A. (2020). Measuring inequality of opportunity in India: A comprehensive analysis. *Indian Journal of Human Development, 14*(1), 45–63.

Mehta, B. S., Dhote, S., & Srivastava, R. (2023). Decomposition of inequality of opportunity in India: An application of data-driven machine learning approach. *The Indian Journal of Labour Economics, 66*(2), 439–469.

Motiram, S. (2018). Inequality of opportunity and poverty: Evidence from India. *Journal of Economic Inequality, 16*(4), 571–596.

NITI Aayog. (2024). *Multidimensional Poverty Index: India 2022–23*. National Institution for Transforming India.

Rawls, J. (1971). *A theory of justice*. Harvard University Press.

Roemer, J. E. (1993). A pragmatic theory of responsibility for the egalitarian planner. *Philosophy & Public Affairs, 22*(2), 146–166.

Roemer, J. E. (1998). *Equality of opportunity*. Harvard University Press.

Roemer, J. E. (2006). Equalizing opportunity. *The Journal of Economic Perspectives, 20*(1), 11–24.

Roemer, J. E., & Trannoy, A. (2015). Equality of opportunity. In *The handbook of income distribution* (Vol. 2, pp. 217–300). Elsevier.

Sen, A. (1980). *Equality of what? The Tanner Lectures on human values* (Vol. 1). University of Utah Press.

Sen, A. (1985). Well-being, agency and freedom: The Dewey Lectures 1984. *Journal of Philosophy, 82*(4), 169–221.

Sen, A. (1992). *Inequality reexamined*. Harvard University Press.

Sen, A. (1999). *Development as freedom*. Oxford University Press.
Singh, S. (2012). Inequality of opportunity and poverty in India. *Economic & Political Weekly, 47*(44), 49–56.
Taubenböck, H., Wurm, M., & Pahl, S. (2018). Socio-economic information extraction from remote sensing data. *ISPRS Journal of Photogrammetry and Remote Sensing, 144*, 110–125.
World Bank. (2020). *Poverty and shared prosperity 2020: Reversals of fortune*. World Bank.
Wurm, M., & Taubenböck, H. (2018). Satellite data and machine learning for socio-economic analysis. *Remote Sensing of Environment, 211*, 229–244.

Chapter 2
Concept and Measurement of IOp

Keywords Mean Log Deviation · Regression · Inequality of Opportunity · Equality · Circumstances · Regression trees

2.1 Introduction

Inequality, whether economic, social, or political, has consistently been a major concern globally. Over the past three decades, the rising economic inequality across nations has drawn significant attention from policymakers and scholars alike (Morelli & Rohner, 2015). This growing interest has led to numerous studies on the measurement of inequality focusing predominantly on income or consumption expenditure. In other words, traditionally, the past studies employed a welfarist approach to measure income inequality, with inequality in outcomes as their primary focus. This classical approach, while valuable, has faced several criticisms for its insufficient consideration of the multifaceted factors that contribute to inequality (Dworkin, 1981b). This critique sparked a philosophical debate in the late twentieth century, emphasizing responsibility-sensitive egalitarian justice (Roemer, 1993,

Disclaimer: The presentation of material and details in maps used in this chapter does not imply the expression of any opinion whatsoever on the part of the Publisher or Author concerning the legal status of any country, area or territory or of its authorities, or concerning the delimitation of its borders. The depiction and use of boundaries, geographic names and related data shown on maps and included in lists, tables, documents, and databases in this chapter are not warranted to be error free nor do they necessarily imply official endorsement or acceptance by the Publisher or Author.

Earlier version of this chapter was published as a working paper by Institute for Human Development (IHD), and in the IASSI Quarterly.

B. S. Mehta et al., *Predicting Inequality of Opportunity and Poverty in India Using Machine Learning*, India Studies in Business and Economics,
https://doi.org/10.1007/978-981-96-2544-4_2

1998). This approach differentiates between 'fair' and 'unfair' inequalities, highlighting the role of individual responsibility in distributive justice. It shifts the focus from merely examining 'inequality of outcomes' to addressing 'inequality of opportunities (IOp)'. This notion of IOp provides a framework to distinguish between 'good' and 'bad' inequalities in a society, crucial for achieving both economic efficiency and social cohesion. Unequal societies may inadvertently hinder certain segments of the population while favouring others, making it essential to understand how IOp influences these dynamics.

In this background, it is important to understand to what extent the inequality is driven by IOp. However, the traditional methods and data sources for measuring IOp have several limitations. These conventional approaches often struggle to capture the complexity of IOp and its determinants accurately. To address these shortcomings, the application of Machine Learning (ML) algorithms emerges as a promising solution. ML techniques offer advanced analytical capabilities, potentially providing more nuanced and robust estimates of IOp by analysing large and complex datasets. In this light, the first objective of this chapter is to explore the theoretical evolution of the concept of IOp, while second objective is how emerging ML techniques can offer new and insightful perspectives on IOp. By leveraging ML algorithms. The aim is to overcome the constraints of traditional methods and enhancing the understanding of the contribution of IOp in overall inequality, and factors contributing to IOp.

This issue is particularly important in developing countries, where income inequality has been widening over the last few decades, with some recent reversals in countries like India. As discussed in the introductory chapter, despite the impressive economic growth witnessed in India since the economic reforms of the 1990s, the benefit of growth has not led to equitable improvements in economic and social welfare of the people (Sharma, 2015). This persistent and widening inequality underscores the importance of addressing IOp to achieve meaningful reductions in overall inequality. Existing studies have extensively analysed outcome-based inequality in India, but research specifically focusing on IOp remains limited. This gap in the literature highlights the need for a comprehensive examination of IOp within the Indian context, serving as a case study for developing countries. Thus, the third objective of this chapter is to measure and identify the factors contributing to IOp in India, utilizing both conventional methods and ML algorithms. By integrating these approaches, this chapter aims to provide a clearer understanding of IOp in India and offer insights that can guide policy development for India as well as other developing countries. This can help in addressing the root causes of inequality and create equal opportunities for all individuals in society.

The remainder of this chapter is structured as follows: Sect. 2.2 outlines the evolution and theoretical underpinnings of IOp. Section 2.3 details the methodologies and approaches used in the analysis. Section 2.4 discusses about the data sources, and Sect. 2.5 presents the findings from the India-based analysis, and Sect. 2.6 concludes with summary, policy recommendations and future research directions.

2.2 Evolution of IOp Concept

The concept of IOp has evolved significantly over time, influenced by broader philosophical and economic debates on justice and fairness. To understand the development of IOp, it is essential to trace its roots and the theoretical shifts that have shaped its current interpretation as briefly reviewed below.

Origins and Early Theoretical Frameworks: The idea of equality of opportunity is deeply rooted in the principle of distributive justice. Historically, this principle has often been associated with welfarist approaches, where equity assessments are based on the distribution of individual achievements—such as welfare, utility, or satisfaction—across a population. Utilitarianism, a prominent version of this tradition, aggregates individual achievements to form a social objective function, aiming to maximize overall utility. However, utilitarianism and its welfarist foundations faced significant challenges in political philosophy and normative economics (Dworkin, 1981b).

John Rawls and Egalitarianism: John Rawls (1958, 1971) introduced a critical shift with his egalitarian perspective, challenging utilitarianism. Rawls proposed the concept of primary goods—basic liberties, rights, income, and wealth—as central to justice. He argued that justice requires institutions that maximize the distribution of these primary goods to the least advantaged people of the society, ensuring a fair starting point for all individuals. Rawls's theory posits that true equality of opportunity is achieved when individuals have equal access to the basic goods necessary to pursue their interests and ambitions.

Critiques and Alternatives: The notion of equality of opportunity faced critiques from scholars like Ronald Dworkin (1981b, 1981c). Dworkin questioned the feasibility of equalizing welfare, noting that individuals have diverse material needs and preferences. He argued that achieving equality of welfare might require different amounts of wealth or income for different individuals. Dworkin introduced the concept of 'equality of resources', which extends beyond tangible goods to include biological traits and personal talents. Arneson (1989) and Cohen (1989) further critiqued Dworkin's approach. Arneson proposed 'equal opportunity for welfare,' suggesting that equality is achieved when every individual has the same set of possibilities to satisfy their preferences. Cohen's 'equal access to advantage' aligns closely with Arneson's view but includes a broader range of advantages beyond mere welfare.

Amartya Sen Capability Approach: Amartya Sen (1985, 1992, 1999) contributed another significant perspective with his 'capability approach.' Sen argued that focusing on individuals' capabilities—their ability to achieve desired functioning or states of being—provides a more comprehensive measure of equality. This approach integrates elements of Arneson and Cohen's proposals, emphasizing the freedom and capability to achieve various life outcomes rather than just the distribution of resources or goods.

Roemer's Conceptualisation: The work of John Roemer (1998, 2002) represents a critical development in the formalisation of IOp concept. Roemer conceptualised IOp as the outcome resulting from two sets of factors: those within an individual's control (efforts) and those beyond their control (circumstances). Efforts include factors like the number of hours worked or educational choices, while circumstances encompass aspects such as family background, socio-economic status, gender, and ethnicity. Roemer's framework provides a clear distinction between what individuals can be held accountable for and what they cannot, thus defining IOp as inequality arising from circumstances rather than efforts (Roemer & Trannoy, 2016a, 2016b).

Empirical Developments and Methodological Approaches: The theoretical underpinnings of IOp have spurred considerable empirical research. Scholars have developed various methods to estimate IOp and analyse its impact on economic outcomes. Important contributions include: Bourguignon et al. (2007): provided early empirical work on estimating IOp and its relation to economic inequality. Ferreira and Gignoux (2008, 2011, 2014): offered methodologies for measuring IOp and its effect on income inequality. Barros et al. (2009a; 2009b) explored the role of IOp in shaping consumption and income disparities. Fleurbaey and Schokkaert (2009) contributed to the understanding of how IOp affects welfare outcomes. Cecchi and Peragine (2010) expanded on methods to quantify IOp and its implications. These studies have advanced the measurement of IOp, offering valuable insights into its determinants and consequences. The next section delves deeper into the concept and measurement of IOp, reviewing the existing literature and discussing methodological advancements.

2.3 Measurement of IOp

The measurement of IOp hinges on two fundamental ethical principles: the principle of reward and the principle of compensation. These principles guide how we understand and evaluate inequality in relation to individual efforts and circumstances.

Principle of Reward and Principle of Compensation: The principle of reward is rooted in the idea that differential rewards should be preserved when they arise from individual responsibility and effort. In contrast, the principle of compensation asserts that individuals should be compensated for disadvantages arising from circumstances beyond their control (Fleurbaey, 1994). These principles shape how one should categorize and address IOp. To refine these concepts, the literature distinguishes between two key groups: *types* and *tranches*. *Types* refer to groups of individuals who share the same set of circumstances or opportunities. In contrast, *tranches* denote groups of individuals who exert the same level of effort. According to Peragine (2004a; 2004b), '*within-type*' inequality arises from differences in individual effort, which is considered morally permissible. Conversely, '*between-type*' inequality is driven by disparities in circumstances and is seen as inequitable, thus warranting compensation. Roemer (1998) contends that the principle of reward, or the concept of 'within-type' inequality, is less central to the measurement of IOp. His focus is primarily on the principle of compensation, which emphasizes the need to address inequality arising from circumstances beyond an individual's control. Consequently, while empirical evidence on ‘within-type’ inequality is limited, substantial research supports the principle of compensation in understanding and measuring IOp.

Ex-Ante and Ex-Post Approaches: The measurement of IOp is further informed by two distinct perspectives: the *ex-ante* and *ex-post* approaches (Fleurbaey & Peragine, 2013a; 2013b). The *ex-ante* approach examines inequality between types—groups of individuals who have identical circumstances. This approach is predicated on the idea that individuals should have equal opportunities to achieve similar outcomes, given the same circumstances. In contrast, the *ex-post* approach focuses on inequality between tranches—groups of individuals who have exerted the same level of effort. This perspective assesses how different efforts yield varying outcomes and the role of individual responsibility in these outcomes. The distinction between these approaches arises from differing views on the nature and measurement of effort. The ex-post approach has been less popular due to challenges in accurately measuring effort, which requires strong assumptions and is often difficult to operationalize (Fleurbaey & Peragine, 2013; Ramos & Van de Gaer, 2016). As a result, most empirical applications and studies predominantly utilize the ex-ante approach. This approach is more straightforward, as it focuses on comparing outcomes based on equal circumstances, without delving into the complexities of effort measurement.

Overall, the measurement of IOp involves navigating between the principles of reward and compensation and choosing between ex-ante and ex-post approaches. The ex-ante approach, focusing on inequalities between types, is more prevalent due to its relative simplicity and fewer methodological challenges compared to the ex-post approach. This framework guides our discussion and analysis of IOp, aligning with the predominant empirical focus in the field.

Regression Approach to Measuring IOp: Over time, various methods have been proposed to assess ex-ante IOp, with the regression approach emerging as one of the most popular and widely utilized techniques across different countries and outcomes. This has become a widely adopted method because of its flexibility and applicability across different contexts and outcomes. This method primarily involves relating an outcome variable to a matrix of circumstances, either through parametric or non-parametric regression methods. Ferreira and Gignoux (2011) applied this method using income as the dependent variable, estimating the relationship with both ordinary least squares (OLS) regression and non-parametric methods, such as averaging over types. The method can be summarized as follows: Let y represent the outcome variable of interest, such as individual earnings or income, and X denote the matrix of circumstances beyond an individual's control, such as race, gender, parental education, and occupation. The relationship between the outcome variable and the vector of circumstances can be described by the expected conditional outcome, represented by the equation:

$$y_i = f(X_i) + \epsilon_i \tag{2.1}$$

where $f(X_i)$ denotes the function that captures the impact of circumstances X_i on the outcome y_i, and ϵ_i represents the error term. This relationship can be estimated using various methods depending on the research question and the nature of the dependent variable. Regardless of the estimation method used, IOp is computed using a common inequality measure applied to the outcomes derived from the regression model as expressed in Eq. 2.1. This involves comparing the inequality observed in the outcome variable to the inequality attributed to circumstances. The measure of IOp can be quantified by:

$$\theta_r = I(\hat{y})/I(y) \tag{2.2}$$

where θ_r is IOp, $I(\hat{y})$ denotes the inequality measure applied to the predicted outcomes based on circumstances, and $I(y)$ represents the inequality measure of the actual outcomes. The choice of inequality measure—such as the dissimilarity index (Barros et al., 2009), mean logarithmic deviation (Ferreira & Gignoux, 2011), or variance (Ferreira & Gignoux, 2014)—depends on the nature of the outcome variable. For instance, binary outcomes may require different inequality metrics compared to continuous outcomes.

Decomposition of IOp Measure: To understand the extent to which various circumstances contribute to overall IOp, decomposition methods are employed. One important decomposition method is the Shapley value, derived from cooperative game theory, which offers a way to quantify the contribution of each circumstance to the total inequality observed. The Shapley value method involves two steps: the first step is estimating inequality measures by computing the inequality measure for all possible permutations of circumstance variables (Shapley, 1953). The second step is computing marginal effects by calculating the average marginal effect of each circumstance on the IOp measure. The Shapley decomposition is computationally intensive, requiring 2^K permutations where K represents the number of circumstances. Its advantages include being order-independent and ensuring that the sum of individual contributions equals the total value of IOp.

Machine Learning Algorithm—Conditional Inference Trees: Traditional regression methods face limitations, such as the challenge of selecting which variables to include in the model. Omitting relevant variables can lead to downward bias while including too many can introduce upward bias (Brunori et al., 2019a; 2019b, Hufe et al., 2017). Machine Learning (ML) algorithms address these issues by learning from data and making decisions based on patterns identified during the training phase. ML methods, including conditional inference regression trees, are gaining popularity for their ability to mitigate biases associated with model selection and to provide standardized approaches for estimating IOp. These methods offer several advantages such as reduction of bias: ML algorithms minimize arbitrary choices in model specification and address issues of upward and downward biases in IOp estimation, and improved interpretability: Conditional inference trees, a type of supervised ML method, provide clear graphical representations of opportunity structures, enhancing the comprehensibility of IOp analysis. Conditional inference trees improve upon traditional methods by using recursive binary splitting to identify relevant splits in the data based on circumstance factors. The algorithm operates through two stages: first step is initial splitting: Performs a hypothesis test (e.g. t-test) for each circumstance to determine if there is a significant split, while second step is tree growth: If the hypothesis test suggests a significant split, the algorithm uses this circumstance to partition the data and grows the tree accordingly. As if the p-value is greater than the pre-specified significance level or alpha level, no split is made. Otherwise, the selected circumstance becomes the splitting variable, and the tree is expanded accordingly, producing a visually interpretable hierarchical opportunity structure.

This approach generates opportunity trees that visually represent how different circumstances contribute to inequality. It allows for an in-depth, hierarchical analysis of opportunities, making the results accessible to a broader audience (Brunori & Neidhofer, 2020; Brunori et al., 2018a, 2018b; Lefranc & Kundu, 2020).

2.4 Data Sources and Variables

This analysis utilizes household-level survey data from several key sources: the Employment and Unemployment Surveys (EUS) for the years 2004–05 and 2011–12, and the Periodic Labour Force Survey (PLFS) for the years 2019–20 and 2022–23. These surveys are conducted by the National Statistical Office (NSO), Government of India. The cross-sectional data from these surveys are representative at both the national and state levels. The outcome variables used in this analysis include household consumption expenditure, total household income, monthly wage income (both regular and casual), regular salaried/wage income, self-employed income, and casual wage income. It is important to note that data on the earnings of self-employed individuals is not available for the years 2004–05 and 2011–12. Additionally, the weekly wages or earnings of casual and regular workers have been converted into monthly earnings for consistency in the analysis.

The circumstance variables considered in this study include: *Parent's Education*: Categories include no education, primary education, secondary education, higher secondary education, and graduate or higher. *Parent's Occupation*: Classified as high-skilled, medium-skilled, low-skilled, and unskilled. *Social Group*: Divided into scheduled castes, scheduled tribes, other backward classes, and others. *Gender*: Male or female. *Place of Birth*: Regions include north, east, central, northeast, south, and west, and *Location*: Rural or urban. The analysis focuses on individuals within the working-age range of 15–64 years. The final sample sizes, after excluding cases with missing parental background information,[1] are as follows: 149,909 individuals in 2004–05; 112,103 individuals in 2011–12; 105,020 individuals in 2019–20; and 75,708 individuals in 2022–23. These samples represent approximately one-third of the total sample covered in each respective survey year (34% in 2022–23, 35% in 2019–20, 33% in 2011–12, and 33% in 2004–05).

[1] Whenever available, information for parents (both father and mother) has been used; however, in few cases, data is available for only either father or mother.

2.5 Findings and Discussions

2.5.1 Characteristics of the Sample Population

This section examines the profile of the working-age population (15–64 years) based on various factors, including location, region, social group, and parental background, and their relation to outcome variables such as consumption expenditure, total income, wage income, regular salaried income, casual labour income, and self-employed income. Detailed procedures for sample and variable selection are outlined in Appendix 1.

Table 2.1 Profile of sample population (in %)

		2004–05	2011–12	2019–20	2022–23
Sector	Rural	73.6	70.2	68.5	62.5
	Urban	26.4	29.8	31.5	37.5
	Total	100.0	100.0	100.0	100.0
Region (zone)	North	12.3	13.2	14.5	17.8
	East	20.3	20.7	19.5	17.3
	Central	24.0	24.5	26.2	21.6
	North East	3.7	3.5	3.9	14.5
	South	24.2	22.8	20.8	17.2
	West	15.4	15.3	15.1	11.5
	Total	100.0	100.0	100.0	100.0
Gender	Male	75.8	73.9	71.7	66.1
	Female	24.2	26.1	28.3	33.9
	Total	100.0	100.0	100.0	100.0
Social group	ST	7.9	8.0	8.5	15.9
	SC	19.6	19.1	20.5	18.5
	OBC	40.8	43.4	43.5	41.4
	Others (general)	31.8	29.5	27.5	24.3
	Total	100.0	100.0	100.0	100.0

Source Authors calculations from EUS, 2004–05 and 2011–12, and PLFS, 2019–20 and 2022–23

Geographic Distribution and Demographic Characteristics: A significant portion of the sample population having individuals with parental information resides in rural areas, although this proportion has decreased over time. In 2004–05, 73.6% of the population lived in rural India, whereas this figure declined to 62.5% by 2022–23 (Table 2.1). This shift reflects broader socio-economic changes and urbanization trends in India. The distribution across regions shows that the central region has the highest proportion of the sample population (21.6% in 2022–23), followed by the north, east, south, northeast, and west regions (Table 2.1). This regional distribution highlights the demographic diversity within the country and the varying economic conditions across regions. In terms of gender, the sample is predominantly male, with males constituting 66.1% of the population in 2022–23, reflecting the tendency to record the household head, who is often male, in these surveys. The representation of women has increased over time, but males remain the majority. Regarding social groups, Other Backward Classes (OBC) represent the largest share (41.4%), followed by the general caste (24.3%), Scheduled Castes (SC) (18.5%), and Scheduled Tribes (ST) (15.9%) (Table 2.1). This distribution indicates the significant presence of historically disadvantaged groups in the sample population.

Parental Education and Occupation Profile: The educational attainment of parents has seen notable changes over the years. In 2022–23, more than three-quarters of parents (75.3%) had education levels below secondary, including those who were

Table 2.2 Parents' education and occupation profile (in percentage)

		2004–05	2011–12	2019–20	2022–23
Education	No education	*49.3*	*42.0*	*37.3*	*26.3*
	Below secondary	*34.5*	*37.3*	*38.3*	*49.0*
	Secondary/higher secondary	*11.7*	*14.7*	*17.2*	*17.4*
	Graduate and above	*4.5*	*6.0*	*7.2*	*7.3*
	Total	*100.0*	*100.0*	*100.0*	*100.0*
Occupation	High skilled	2.1	3.8	4.6	5.4
	Medium skilled	3.0	3.4	4.1	2.2
	Low skilled	67.0	62.9	66.3	68.7
	Unskilled	27.9	29.9	25.0	23.7
	Total	100.0	100.0	100.0	100.0

Note 'High Skilled' includes, Professionals; 'Medium Skilled' includes Associate Professionals; 'Low Skilled' includes Clerks, Service Workers, Skilled Agricultural Workers, Craft workers, and Plant and Machinery Operators; 'Unskilled' includes workers in elementary occupations
Source Authors calculations from EUS, 2004–05 and 2011–12, and PLFS, 2019–20, and 2022–23

illiterate (26.3%) (Table 2.2). However, there has been an increase in the proportion of parents with higher secondary education (from 11.7% in 2011–12 to 17.4% in 2022–23) and those with graduate-level education (from 4.5% in 2011–12 to 7.3% in 2022–23). This trend reflects improvements in educational attainment over the past two decades. The occupational profile of parents reveals a predominance of low-skilled and unskilled jobs. The share of parents in low-skilled jobs increased marginally from 67% in 2004–05 to 68.7% in 2022–23, while the share of those in unskilled manual jobs declined from 27.9% to 23.7% during the same period. Conversely, the proportion of parents in high-skilled jobs has consistently increased, rising from 2.1% in 2004–05 to 5.4% in 2022–23, whereas their share in medium-skilled jobs has declined marginally over the same period. However, the increasing share of high-skilled jobs and the declining share of unskilled manual jobs indicate a growing demand for high-skilled positions and a decreasing demand for unskilled ones in the economy. This trend also highlights a growing disparity in job quality and skill levels among parents, potentially affecting the socio-economic outcomes for their children.

Household Monthly Consumption Expenditure (MPCE): In 2022–23, the average Monthly Consumption Expenditure (MPCE) for households was INR 12,646, with a marginal disparity between rural and urban areas. Rural households reported an average MPCE at INR 11,439, while urban households average MPCE stands at INR 15,939 on average (Table 2.3). The real value of average MPCE has fluctuated over time. It increased from INR 11,391 in 2004–05 to INR 13,173 in 2011–12, before declining to INR 10,652 in 2019–20, and increased to 12,646 in 2022–23. This decrease in average MPCE in 2019–20 may be attributed to the economic impact of the COVID-19 pandemic, which included a nationwide lockdown for several months in 2020 aimed at curbing the spread of the virus, the increase in average

Table 2.3 Average monthly consumer expenditure and income in real value[2] (in INR) in 2004–05, 2011–12, and 2019–20

	Rural	Urban	Total
Average monthly consumer expenditure			
2022–23	11,493	15,839	12,646
2019–20	8839	14,587	10,652
2011–12	10,758	18,864	13,173
2004–05	9863	15,662	11,391
Average monthly income (Self-employed + Regular salaried + Casual labour)			
2022–23	10,018	17,647	12,135
2019–20	13,812	24,078	17,049

Source Authors calculations from EUS, 2004–05 and 2011–12, and PLFS, 2019–20, PLFS, 2022–23

MPCE can be attributed to the post pandemic recovery. The lockdown likely led to reduced consumer spending due to restricted mobility and economic uncertainty. Conversely, the average monthly income of households in 2022–23 was, at INR 12,135, marginally lower the average monthly consumption expenditure.

This disparity indicates that households had a lower income relative to their expenditure during 2004–05 to 2022–23. The fall in incomes is mainly attributed to a decline in income in regular and casual work (Table 2.3). Higher consumption compared to income also could be due to the various welfare schemes, such as free rations, launched by the government to absorb the economic shocks of the pandemic.

Employment Status and Trends: In 2022–23, the employment status among the sample with parental information in the working-age population reveals that approximately 51.4% were engaged in self-employment, 28.9% in regular salaried jobs, and 19.7% in casual labour (Table 2.4). Over time, there has been a significant shift in employment patterns: The proportion of individuals in regular salaried jobs has increased substantially from 13.0% in 2004–05 to 28.9% in 2022–23. Conversely, the share of those engaged in casual labour has decreased from 32.1% in 2011–12 to 19.7% in 2022–23. The percentage of individuals in self-employment has also declined, from 54.9% in 2011–12 to 51.4% in 2022–23. These shifts indicate a growing trend towards regular employment, though self-employment remains a significant component of the labour market.

Income Analysis by Status of Employment: In 2022–23, the average monthly income varied significantly by type of employment among the sample of individuals having parental information. Regular salaried jobs offered the highest average income at INR 14,431, followed by self-employment at INR 12,876, and casual labour at INR 5020 (Table 2.5). Over the years, there have been notable changes in average monthly income: For regular salaried jobs, income increased from INR 11,407 in 2004–05 to INR 15,801 in 2011–12, but then declined slightly to INR 15,505 in

[2] Nominal values are converted into real values by using CPI-Rural and CPI Urban retrieved from https://cpi.mospi.gov.in/Default1.aspx.

Table 2.4 Status of employment of working sample (in percentage) in 2004–05, 2011–12, and 2022–23

Status of employment	2004–05	2011–12	2019–20	2022–23
Self-employed	54.9	50.2	49.2	51.4
Regular	13.0	18.2	29.4	28.9
Casual labour	32.1	31.6	21.4	19.7
Total	100.0	100.0	100.0	100.0

Source Authors calculations from EUS, 2004–05 and 2011–12, and PLFS, 2019–20 and 2022–23

Table 2.5 Average monthly income in real value[3] (in INR) by status of employment in 2004–05, 2011–12, and 2022–23

	Location		Gender		Total
	Rural	Urban	Male	Female	
Average monthly self-employed (SE) income					
2022–23	11,735	15,413	13,953	5799	12,876
2019–20	10,214	17,312	12,475	6055	12,133
Average monthly regular salaried (RE) income					
2022–23	13,441	15,322	14,607	13,482	14,431
2019–20	12,849	17,729	15,756	13,940	15,505
2011–12	11,500	18,595	16,283	12,375	15,801
2004–05	8979	13,216	11,842	8373	11,407
Average monthly casual labour (CL) income					
2022–23	4865	5613	5133	3087	5020
2019–20	7155	8549	7581	4865	7392
2011–12	5926	7062	6291	3987	6106
2004–05	3504	4586	3842	2291	3651

Source Authors calculations from EUS, 2004–05 and 2011–12, and PLFS, 2019–20, and 2022–23

2019–20 and further to INR 14,431 in 2022–23. This decline, particularly in the urban sector and for males, may be linked to the economic disruptions caused by the COVID-19 lockdown. Casual labour income showed a substantial increase from INR 3651 in 2004–05 to INR 6106 in 2011–12, and INR 7392 in 2019–20, but again decreased to INR 5020 in 2022–23. The fluctuations in casual labour income highlight the vulnerability of this sector to economic instability and policy changes. Overall, these variations highlight the impact of economic conditions on different types of employment, with significant implications for household income stability and consumption patterns.

[3] Nominal values are converted into real values by using CPI-Rural and CPI Urban retrieved from https://cpi.mospi.gov.in/Default1.aspx.

2.5.2 Trends of Inequality of Opportunity in India

Overall Inequality and IOp: The trends in inequality and IOp across different outcomes such as consumption, total labour earnings (including self-employed, regular, and casual work), and wage earnings (both regular and casual work) from 2004–05 to 2022–23 are provided in Table 2.6. Inequality is measured using the Mean Log Deviation (MLD)[4] and Relative IOp, with bootstrap standard errors indicating the precision of the estimates.

Consumption Inequality and Relative IOp: The MLD shows that consumption inequality increased from 0.172 in 2004–05 to 0.191 in 2011–12, indicating a rise in inequality during this period. However, it decreased to 0.160 in 2019–20 and further to 0.142 in 2022–23, showing a reduction in consumption inequality in recent years. The Relative IOp remained relatively stable from 2004–05 to 2011–12, slightly decreased in 2019–20, but increased to 0.262 in 2022–23. This indicates that while overall consumption inequality has decreased, IOp in consumption has risen sharply in the most recent period. This suggests that even though consumption levels are becoming more equal, the opportunities leading to those levels are becoming more unequal.

Total Labor Earnings (Income) Inequality and IOp: The MLD for total labour earnings decreased from 0.307 in 2019–20 to 0.260 in 2022–23, indicating a reduction in income inequality over this period. The Relative IOp for total labour earnings increased from 0.241 in 2019–20 to 0.278 in 2022–23. This suggests a rise in IOp in labour earnings, indicating emerging disparities in the opportunities to earn income even though overall income inequality has decreased.

Wage Earnings (Regular and Casual Work) Inequality and IOp: The MLD for wage earnings shows a consistent decline in inequality from 0.465 in 2004–05 to 0.190 in 2022–23, indicating a significant reduction in wage inequality over the years. The Relative IOp for wage earnings increased from 0.184 in 2004–05 to 0.272 in 2011–12, suggesting a rise in IOp during this period. Although it slightly declined to 0.265 in 2019–20, it increased again to 0.282 in 2022–23. This indicates that while wage inequality has substantially declined, the IOp in wages has fluctuated but generally increased, suggesting that factors beyond individual control (such as family background and education) are playing a larger role in determining wage outcomes.

These results align with earlier findings, which also show that relative IOp is higher for wages and total wage earnings compared to consumption (Lefranc & Kundu, 2020; Singh, 2012a; 2012b). Over the past two decades, overall inequality has decreased. However, the persistent and increasing IOp highlights the need for policies that address the underlying factors contributing to these disparities. This includes improving access to quality education, health care, and other essential services to

[4] The mean-log deviation (MLD) is chosen as the measure of inequality because it uniquely satisfies all six of the following properties: (1) anonymity or symmetry, (2) population replication or replication invariance, (3) mean independence or scale invariance, (4) the Pigou-Dalton principle of transfers, (5) additive subgroup decomposability, and (6) path independence.

Table 2.6 Inequality of opportunity in consumer expenditure, income and wages

	Consumption				Income (labour earnings)		Wages earnings (regular and casual work)			
	2004–05	2011–12	2019–20	2022–23	2019–20	2022–23	2004–05	2011–12	2019–20	2022–23
Inequality (MLD)	0.172	0.191	0.160	0.142	0.307	0.260	0.465	0.394	0.291	0.190
Relative IOp	0.236	0.235	0.222	0.262	0.241	0.278	0.184	0.272	0.265	0.282
	(0.007)	(0.010)	(0.014)	(0.015)	(0.007)	(0.009)	(0.013)	(0.015)	(0.019)	(0.017)

Note Figures in parentheses are Bootstrap standard error
Source Authors calculation from EUS, 2004–05 and 2011–12, and PLFS, 2019–20 and 2022–23

ensure a more level playing field for all individuals, regardless of their circumstances. These issues are explored in detail in the subsequent chapters of the book.

Overall Inequality and IOp by Status of Employment: Further, Table 2.7 presents data on Inequality and IOp in income and wages, by employment status—regular salaried jobs, self-employment, and casual labour from 2004–05 to 2022–23. The data shows that income inequality, as measured by MLD, is highest among regular salaried employees, followed by those who are self-employed, with the lowest among casual workers. This pattern is consistent across the different time periods analysed. On the other hand, the Relative IOp is higher for regular salaried jobs compared to self-employed and casual workers.

Regular Salaried Jobs: MLD for regular salaried jobs indicate inequality decreased from 0.500 in 2004–05 to 0.208 in 2022–23. This shows a significant reduction in income inequality for regular salaried jobs over this period. The Relative IOp increased from 0.163 in 2004–05 to 0.242 in 2019–20, and slightly decreased to 0.229 in 2022–23. This indicates that the IOp has increased for regular salaried jobs over the years, suggesting that income inequality for regular workers is influenced relatively more by differences in opportunities rather than just income levels.

Self-Employed: MLD for self-employed individuals decreased from 0.269 in 2019–20 to 0.239 in 2022–23. This indicates a modest decline in income inequality among the self-employed. The Relative IOp for self-employed individuals was relatively stable, ranging from 0.179 in 2019–20 to 0.194 in 2022–23. This suggests a moderate level of IOp among self-employed that did not change drastically over time.

Casual Labour: MLD for casual workers remained relatively stable, decreasing slightly from 0.186 in 2004–05 to 0.113 in 2022–23. Casual workers have consistently experienced lower levels of income inequality compared to regular salaried and self-employed individuals. The Relative IOp for casual workers increased slightly from 0.153 in 2004–05 to 0.208 in 2022–23. Despite the small increase, casual workers generally experienced lower levels of IOp compared to those in regular salaried and self-employed roles.

The analysis reveal that increase in Relative IOp among regular salaried jobs suggests that most of the rise in income inequality can be attributed to growing disparities in opportunities within this employment category. This indicates that addressing IOp in regular salaried jobs could be crucial for reducing overall income inequality. In contrast, self-employment and casual workers has had more stable opportunities, but the overall lower inequality in these categories suggests fewer barriers to equitable access in this type of employment.

2.5.3 Contribution of the Factors

To relative contribution of various circumstances to IOp has been calculated by using Shapley decomposition (Fig. 2.1). The results indicate that parental background is the most significant factor contributing to IOp in consumption (MPCE), accounting

Table 2.7 Inequality of opportunity in income/wages by employment status

	Regular salaried				Self- employed)		Casual worker			
	2004–05	2011–12	2019–20	2022–23	2019–20	2022–23	2004–05	2011–12	2019–20	2022–23
Inequality (MLD)	0.500	0.457	0.306	0.208	0.269	0.239	0.186	0.155	0.117	0.113
Relative IOp	0.163	0.238	0.242	0.229	0.179	0.194	0.153	0.173	0.162	0.208
	(0.012)	(0.018)	(0.024)	(0.019)	(0.017)	(0.011)	(0.009)	(0.013)	(0.014)	(0.0100)

Note Figures in parentheses are Bootstrap standard error
Source Authors calculations from EUS, 2004–05 and 2011–12, and PLFS, 2019–20, and 2022–23

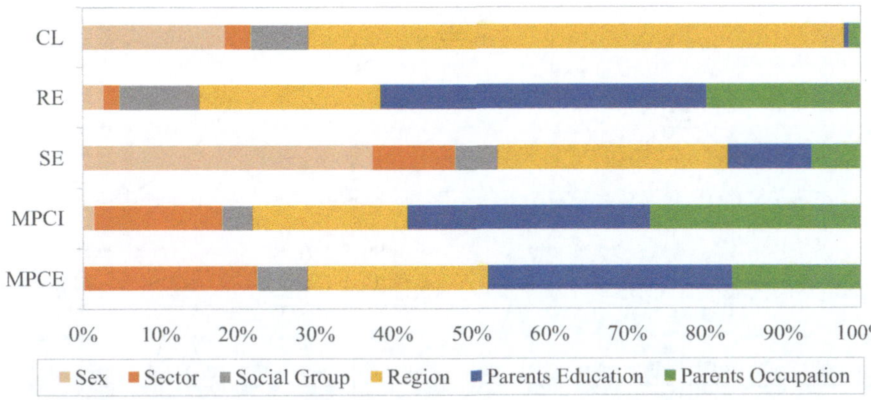

Fig. 2.1 Shapley decomposition of IOp in 2022–23. *Source* Authors calculations from EUS, 2004–05 and 2011–12, and PLFS, 2019–20, and 2022–23

for 47.9%. This includes parental education (31.4%) and occupation (16.5%). The region contributes 23.1% to consumption IOp. For total labour earnings (MPCI) IOp, parental background remains the most significant factor, contributing 58.1%, followed by region at 19.9%. These findings highlight the substantial impact of familial and regional circumstances on economic outcomes, emphasizing the need for policies targeting these fundamental sources of inequality.

Further, the contributing factors by status of employment reveal that parental background also significantly influences IOp in various forms of employment. For regular salaried workers, parental education and occupation combined contribute approximately 61.5% to their income IOp. This substantial impact arises because the likelihood of securing a regular salaried position is heavily influenced by an individual's educational attainment, which in turn is shaped by their parents' educational levels and occupational status (Das & Biswas, 2022). In essence, parents' educational and occupational backgrounds play a crucial role in determining access to better-paying, stable employment, highlighting a key area where inequality of opportunity is perpetuated across generations. Conversely, regional differences emerge as the primary factor contributing to income IOp in casual wage employment, accounting for 68.7%.

This suggests that geographic location and regional economic conditions are pivotal in determining the opportunities available to casual workers. Additionally, gender disparities play a significant role in self-employment, where gender accounts for 37.5% of income IOp, and regional factors contribute 29.6%. Social identity, including caste or social group, contributes to income IOp as well, though its impact is more pronounced in regular salaried positions (10.4%) compared to casual (7.4%) and self-employment (5.4%) (Das & Biswas, 2022). These findings underscore that while parental background is a major factor in regular employment, gender and regional factors are more influential in self-employment and casual wage work, respectively.

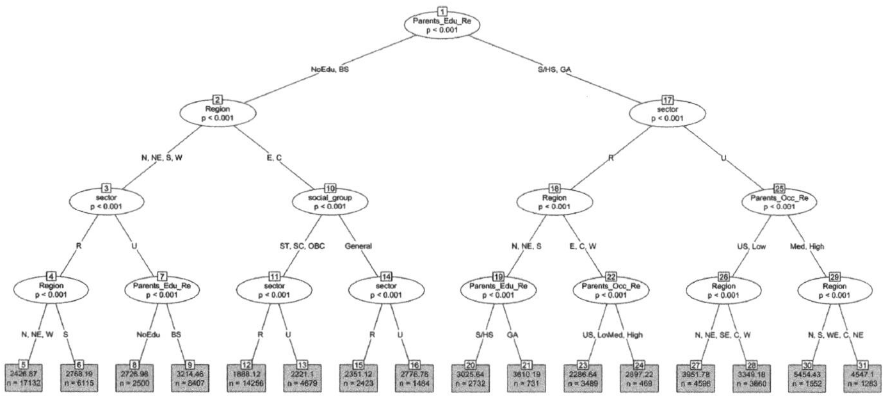

Fig. 2.2 Monthly consumption expenditure tree. *Note* R: Rural; U: Urban; N: North; NE: North East; S: South; W: West E: East; C: Central; Sec/HS: Secondary/Higher Secondary; GradAbv: Graduate and Above; NoEdu: Illiterate or Nor Formal Schooling; BS: Below Secondary; US: Unskilled; Low: Low Skilled; Med: Medium Skill; High: High Skilled; M: Male; F: Female. *Source* Authors calculations from PLFS, 2022–23

2.5.4 Conditional Inference Regression Tree

Conditional inference regression trees provide a nuanced understanding of how various circumstances affect IOp in consumption expenditure and income. The analysis based on MLD reveals that tree-based methods yield estimates for consumption IOp at 0.240 and income IOp at 0.282 that are slightly higher but closely aligned with parametric estimates. The conditional inference regression tree visually represents the types and conditions that most significantly impact IOp.

Conditional Inference Regression Tree for Consumption Expenditure: The conditional inference regression tree for consumption expenditure (MPCE), as shown in Fig. 2.2, identifies parental education as the most critical factor or circumstances influencing consumption IOp. For individuals whose parents have attained secondary or higher levels of education, the sector (rural or urban) emerges as the second most significant factor, followed by parental occupation for urban residents and geographical region for rural residents. Specifically, individuals with parents in high or medium-skilled occupations in urban areas, particularly in the central and northeastern regions, exhibit the highest outcome value (MPCE), which is followed by those belonging to the northern, southern, and western regions of India. This pattern indicates that individuals with parents with secondary or higher education, residing in urban areas, and engaged in skilled jobs, experience the highest MPCE values and the lowest levels of consumption IOp.

Conversely, for individuals whose parents have less than secondary education or no formal schooling, the region becomes the second most important factor influencing consumption IOp. In these cases, the third most significant factor is sector (rural or urban) for individuals from NNESW (northern, northeastern, southern, and western)

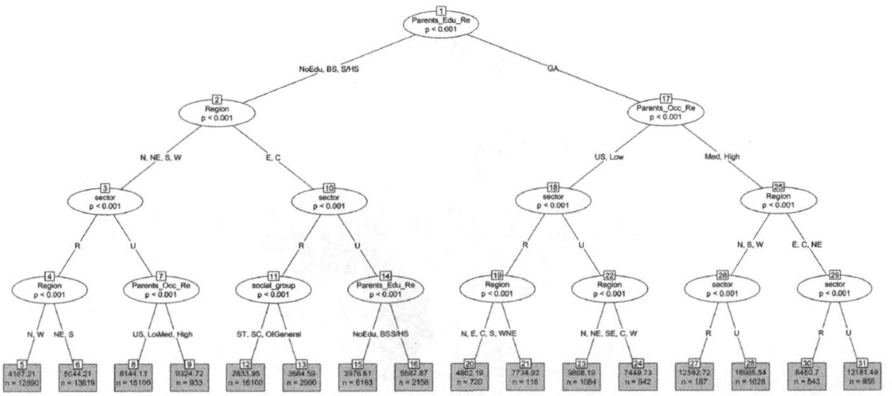

Fig. 2.3 Conditional inference regression tree for HH total labour income. *Note* R: Rural; U: Urban; N: North; NE: North East; S: South; W: West: E: East; C: Central; Sec/HS: Secondary/ Higher Secondary; GradAbv: Graduate and Above; NoEdu: Illiterate or Nor Formal Schooling; BS: Below Secondary; US: Unskilled; Low: Low Skilled; Med: Medium Skill; High: High Skilled; M: Male; F: Female. *Source* Authors calculations from PLFS, 2022–23

regions, and social group (caste) for those from the eastern and central regions. Further, the analysis highlights that individuals residing in rural parts of NNESW regions have the lowest MPCE values, indicating the highest levels of consumption IOp.

Conditional Inference Regression Tree for Income (Total Labour Earnings): The conditional inference regression tree for labour income or earnings, presented in Fig. 2.3, reveals that parental education is the most significant factor determining income IOp. For individuals with parents who have a graduate-level education or higher, parental occupation becomes the second most important factor. In contrast, for those with less educated parents, the region becomes the second significant factor influencing income IOp. For individuals whose parents have graduate or higher education and are engaged in high or medium-skilled jobs, geographical region is the next crucial factor, followed by the sector (rural or urban). Further, individuals from the eastern, central, and northeastern regions who reside in urban areas exhibit the highest labour income values or the lowest income IOp, followed by those from northern, southern, and western regions.

Conversely, for individuals with parents who have less than a graduate-level education, the sector is the third most important determinant of income IOp across all regions. In rural areas, social group (caste) is the next critical factor, particularly in the eastern and central regions, where those belonging to Scheduled Castes (SC) and Scheduled Tribes (ST) have the lowest total labour income values or highest income IOp. In urban areas, parental education remains a significant factor. In the NNESW (north, northeast, south, and west) regions, geographical region for individuals residing in rural areas, and parental occupation for those residing in urban areas emerge as key factors influencing labour income IOp. Among these groups, individuals with parents who have below secondary education or no formal schooling, for

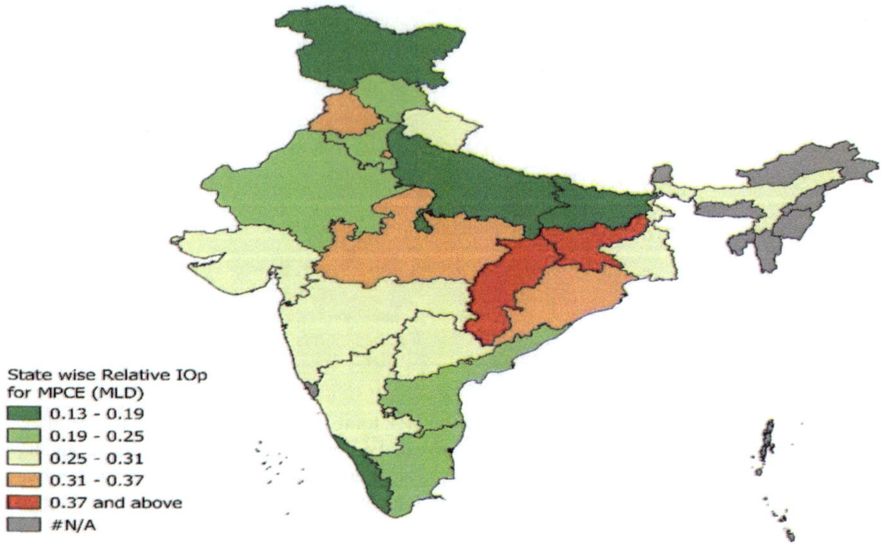

Map 2.1 Regional consumption IOp (MLD). *Source* Authors calculations from PLFS, 2022–23

those residing in rural parts of the NNESW regions, experience the lowest labour income values or the highest income IOp.

2.5.5 Regional Analysis

Consumption IOp: A regional analysis of consumption IOp reveals significant differences across Indian states. Chhattisgarh has the highest consumption IOp (42%), while Bihar has the lowest (14%) (Map 2.1 and Table 2.8). In the Central region, Chhattisgarh and Madhya Pradesh (31%) have high IOp, while Uttar Pradesh (18%) and Uttarakhand (28%) have lower levels. In the Northern region, Delhi (33%) and Punjab (32%) have higher IOp compared to Rajasthan, Haryana, and Himachal Pradesh (19–25%), with Jammu and Kashmir having the lowest (19%). The high IOp in Delhi and Punjab is due to diverse economies and significant urban populations, which may lead to greater disparities in consumption opportunities (Bourguignon et al., 2007). In the Western region, Gujarat (29%) and Maharashtra (27%) show relatively higher IOp. Among the Southern states, Telangana (30%) has the highest IOp, while Kerala has the lowest (16%), with Andhra Pradesh, Tamil Nadu (22.8%), and Karnataka ranging between 23 and 26%. The progressive social policies in Kerala may contribute to lower IOp by promoting a more equal distribution of resources and opportunities (World Bank, 2021).

However, it is surprising that the relatively less developed states in the Eastern region, Odisha and Jharkhand indicate high IOp, while Bihar and also Uttar Pradesh in the Central region show low IOp. The reasons could be that states like Odisha, Jharkhand, and Chhattisgarh are rich in natural resources, which can lead to unequal wealth distribution and high IOp. The mining industry often benefits a small elite, leaving the majority with limited economic opportunities (Singh, 2012). These states have underdeveloped infrastructure and limited access to education and health care, exacerbating inequality. The lack of social services and infrastructure perpetuates disparities in consumption opportunities (World Bank, 2016). On the other hand, despite overall poverty, the more uniform socio-economic conditions in Uttar Pradesh and Bihar may result in lower consumption IOp. The widespread poverty reduces the gaps in consumption opportunities (Singh & Mohapatra, 2019).

Income IOp: A regional analysis of income IOp shows significant variations across Indian states.[5] Jharkhand has the highest income IOp at 43%, while Himachal Pradesh has the lowest at 16% (Map 2.2 and Table 2.9). High levels of income IOp are particularly seen in the eastern (Jharkhand and Odisha), northeastern (Assam), and central (Madhya Pradesh and Chhattisgarh) regions of India. In the eastern region, Jharkhand tops the list with an income IOp of 43%, followed by Odisha at 36%. West Bengal has an income IOp of 26%, while Bihar has the lowest among the eastern states at 20%. The high income IOp in Jharkhand and Odisha is largely due to their rich natural resources, such as coal and minerals. These resources often lead to income disparities as the wealth tends to benefit a small, elite group, leaving the majority with fewer economic opportunities (Deaton & Dreze, 2002). In central India, Chhattisgarh leads with an income IOp of 36%, followed by Madhya Pradesh at 33%. Uttarakhand and Uttar Pradesh have lower income IOp at 21% and 18%, respectively. The high IOp in Chhattisgarh and Madhya Pradesh is also attributed to resource concentration issues, similar to those in Jharkhand and Odisha (World Bank, 2016).

In Northern India, Delhi and Punjab have high income IOp of 34% and 32%, respectively. This is due to their diverse economies and large urban populations, which contribute to greater income disparities (Singh, 2012). Haryana and Jammu and Kashmir also have high income IOp at 29% and 27%. Rajasthan has a lower income IOp of 24%, and Himachal Pradesh has the lowest in the north at 16%. In Western India, Gujarat has an income IOp of 26%, and Maharashtra has 23%. These states show relatively high income IOp due to their advanced economic development and industrialization. In Southern India, Karnataka and Telangana have higher income IOp at 28% and 26%, respectively, followed by Andhra Pradesh at 22%. Tamil Nadu and Kerala have lower income IOp at 19% and 18%, respectively. Kerala's lower income IOp is attributed to its progressive social policies and better distribution of resources (World Bank, 2021). Overall, the patterns of income IOp across states generally mirror those of consumption IOp, reflecting similar underlying regional disparities (Das & Biswas, 2022).

[5] For the analysis IOp, only major states of India with a sufficient sample size (3,600 or more) have been considered to ensure robust state-level estimates.

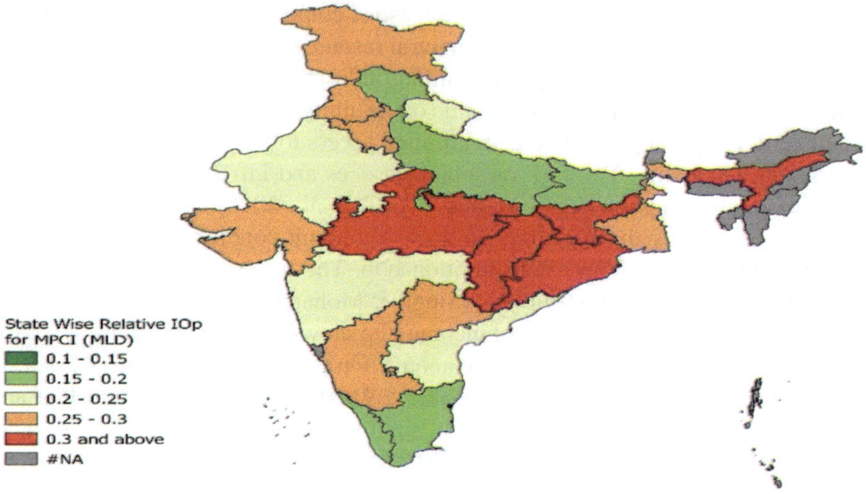

Map 2.2 Regional income IOp (MLD). *Source* Authors calculations from PLFS, 2022–23

2.6 Summary and Conclusion

The analysis reveals that unequal circumstances account for a substantial portion of inequality in consumption and income in India. Specifically, about 26.2% of consumption inequality, 27.8% of income inequality, and 28.2% of wage earnings inequality can be attributed to these unequal circumstances. Similarly, using the conditional inference tree, around 24% of consumption inequality and 28% of income inequality can be attributed to circumstances. Despite a significant decline in overall inequality in consumption, income and wages in recent years, the relative contribution of IOp has increased significantly. This suggests that while the outcomes have improved, the disparities in opportunities themselves have persisted or even widened in recent years.

The findings highlight the need for a policy shift towards addressing IOp rather than focusing solely on outcome-based metrics. This shift is crucial given that IOp in regular salaried employment is notably higher and has increased significantly over the past two decades. Conversely, IOp in casual wage employment and self-employment has almost stable or decline, reflecting differing dynamics across employment types. Machine learning (ML) algorithms have provided deeper insights into the factors contributing to IOp, revealing that parental background—specifically, education and occupation—plays a pivotal role in determining unequal opportunities in labour income as well as for regular salaried jobs. Gender disparities are more pronounced in casual wage employment and self-employment.

Regional analyses of consumption and income IOp reveal significant differences across Indian states. Chhattisgarh and Jharkhand have the highest consumption IOp, while Kerala, Himachal Pradesh, and also Bihar has the lowest IOp. In both cases, states with rich natural resources, like Jharkhand and Odisha, exhibit higher IOp due to uneven wealth benefits, while some underdeveloped states like Uttar Pradesh and Bihar show lower IOp attributed to high poverty with low consumption and income. On the other hand, the developed states such as Kerala and Tamil Nadua have lower IOp, while Maharashtra and Gujarat show higher IOp. These contradictory results indicate uneven distribution of resources in industrialised states, and progressive social policy and better resource distribution in other developed states.

To mitigate these deep-rooted inequalities, policies must be customized to meet the unique needs of different geographical regions and groups. It is important to focus on improving access to quality education for children from disadvantaged backgrounds, as equitable educational opportunities can significantly reduce IOp and lead to better overall outcomes. Additionally, regional policies should aim to improve infrastructure and implement progressive social measures to ensure fair distribution of resources and result in lower income, and consumption IOp.

Notes

1. "Types" is defined as a group of individuals sharing the same circumstances.
2. The place of birth representing by States/UTs of India are divided into broad five zone or regions as North: Jammu & Kashmir, Himachal Pradesh, Punjab, Haryana and Uttarakhand; East:Bihar, Jharkhand, Orissa, West Bengal; Central: Uttar Pradesh, Rajasthan, Madhya Pradesh, Chattisgarh; North East: Sikkim, Arunachal Pradesh, Assam, Nagaland, Meghalaya, Manipur, Mizoram, Tripura—Northeast; South: Karnataka, Andhra Pradesh, Tamilnadu, Pondichery, Kerala, Lakshadeep; and West: Gujrat, Daman & Diu, Dadra & Nagar Haveli, Maharashtra, Goa.
3. The consumer expenditure is converted from nominal to real values by using Consumer Price Index (CPI), CPI-agriculture labour for rural areas, and CPI-industrial workers for urban areas.
4. The self-employed income, regular salaried income, and casual labour income expenditure are converted from nominal to real values by using Consumer Price Index (CPI), CPI-agriculture labour for rural areas, and CPI-industrial workers for urban areas.
5. The bootstrap standard errors are based on 100 replication and nearly zero, which suggest the robustness of the estimate.

Appendices

Appendix 1: Sample Selection and Variable Construction

Variable Selection

From the 2018–19 PLFS survey, six key variables were selected for analysis. These include three variables used in their original form—sector, caste, and gender—and three variables that were modified or created—states, parents' education, and parents' occupations.

- Sector is categorized into two groups: rural and urban.
- Gender is classified as male and female; the transgender category was excluded from this analysis.
- Caste is divided into four categories: Scheduled Caste (SC), Scheduled Tribe (ST), and Other Backward Classes (OBC), and General.

For the **state** variable, which originally covered 36 states and union territories in India, we have consolidated these into six broad geographical regions:

- North: Jammu & Kashmir, Himachal Pradesh, Punjab, Haryana, and Rajsthan
- East: Bihar, Jharkhand, Odisha, and West Bengal
- Central: Uttar Pradesh, Uttarakhand, Madhya Pradesh, and Chhattisgarh
- Northeast: Sikkim, Arunachal Pradesh, Assam, Nagaland, Meghalaya, Manipur, Mizoram, and Tripura
- South: Karnataka, Andhra Pradesh, Tamil Nadu, Puducherry, Kerala, and Lakshadweep
- West: Gujarat, Daman & Diu, Dadra & Nagar Haveli, Maharashtra, and Goa

The **education** variable is categorized into four broad groups:

- Illiterate or No Education: Code 1 (Illiterate)
- Below Secondary: Codes 2–7 (Literate to up to middle school)
- Secondary and Higher Secondary: Codes 8–10 (Secondary to higher secondary)
- Graduate and Above: Codes 12–13 (Graduate and post-graduate)

The **occupation/skill level** variable is classified into four categories based on the National Classification of Occupations (NCO) at one digit, as per the OECD Employment Outlook 2014 and the NCO 2015 from the Ministry of Labour and Employment, Government of India:

- Unskilled or Routine Manual Tasks: Involves simple and routine physical or manual tasks (NCO code 9—Elementary Occupations), such as domestic helpers, cleaners, street vendors, and garbage collectors.
- Low Skilled or Non-Routine Manual Tasks: Includes tasks like operating machinery, driving vehicles, maintenance, and repair (NCO codes 4–8), such as clerical jobs, service workers, sales workers, and craft and trade workers.

- Medium Skill or Non-Routine Cognitive Tasks: Involves complex technical and practical tasks requiring extensive knowledge in a specialized field (NCO code 3—Professional and Technical Associates).
- High Skill or Cognitive Tasks: Requires complex problem-solving, decision-making, and creativity based on substantial theoretical and factual knowledge (NCO code 2—Professionals and Technicians).

For NCO code 1 (e.g. legislators, managers), skill levels are not applied due to the wide variation in skills required for these occupations, making classification into the four broad skill levels impractical.

Sample Selection

The sample selection process follows a multi-stage procedure:

- Identification of Parents[6]: Initially, each respondent's parents were identified using the "relation to head" variable. For individuals classified as "self" (code 1), the household member labelled as "Father/Mother/Father-in-Law/Mother-in-Law" (code 7) was considered the parent. This generated the first set of data, linking children with their parents.
- Categorization of Children: In the second stage, individuals were categorized as unmarried children (code 5) or married children (code 3). The parents of these children, identified as household heads labelled "self" (code 1), were then used to create the second set of data.
- Handling Duplicates: Duplicate records were carefully reviewed and removed. For instance, if records for both males and females existed for the same individual, the duplicates were deleted to ensure accuracy. After cleaning both data files, they were merged based on key variables as described above.

This systematic approach ensures a comprehensive and accurate dataset for analysing inequality and related factors.

---

[6] Whenever available, information for parents (both father and mother) has been used; however, in few cases, data is available for only either father or mother.

Appendix 2: Consumption and Income IOp Across States

Table 2.8 Consumption IOp across major states

State name	Overall inequality MLD MPCE	Absolute IOp MLD MPCE	MLD MPCE relative IOp
Chhattisgarh	0.109	0.046	0.421
Jharkhand	0.123	0.051	0.413
Odisha	0.112	0.041	0.363
Delhi	0.101	0.034	0.339
Punjab	0.116	0.037	0.324
Madhya Pradesh	0.095	0.030	0.321
Telangana	0.098	0.030	0.303
Gujarat	0.126	0.037	0.293
Uttarakhand	0.096	0.027	0.285
West Bengal	0.098	0.027	0.279
Maharashtra	0.158	0.044	0.275
Karnataka	0.136	0.035	0.256
Assam	0.072	0.018	0.256
Haryana	0.099	0.023	0.235
Tamil Nadu	0.111	0.025	0.228
Himachal Pradesh	0.090	0.020	0.227
Andhra Pradesh	0.084	0.019	0.221
Rajasthan	0.104	0.020	0.197
Jammu & Kashmir	0.155	0.029	0.189
Uttar Pradesh	0.106	0.019	0.183
Kerala	0.084	0.013	0.158
Bihar	0.064	0.009	0.136

Source Authors calculations from PLFS, 2022–23

Table 2.9 Income IOp across major states

State Name	Overall inequality MLD MPCI	Absolute IOp MLD MPCI	MLD MPCI relative IOp
Jharkhand	0.28	0.121	0.43
Odisha	0.29	0.104	0.36
Chhattisgarh	0.32	0.114	0.36
Assam	0.16	0.053	0.33
Madhya Pradesh	0.24	0.080	0.33

(continued)

Table 2.9 (continued)

State Name	Overall inequality MLD MPCI	Absolute IOp MLD MPCI	MLD MPCI relative IOp
Delhi	0.27	0.080	0.30
Haryana	0.21	0.061	0.29
Telangana	0.21	0.057	0.28
Jammu & Kashmir	0.23	0.063	0.27
Karnataka	0.21	0.055	0.26
West Bengal	0.19	0.051	0.26
Punjab	0.25	0.063	0.26
Gujarat	0.20	0.050	0.26
Rajasthan	0.29	0.070	0.24
Maharashtra	0.32	0.073	0.23
Andhra Pradesh	0.22	0.048	0.22
Uttarakhand	0.20	0.042	0.21
Bihar	0.15	0.030	0.20
Tamil Nadu	0.20	0.039	0.19
Kerala	0.23	0.042	0.18
Uttar Pradesh	0.29	0.052	0.18
Himachal Pradesh	0.39	0.062	0.16

Source Authors calculations from PLFS, 2022–23

References

Arneson, R. J. (1989). Equality and equality of opportunity for welfare. *Philosophical Studies, 56*(1), 77–93.

Bourguignon, F., Ferreira, F. H., & Lucchetti, L. (2007). Inequality of opportunity in Brazil. *Review of Income and Wealth, 53*(4), 583–604.

Brunori, P., Hufe, P., & Mahler, D. G. (2018a). *The roots of inequality: Estimating inequality of opportunity from regression trees* (World Bank Policy Research Working Paper, 8349).

Brunori, P., Hufe, P., & Mahler, P. (2018b). Machine learning methods in inequality measurement: An overview. *Journal of Economic Inequality, 16*(2), 145–168.

Brunori, P., Hufe, P., & Mahler, P. (2019a). Comparative analysis of inequality of opportunity using machine learning techniques. *Review of Income and Wealth, 65*(3), 523–548.

Brunori, P., Peragine, V., & Serlenga, L. (2019b). Upward and downward bias when measuring inequality of opportunity. *Social Choice and Welfare, 52*(4), 635–661.

Brunori, P., & Neidhofer, G. (2020). Conditional inference trees for inequality of opportunity analysis. *Economics Letters, 191*, 108799.

Cecchi, L., & Peragine, V. (2010). Measuring inequality of opportunity with generalized entropy measures. *Journal of Economic Inequality, 8*(4), 579–598.

Cohen, G. A. (1989). On the currency of egalitarian justice. *Ethics, 99*(4), 906–944.

Das, P., & Biswas, S. (2022). Social identity, gender and unequal opportunity of earning in urban India: 2017–2018 to 2019–2020. *The Indian Journal of Labour Economics, 65*(1), 39–57.

Deaton, A., & Dreze, J. (2002). Poverty and inequality in India: A re-examination. *Economic and Political Weekly, 37*(36), 3729–3748.

De Barros, R. P., Ferreira, F. H., & Sátyro, N. (2009a). *Measuring inequality of opportunity in Brazil*. Proceedings of the Annual Bank Conference on Development Economics.
De Barros, R. P., Ferreira, F., Vega, J., & Chanduvi, J. (2009b). *Measuring inequality of opportunities in Latin America and the Caribbean*. World Bank Publications.
Dworkin, R. (1981b). What is equality? Part 1: Equality of welfare. *Philosophy & Public Affairs, 10*(3), 185–246.
Dworkin, R. (1981c). What is equality? Part 2: Equality of resources. *Philosophy & Public Affairs, 10*(4), 283–345.
Ferreira, F. H., & Gignoux, J. (2008). The measurement of inequality of opportunity: Theory and an application to Latin America. *Review of Income and Wealth, 54*(4), 582–608.
Ferreira, F. H., & Gignoux, J. (2011). The measurement of inequality of opportunity: Theory and an application to Latin America. *Review of Income and Wealth, 57*(4), 627–646.
Ferreira, F. H., & Gignoux, J. (2014). A distributional analysis of the impact of inequality of opportunity on income inequality. *Journal of Economic Inequality, 12*(4), 433–455.
Fleurbaey, M. (1994). On fair compensation. *Theory and Decision, 36*(3), 277–307.
Fleurbaey, M., & Peragine, V. (2013a). Ex-ante and Ex-post approaches to inequality of opportunity. In A. B. Atkinson & F. Bourguignon (Eds.), *Handbook of income distribution* (Vol. 2, pp. 1120–1150). Elsevier.
Fleurbaey, M., & Peragine, V. (2013b). Inequality of opportunity. In A. B. Atkinson & F. Bourguignon (Eds.), *Handbook of income distribution* (Vol. 2, pp. 1225–1260). Elsevier.
Fleurbaey, M., & Schokkaert, E. (2009). Unfair inequality and the moral point of view. *The Journal of Political Philosophy, 17*(1), 1–25.
Hufe, P., Peichl, A., Roemer, J., & Ungerer, M. (2017). Inequality of income acquisition: The role of childhood circumstances. *Social Choice and Welfare, 49*(3), 499–544.
Lefranc, A., & Kundu, S. (2020). Machine learning approaches to inequality of opportunity measurement: A comparative study. *Applied Economics, 52*(16), 1723–1741.
Morelli, M., & Rohner, D. (2015). Economic inequality and political instability. *American Economic Review, 105*(5), 184–188.
Peragine, V. (2004a). Ranking income distributions according to equality of opportunity. *The Journal of Economic Inequality, 2*(1), 11–30.
Peragine, V. (2004b). The measurement of inequality of opportunity: A survey of the literature. In P. Anand, P. Segal, & J. E. Stiglitz (Eds.), *Choice, welfare and development: A festschrift in honour of Amartya Sen* (pp. 75–90). Oxford University Press.
Ramos, X., & Van de Gaer, D. (2016). Approaches to inequality of opportunity: Principles, measures and evidence. *Journal of Economic Surveys, 30*(5), 855–883.
Rawls, J. (1958). Justice as fairness. *The Journal of Philosophy, 35*(5), 185–225.
Rawls, J. (1971). *A theory of justice*. Harvard University Press.
Roemer, J. E. (1993). A pragmatic theory of responsibility for the egalitarian planner. *Philosophy & Public Affairs, 22*, 146–166.
Roemer, J. E. (1998). *Equality of opportunity*. Harvard University Press.
Roemer, J. E. (2002). Equality of opportunity: A progress report. *Social Choice and Welfare, 19*(2), 455–471.
Roemer, J. E., & Trannoy, A. (2016a). Equality of opportunity: Theory and measurement. *Journal of Economic Literature, 54*(4), 1288–1332.
Roemer, J. E., & Trannoy, A. (2016b). Equality of opportunity. In J. E. Roemer (Ed.), *Handbook of income distribution* (Vol. 2, pp. 217–300). Elsevier.
Sen, A. (1985). Well-being, agency and freedom: The Dewey lectures 1984. *The Journal of Philosophy, 82*(4), 169–221.
Sen, A. (1992). *Inequality re-examined*. Clarendon Press.
Sen, A. (1999). *Development as freedom*. Oxford University Press.
Shapley, L. S. (1953). A value for n-person games. In H. W. Kuhn & A. W. Tucker (Eds.), *Contributions to the theory of games* (Vol. 2, pp. 307–317). Princeton University Press.

Sharma, A. (2015). Economic reforms and inequality in India. *Economic and Political Weekly, 50*(30), 45–53.
Singh, A. (2012a). Inequality of opportunity in earnings and consumption expenditure: The case of Indian men. *Review of Income and Wealth, 58*(1), 79–106.
Singh, K. (2012b). Inequality of opportunity in India: An analysis of the impact of parental background on educational and labor market outcomes. *Indian Economic Review, 47*(2), 215–234.
Singh, A., & Mohapatra, S. (2019). Inequality of opportunity in consumption: Evidence from India. *Economic and Political Weekly, 54*(10), 42–49.
World Bank. (2016). *India development update: Financing double-digit growth.*
World Bank. (2021). *Fair progress? Economic mobility across generations around the world.*

Chapter 3
Decomposition of Inequality of Opportunity

3.1 Introduction

The interplay between economic growth and income distribution has been a central topic in economic research for several decades. A landmark study by Kuznets (1955) introduced the concept that as countries experience early stages of rapid economic growth, income inequality initially widens. This phenomenon occurs because the benefits of growth are not evenly distributed. However, as economies mature and achieve higher levels of income, the advantages of growth become more widely shared, leading to a reduction in income inequality. This creates an inverted U-shaped relationship between economic growth and inequality, known as Kuznets's inverted-U hypothesis. This hypothesis has sparked extensive debate and research. While some empirical studies support the inverted-U relationship, others challenge it. Critics argue that economic growth alone is insufficient to address poverty and inequality. Instead, they stress the need to differentiate between the 'growth effect' and the 'inequality effect' within an economy (Bourguignon, 2004; Ravallion & Chen, 2003). In the contemporary global context, many countries are grappling with this dual challenge of reducing poverty while addressing rising income inequality amid their growth trajectories.

Disclaimer: The presentation of material and details in maps used in this chapter does not imply the expression of any opinion whatsoever on the part of the Publisher or Author concerning the legal status of any country, area or territory or of its authorities, or concerning the delimitation of its borders. The depiction and use of boundaries, geographic names and related data shown on maps and included in lists, tables, documents, and databases in this chapter are not warranted to be error free nor do they necessarily imply official endorsement or acceptance by the Publisher or Author.

Earlier version of this chapter was published as a working paper by Institute for Human Development (IHD), and in the *Indian Journal of Labour Economics* (Mehta et al., 2023). Excerpts have been re-used here with permission.

B. S. Mehta et al., *Predicting Inequality of Opportunity and Poverty in India Using Machine Learning*, India Studies in Business and Economics,
https://doi.org/10.1007/978-981-96-2544-4_3

According to the latest World Inequality Report (WIR, 2022) by Chancel et al. (2022), income and wealth disparities have markedly increased since the 1980s. This rise in inequality is linked to various deregulation and liberalization policies implemented across different countries. The report highlights a widening gap between the rich and the poor: the wealthiest 10% of the global population now captures 52% of global income, while the poorest 50% own only 8.5%. Wealth inequality is even more pronounced, with the poorest 50% holding just 2% of total wealth, while the richest 10% control an astounding 76%. Although global income inequality between countries has reduced since the 1990s—evidenced by a significant reduction in the income gap between the richest and poorest countries—within-country inequalities have intensified. The income disparity between the richest 10% and the poorest 50% within countries has nearly doubled, from a ratio of 8.5–15 times. This trend is particularly evident in developing nations like India and China, which face the challenge of reducing inequality and poverty concurrently during periods of rapid economic growth.

India, in particular, has witnessed substantial economic growth over the past two decades, averaging an annual growth rate of 7% (Anand & Thampi, 2016; Chancel & Piketty, 2019). Despite this growth, income inequality has worsened. The benefits of economic progress have not been equitably distributed, leading to India being categorized as one of the 'most unequal countries in the world' (Chancel et al., 2022). Research by Chancel and Piketty (2019) reveals that the richest 10% of the Indian population holds 57% of the national income, whereas the poorest 50% hold only 13%. Household surveys show significant income disparity, with a Gini coefficient of 0.543 in 2012 (Anand & Thampi, 2016), and a higher Gini coefficient of 0.587 for per capita income among agricultural households in 2013. The Institute for Competitiveness's inequality report indicates a substantial divergence in earnings, with the cumulative annual earnings of the top 1% being nearly three times larger than those of the bottom 10%. Between 2017–18 and 2019–20, the share of income captured by the richest 1% increased from 6.1% to 6.8%, while the share of the poorest 50% remained stagnant at around 22%. During this period, the income of the richest 1% grew by 15%, and the income of the richest 10% rose by 8.1%, whereas the income of the poorest 10% declined by 1% (Chancel et al., 2022). These trends suggest that the concept of 'trickle-down economics' is not applicable in the Indian context. Studies have also highlighted the negative consequences of uneven growth processes in India. Anand and Thampi (2016) discuss the rising wealth inequality during the neoliberal era, and Chancel and Piketty (2019) emphasize the increase in the income share of the wealthiest 1%. Deaton and Stone (2013) argue that when income is concentrated at the top without a simultaneous rise in average income levels at the bottom, income inequality inevitably increases.

In India, rising income inequality is not merely a result of skewed income distribution but is also driven by entrenched social disparities and hierarchies. The persistence of resource inequalities, such as land ownership and income, along with ongoing caste-based discrimination, exacerbates this issue (Tagade et al., 2018). Gender disparities are evident in women's limited participation in the labour market and the disproportionate burden of unpaid work (Ghose, 2021). Additionally, rural–urban wage gaps and gender-based wage disparities highlight persistent gender discrimination (Deshpande et al., 2018; IHD, 2014). Addressing these issues is crucial for creating a society that ensures equal opportunities for all individuals, bridges gaps between identity groups, and provides greater representation for historically marginalized populations (Weisskopf, 2011).

In rapidly growing countries like India, the persistent trend of rising income inequality has prompted increased research to identify its main causes. There is a consensus that equal opportunities for success are vital. Literature also highlights the connection between inequality of opportunity (IOp) and income inequality, particularly with the growing accumulation of income at the top where inheritances are more prevalent (Piketty, 2011; Piketty & Zucman, 2015). As discussed in Chapters 1 and 2, Roemer (1998) argues that IOp results from the interplay between 'circumstances' and the 'efforts' exerted by individuals (also discussed in detail later section). The study of IOp has gained prominence in empirical research, focusing on the unfair aspects of societal inequality (Brunori & Neidhöfer, 2021a; Brunori et al., 2019; Checchi & Peragine, 2010; Ferreira & Gignoux, 2011; Ferreira & Peragine, 2015; Fleurbaey, 2008; Hothorn & Zeileis, 2021; Roemer & Trannoy, 2016; Salas-Rojo & Rodríguez, 2022).

Most research on IOp has primarily concentrated on developed nations, with comparatively limited attention given to developing countries like India. Addressing inequality in India necessitates substantial redistribution of income and wealth due to the country's pronounced social and spatial inequalities. Historical and socio-cultural factors—such as social groups, religions, locations, and geographical regions—have contributed to a fragmented society in India, resulting in unequal privileges across different groups (Das & Biswas, 2022; Singh, 2012). Moreover, gender disparities further exacerbate this inequality at the individual level. Some select studies have assessed IOp in India by analysing consumption and earnings while considering various circumstances such as social groups, gender, place of birth, rural versus urban locations, parental education, and occupation (Asadullah & Yalonetzky, 2012; Choudhary et al., 2019; Das & Biswas, 2022; Lefranc & Kundu, 2020; Motiram, 2018). These studies highlight that a significant portion of income or consumption inequality is attributable to unequal circumstances, with parental education emerging as a crucial determinant as also highlighted in Chapter 2. However, many of these studies rely on statistical assumptions and potentially biased or arbitrary model selection approaches. Notably, the empirical research to date has often overlooked the role of effort—a critical component of Roemer's theory (Ramos & Van de Gaer, 2021). Incorporating effort into IOp estimates would offer a more nuanced understanding of the factors influencing inequality and help shape more effective policy interventions aimed at reducing it. This chapter aims to explore this aspect of IOp in detail through a case study of India.

The structure of the rest of the chapter is as follows: Sect. 3.2 outlines the conceptual framework and methodology, while Sect. 3.3 delves into the measurement approaches for IOp. Section 3.4 provides details on the data sources and variables utilized in the analysis. Section 3.5 presents descriptive statistics of the sample, discusses the results, and explores key variables contributing to IOp through conditional inference regression trees and transformation trees. Finally, Sect. 3.6 concludes the chapter by summarizing the main findings and offering policy recommendations.

3.2 Conceptual Framework

John Rawls (1958a, 1958b, 1971) argued that justice in an egalitarian society could be achieved through the principle of equality of opportunity, often represented by metaphors such as 'leveling the playing field' or 'equality at the starting gate.' In Rawls' vision of a just society, individuals are granted fair and equal chances to pursue their interests, with a particular focus on 'primary goods'. This ethical justification for equality of opportunity spurred significant philosophical debate and reshaped the understanding of equality (Arneson, 1989; Cohen, 1989; Dworkin, 1981a, 1981b; Sen, 1980). Building on Rawls' work, Roemer (1993, 1998) and Fleurbaey (1995, 2008) developed a systematic approach to measuring inequality of opportunity (IOp). They identified two main factors influencing individuals' outcomes: effort and circumstances.

Effort refers to variables within an individual's control, such as the hours devoted to work or study, the quality of their work, and their occupational choices. Circumstances, in contrast, include factors beyond individual control, such as family background, socio-economic status, ethnicity, gender, and age (Roemer & Trannoy, 2016). Mathematically, this relationship can be expressed as follows: In a population of individuals indexed from $1, \ldots N$, the outcome of individual I, denoted as y_i, as a result of the interaction between circumstances (C_i) and effort (e_i).

$$y_i = g(C_i, e_i), \quad \forall i = 1, \ldots N \tag{3.1}$$

In this Eq. (3.1), the function g represents how circumstances and effort collectively determine the outcome for each individual.

Roemer's framework for achieving equality of opportunity involves categorizing the population into groups based on circumstances (types) and effort levels (tranches). Types are defined so that individuals within the same type share identical circumstances, while individuals within the same tranche exhibit similar effort levels. Under this framework, equal opportunity requires that individuals within the same type have equal potential to convert resources into outcomes, making it essential to address between-type inequality while disregarding within-type variability due to individual effort (Roemer, 2002).

As discussed in Chapter 2, the literature on IOp frequently discusses two ethical principles: the 'compensation' principle and the 'reward' principle. The compensation principle advocates for addressing inequalities arising from circumstances, while the reward principle emphasizes individual responsibility, suggesting that higher outcomes should be awarded for greater effort (Plassot et al., 2022). The reward principle accepts variations in outcomes based on effort, whereas the compensation principle focuses on rectifying unjust inequalities. The compensation principle can be approached through either the ex-ante or ex-post method (Fleurbaey & Peragine, 2013; Plassot et al., 2022). The ex-ante approach addresses inequalities between individuals of different circumstances or types, while the ex-post approach focuses on individuals with the same effort levels or tranches. These differing approaches arise from varying perspectives on the nature of effort (Fleurbaey & Peragine, 2013; Ramos & Van de Gaer, 2016).

In the ex-post approach, equality of opportunity is realized when individuals who exert the same effort achieve the same outcome, regardless of their type. This principle is assessed by comparing outcomes of individuals with the same effort but different circumstances (Brunori & Neidhöfer, 2021a, 2021b). Given that effort is often unobservable, Roemer (2002) proposed a method based on three key assumptions: firstly, individuals are categorized into types; secondly, outcomes increase monotonically with effort. This means that higher effort within each type should correspond to better outcomes, mathematically expressed as:

$$y^k(e_i) \geq y^k(e_j) \Leftrightarrow e_i^k \geq e_j^k, \quad \forall k = 1, \ldots K; \; \forall e_i, e_j \in R \tag{3.2}$$

where $y^k(e_i)$ denotes the outcome of an individual in type k with degree of effort i represented by e_i, while by $y^k(e_j)$ indicate the outcome of individual in type k with degree of effort j represented by e_j, and K signifies the total number of types. It is assumed that the distribution of effort is a characteristic of the type, meaning that when comparing efforts across individuals in different types, adjustments should be made to account for the fact that these efforts are drawn from different distributions, for which individuals should not be held responsible.

Roemer distinguishes between 'level of effort' and 'degree of effort'. The 'degree of effort' is a morally relevant measure, identified as the quantile of the effort distribution for the specific type to which an individual belongs. The assumption is that all circumstances are identified and are exogenous to individual control. If different types face varied incentives and constraints in exerting effort, this is considered a characteristic of the type, falling under circumstances beyond individual control (Brunori et al., 2023). For instance, a student with educated parents might find it easier to dedicate long hours to studying compared to a student from a less favourable background.

The distribution of effort within type k and quantiles $\pi \in [0, 1]$ is denoted as $G^k(e)$.. When effort is unobservable but the outcome monotonically increases with effort, Roemer suggests defining the 'degree of effort' by the quantile position in the type-specific outcome distribution (y), represented as $y^k G^k(e) = y^k(\pi)$. This definition adjusts for differences in absolute effort levels, allowing for comparison across types. This requirement that outcomes should be identical for individuals exerting the same effort is expressed as:

$$y^k(\pi) = y^l(\pi) \Leftrightarrow F^k(y) = F^l(y), \quad \forall k, l = 1, \ldots K, \text{ and } \pi \in [0, 1] \tag{3.3}$$

where $F^k(y)$ denotes the type-specific cumulative distribution of outcomes in type k.

Checchi and Peragine (2010) and Ferreira and Gignoux (2011) propose an ex-post IOp measure that evaluates inequality within a standardized distribution. This measure accounts for variability in outcomes among individuals exerting the same effort. When Eq. (3.3) is satisfied, indicating that individuals with the same effort achieve the same outcome, the measure equals zero. As disparities in outcomes among similarly exerted efforts increase, the IOp measure rises accordingly. The standardized distribution, $\overline{\mathrm{Y}}_{\mathrm{EP}}$, is computed by replacing individual outcomes with standardized values, as:

$$\acute{y}_i^k(\pi) = y_i^k(\pi)\frac{\mu}{\mu^\pi}, \quad \forall i = 1, \ldots N;\ k = 1, \ldots K;\ \forall \pi \in [0, 1] \tag{3.4}$$

where $y_i^k(\pi)$ represents the outcome of individual i in the type k at quantile π of the type-specific effort distribution, μ^π denotes the average outcome of individuals at quantile π across all types, and μ is the population mean outcome. In the standardized distribution, the average value for individuals in all the quantiles is uniform, eliminating between quantile inequality, while preserving relative distance within-quantile. Hence, the ex-post measure of IOp, is given by:

$$\text{Ex-post IOp}_{\mathrm{EP}} = I(\overline{\mathrm{Y}}_{\mathrm{EP}}) \tag{3.5}$$

where I is an inequality measure satisfying standard properties, including scale invariance. Notably, ex-post measures of IOp are less commonly used in empirical studies compared to ex-ante measures. The ex-ante IOp measure, proposed by Van de Gaer (1993), also known as the 'weak equality of opportunity' criterion, allows for some within-group inequality but requires that mean advantage levels are equal across types (Ferreira & Gignoux, 2011). This approach defines the opportunity set for each type by the type-specific outcome distribution. The value of the opportunity set for each type is determined by the mean outcome of that type. Consequently, in this framework, IOp is essentially the inequality between types. The counterfactual distribution, denoted as $\bar{\mathrm{Y}}_{\mathrm{EA}}$, is derived by substituting individual outcomes with the mean outcome, expressed as:

$$\acute{y}_i^k(\pi) = \mu^k, \quad \forall i = 1, \ldots N;\ \forall k = 1, \ldots K;\ \forall i, \pi \in [0, 1] \tag{3.6}$$

where μ^{k} represents the mean outcome of type k. Thus, the ex-ante IOp is given by:

$$\text{Ex-ante IOp}_{\mathrm{EA}} = I(\acute{y}_{\mathrm{EA}}) \tag{3.7}$$

These measures offer different perspectives on IOp. The ex-post measure focuses on within-group inequality among individuals exerting the same effort while the ex-ante measure examine inequality between types based on average advantage levels.

3.3 Measurement Approaches for Estimating IOp: Data-Driven Machine Learning Techniques

Traditional methods for measuring IOp often face significant limitations, such as the researcher's discretion in selecting variables related to circumstances or effort. This subjective selection process can lead to the exclusion of relevant variables or the inclusion of too many, resulting in biased estimates. Omitting important variables can reduce the model's explanatory power and lead to downward-biased estimates, while including excessive variables may produce upward-biased estimates (Brunori et al., 2019; Ferreira & Gignoux, 2011; Hufe et al., 2017). Machine learning (ML) algorithms provide a promising alternative for measuring IOp by adhering to a data-driven approach. These algorithms minimize arbitrary and ad-hoc selections, thereby reducing the risk of bias. They also standardize the approach to balancing upward and downward biases (Brunori & Neidhöfer, 2021a, 2021b; Brunori et al., 2019; Hothorn & Zeileis, 2021; Hothorn et al., 2006; Salas-Rojo & Rodríguez, 2022).

In this chapter, the ML algorithms employed to estimate IOp using both ex-ante and ex-post approaches. Specifically, the conditional inference regression tree and conditional inference forest algorithms are used to estimate ex-ante IOp, and the transformation tree algorithm for ex-post IOp. These ML techniques help identify types and the degree of effort needed to calculate IOp through both approaches. It is important to note that the first step in both the ex-ante and ex-post approaches is the identification of types by dividing the sample into subgroups with identical circumstances (Brunori et al., 2023, p. 8).

3.3.1 Identification of Types: Conditional Inference Tree and Conditional Inference Forest

The identification of types based on individual circumstances is crucial for empirical analyses of Inequality of Opportunity (IOp) (Brunori et al., 2019; Ferreira & Gignoux, 2011). To facilitate this, data-driven machine learning algorithms such as conditional inference trees and conditional inference forests are utilized (Brunori & Neidhöfer, 2021a, 2021b). These techniques have been extensively employed in recent empirical studies (Brunori & Neidhöfer, 2021a, 2021b; Brunori et al., 2018, 2019; Lefranc & Kundu, 2020).

Conditional inference trees provide a visually intuitive representation of the structure of opportunities by recursively splitting the range of circumstances and identifying subgroups with similar characteristics. Conditional inference forests, an extension of the conditional inference tree created through bootstrapping, enhance the reliability of IOp estimates by aggregating multiple trees. A key feature of conditional inference forests is their ability to determine the relative importance of factors beyond the structure of the tree.

The algorithm for conditional inference trees involves two stages: (i) selection of the initial splitting circumstance and (ii) growth of the opportunity tree. In the first stage, a hypothesis test (typically a t-test) is performed before each split to assess whether equal opportunities exist within a given sample or subsample. If a split is not warranted (p-value > significance level α), the null hypothesis of equal opportunity is not rejected or it fails to reject null hypothesis. This occurs when the p-value associated with the circumstance being considered (C*) is greater than a pre-determined significance level (α). Conversely, if a split is justified (p-value < α), the selected circumstance (C*) becomes the splitting variable, and the algorithm continues to grow the tree. This process generates a hierarchical arrangement of circumstances, reflecting significant associations with the outcome. The terminal nodes represent the average predicted outcome for each type or group, while internal nodes and branches illustrate the predictor space divisions. The final prediction is the average outcome of each identified group or type.

The conditional inference forest algorithm generates multiple conditional inference trees and combines their results by averaging. The repetitive extraction of subsamples ensures the independence of each tree, resulting in diverse estimates for each subsample. Each tree follows the same two-step structure as the conditional inference tree.

3.3.2 *Identification of Tranches of Effort Degrees: Transformation Trees*

Conditional inference trees and forests primarily estimate the mean differences between types to compute IOp, overlooking higher moments of the within-type distribution and the importance of effort ranks. To address these limitations, the Transformation Tree (TrT) model is employed. This ex-post method uses an algorithm that estimates the outcome distribution within each type using Bernstein polynomial coefficients.[1] The TrT model predicts the shape of the outcome distribution by partitioning the regressors' space and identifying heterogeneity among the distributions defining each type. The process involves estimating the unconditional distribution and searching for binary splitting variables. Splitting is permitted if the resulting conditional distributions exhibit sufficient shape dissimilarity. The distribution shape is approximated using a linear combination of Bernstein basis polynomials, defined as:

$$B_m(\mathrm{y, a, z}) = \sum_{i=0}^{m} \beta_i b_{j,m}(\mathrm{y, a, z}) \tag{3.8}$$

[1] It is widely used in computer graphics to model smooth curves (Farouki, 2012). It outperforms competitors such as kernel estimators, in approximating distribution function (Leblanc, 2012).

For a Bernstein polynomial of order m, $m + 1$ parameters define the shape of the objective distribution. The TrT algorithm involves: (i) setting a confidence level (α) and a polynomial order (m); (ii) estimating the unconditional distribution using Bernstein polynomial approximation; (iii) testing for parameter stability for all possible partitions based on the regressors and storing the p-values. If the parameters are stable (Bonferroni-adjusted p-value > α), the conditional distributions fall into the same terminal node. If unstable (p-value < α), a binary split occurs, and the process repeats until stability is achieved. The TrT generates groups or types, with Bernstein polynomials interpolating the shape of the distributions.

To estimate IOp, each individual's outcome value ($\acute{y}_i^{p,t}$) is multiplied by the ratio of the population mean (μ^p) to the mean within the respective quantile ($\mu^{p,t}$) to obtain the adjusted value. IOp is then measured using any inequality measure applied to the adjusted values. It is denoted as:

$$\acute{y}_i^{p,t} = \mu^{p,t}/\mu^p \quad \forall i, p, t \tag{3.9}$$

IOp is estimated with any inequality measure applied over $\acute{y}_i^{p,t}$.

3.3.3 Decomposition of IOp Measure

The Shapley decomposition method, based on Shapley value in cooperative game theory (Shapley, 1953), estimates the relative contribution of various factors or circumstances to total income IOp also used in Chapter 2. Shapley values are order-independent and compute the value of a function considering all possible combinations of circumstances. The functional form of the index is:

$$\text{IOP} = f(X_{11} \ldots X_{N_1 1}, X_{12} \ldots X_{N_1 2}, X_{13} \ldots X_{N_1 3}) \tag{3.10}$$

where X_{ij} denotes the income of ith individual ($i = 1, \ldots N_j$), within the subgroup $j = 1, 2, 3$.

Additive decomposition considers the impact of inequality within subgroups, between subgroups, ranking, and relative size within each subgroup. Shapley decomposition derives the marginal impact of each circumstance by measuring the difference in the inequality index value between the observed situation and a reference scenario where income does not change with the circumstance (Das & Biswas, 2022).

3.4 Data Sources and Variables

This paper utilizes data from the annual Periodic Labour Force Survey (PLFS) for the year 2022–23 to calculate income Inequality of Opportunity (IOp). The PLFS, conducted by the National Statistics Office (NSO), is a cross-sectional survey representative at both national and state levels. The analysis focuses on household per capita labour income (MPCI), used as a proxy for households' income, which is computed by aggregating the monthly income of regular, self-employed, and casual wage workers within a household and dividing it by the household size. For casual wage workers, the PLFS provides weekly income data, which has been converted into monthly figures. Regular salaried and self-employed individuals' income data are reported monthly. In addition, the monthly per capital expenditure (MPCE) also used in the analysis for comparison with MPCI.

The PLFS data include several circumstances variables: parents' education levels (categorized as no education, primary, secondary, higher secondary, and graduate or above); parents' occupations (classified into non-routine cognitive/high skilled, routine cognitive/medium skilled, non-routine manual/low skilled, and routine manual/unskilled); social group (scheduled caste (SC), scheduled tribes (ST), other backward classes (OBC), and general caste (GC)); gender (male and female); place of birth or region (north, east, central, northeast, south, and west); and location (rural and urban).

A sample of 80,155 individuals with parental information, selected from a total of 419,512 covered in the PLFS 2022–23, has been used for analysis. This sample includes only individuals with available parental background information and is restricted to working-age individuals (15–64 years old). Detailed procedures for sample and variable selection are outlined in Appendix 1 in the previous chapter.

3.5 Results and Discussion

3.5.1 *Sample Profile*

Table 3.1 provides an overview of the sample's demographic characteristics, region, gender, social group, and employment status. The majority of the sample resides in rural areas. Geographically, a quarter of the sample is from the central region, with one-fifth from the eastern and southern regions. The northern and northeastern regions have smaller representations, with around 14.5% and 3.7%, respectively. Males constitute 70% of the sample, while females make up 30%. Approximately 44% of individuals belong to OBC, followed by GC (28%), SC (20%), and ST (9%). Nearly half of the sample is involved in self-employment, about one-third in regular salaried positions, and one-fourth in casual wage work.

Table 3.1 Characteristics of sample individuals (in %)

		%
Sector	Rural	62.5
	Urban	37.5
Region	North	17.8
	East	17.3
	Central	21.6
	North East	14.5
	South	17.2
	West	11.5
Social group	ST	15.9
	SC	18.5
	OBC	41.4
	GC	24.3
Gender	Male	66.1
	Female	33.9
Status of Employment	Self-employment	46.8
	Regular salaried	31.0
	Casual labour	22.2
Total		100.0

Source Authors calculations from PLFS, 2022–23

Table 3.2 outlines the educational qualifications and occupations of the sampled individuals. A larger proportion of them have secondary or higher secondary education, while a smaller percentage have graduate-level education or are illiterate. Regarding the occupations, nearly three-fourth of the sampled individuals engaged in non-routine manual low-skilled jobs, with about one-fifth in routine manual unskilled jobs. On the other hand, only few are engaged in non-routine cognitive high-skilled jobs (5.4%) or routine cognitive medium-skilled jobs (2.2%).

Table 3.3 highlights notable differences in average MPCI of the sample households between urban and rural areas. The households in urban areas exhibit significantly higher average MPCI compared to rural areas, suggesting higher income levels in urban regions. Additionally, the average MPCI varies across social groups, with households belonging to the General Category (GC) having the highest average MPCI, followed by Other Backward Classes (OBC), Scheduled Castes (SC), and Scheduled Tribes (ST). The households in urban areas have relatively higher median value and standard deviation than others.

Table 3.4 presents data on the association between individual's education, occupation, geographical locations, with their household MPCI. The findings reveal substantial differences in average MPCI based on these factors. Individuals with graduate-level educational qualification have nearly two and a half times higher average household level MPCI compared to those without education. The average household MPCI

Table 3.2 Educational qualifications and occupations of the sample (in %)

		%
Education levels	No education	26.3
	Below secondary	49.0
	Secondary/higher secondary	17.4
	Graduate and above	7.3
Occupation by skill levels	Non-routine cognitive (high skilled)	5.4
	Routine cognitive (medium skilled)	2.2
	Non-routine manual (low skilled)	68.7
	Routine manual (unskilled)	23.7
Total		100.0

Source Authors calculations from PLFS, 2022–23

Table 3.3 Per capita household income (MPCI) of the sample

		Mean	Median	SD
Sector	Rural	4030	3284	3039
	Urban	6524	5000	5891
Social group	ST	4720	3536	3993
	SC	4391	3600	3433
	OBC	4691	3700	4118
	GC	6028	4500	5790
Total		4965	3800	4498

Source Authors calculations from PLFS, 2022–23

is also significantly higher for individuals with graduate-level education compared to those with below secondary education or secondary and higher secondary education. Similarly, individuals engaged in high and medium-skilled jobs exhibit significantly higher average household MPCI compared to those involved in low-skilled and unskilled manual jobs. Furthermore, the median value and standard deviation among graduates, those engaged in highly skilled jobs, and sample individuals from the southern regions is relatively higher compared to those from others.

In sum, the sample characteristics provide valuable insights into the factors contributing to variations in household MPCI. Key factors influencing these differences include caste or social groups, sector (rural–urban), education, occupational status, and geographical locations. Categories associated with higher average MPCI values exhibit notable characteristics in terms of median value and standard deviation. Urban areas, southern regions, highly educated individuals, and those from the General and OBC social groups show significantly higher levels of variability, suggesting diverse economic conditions, and opportunities.

Table 3.4 MPCE (in Rs.) by education, occupation, and geographical regions

		Mean	Median	SD
Educational levels	No education	3796	3200	2679
	Below secondary	4457	3700	3117
	Secondary/higher secondary	5864	4545	4805
	Graduate and above	10,412	8000	9607
Occupation by skill levels	Non-routine cognitive (high skilled)	11,410	9000	10,509
	Routine cognitive (medium skilled)	9503	7125	7771
	Non-routine manual (low skilled)	4693	3750	3699
	Routine manual (unskilled)	4083	3442	2925
Region	North	5259	4000	5136
	East	3922	3100	3415
	Central	3527	2800	3018
	North East	5890	4786	4169
	South	6463	5125	5495
	West	5363	4144	4783
Total		4965	3800	4498

Source Authors calculations from PLFS, 2022–23

3.5.2 Ex-ante Inequality of Opportunity

This section presents a comparative analysis of ex-ante Inequality of Opportunity (IOp) results for MPCI (income henceforth) using three distinct approaches: the parametric approach, the conditional inference tree approach, and the conditional forest approach. The parametric approach employs ordinary least squares (OLS) regression to estimate IOp measures for income, modeling the relationship between outcome variables and various circumstances, while accounting for potential confounding factors. This regression analysis helps identify factors significantly contributing to IOp in terms of income.

Parametric Approach: The parametric approach, based on methodologies by Ferreira and Gignoux (2014) and Wendelspiess and Soloaga (2014), utilizes an OLS regression model where MPCI serves as the dependent variable. Sector, gender, caste, parental occupations, parental education, and regions are considered explanatory or circumstance variables. Using the estimated coefficients from the regression, a counterfactual distribution is derived, enabling the decomposition of MPCI inequality

Table 3.5 Parametric: ex-ante income IOp

	Types/IOp
Types	1536
Overall Gini	0.392
Absolute Gini	0.248
Relative IOp	0.632

Source Authors' calculations from PLFS, 2022–23

within the sample population. The Gini coefficient[2] of the predicted income values from the regression provides an absolute measure of IOp, while a relative measure of IOp is obtained by dividing the absolute Gini measure of IOp by the overall Gini measure of inequality.

Table 3.5 shows the results of the parametric approach, with 1536 types representing groups of the sample population with similar circumstances. The overall income inequality is estimated at 0.392, indicating moderate inequality. The opportunity Gini coefficient from the parametric approach is 0.248, suggesting that differences in average income among the 1536 subgroups are lower than the overall Gini coefficient, indicating relatively smaller inequality within these subgroups. The relative IOp is estimated at 0.632, meaning that around 63% of overall income inequality can be attributed to circumstances such as sector, gender, caste, parental occupations, parental education, and regions.

Conditional Inference Tree: As mentioned earlier, tree algorithms divide a dataset into mutually exclusive groups of observations based on sequential and hierarchical criteria. Once all the partitions are completed, the algorithm assigns the average value of the dependent variable to each observation (Salas-Rojo & Rodríguez, 2022). However, one of the main drawbacks of tree-based algorithms is their strong reliance on various factors, including the chosen alpha level, which determines the threshold for accepting or rejecting the null hypothesis. To address this issue, the Grid Search Cross-Validation method has been utilized to obtain an endogenously tuned alpha level (Table 3.9). The alpha level with the lowest root mean squared error (RMSE) is 0.07. The results at an alpha level of 0.07 are also compared with standard measures of alpha ranging from 1% to 5%, as detailed in Appendix "1".

Table 3.6 presents the results based on a conditional inference tree using an endogenously chosen alpha level. The opportunity Gini coefficient for IOp is calculated to be 0.208, indicating that differences in average income among the 16 subgroups of the sample population are significantly less than the overall income inequality. The relative IOp using the conditional inference tree approach is estimated to be 0.532. This suggests that around 53% of the overall income inequality is attributable to various circumstances such as sector, gender, caste, parents' occupations, parents' education, and regions. Nevertheless, the relative IOp estimates

[2] Unlike Chapter 2, which uses the Mean Log Deviation (MLD) for measuring IOp, this chapter uses Gini coefficient to calculate ex-ante and ex-post IOp, for this reason the ex-ante IOp measures for MPCI might not match in Chapter 2 and this chapter.

obtained from the conditional inference tree method are comparatively lower than those obtained from the parametric method. This difference can be attributed to the machine learning (ML) algorithm used in the conditional inference tree method, which automatically generates a smaller number of types compared to the parametric estimates. These types correspond to distinct circumstances contributing to inequality and consequently provide a more robust measure of relative IOp compared to the parametric approach.

Additionally, the conditional inference tree graphically illustrates the key circumstances that influence income IOp, as shown in Fig. 3.1. The results show that parents' education is the most important circumstance determining earnings or income IOp, as indicated by the initial node in Fig. 3.1. Individuals with parents having a graduate or higher level of education tend to have lower income IOp compared to those whose parents are educated below graduate level. For individuals whose parents' education level is graduate or above, parents' occupation becomes the second most important variable in determining income IOp, whereas for individuals whose parents are educated below the graduate level or not educated at all, region becomes the second most important variable, followed by sector as the third most important variable in determining income IOp.

In the case of individuals with parents educated upto the graduate or above level and parents in medium or high-skilled jobs, region becomes the third most important variable in determining income IOp. Those residing in the north, south, and west of India have lower income IOp compared to individuals in the east, central, and northeast India. In both regional groups, individuals in urban areas have lower income IOp compared to their rural counterparts. In the case of individuals with graduate or above-educated parents in low and unskilled jobs, sector becomes the third most important variable in determining income IOp. Individuals in urban areas have lower income IOp compared to those in rural areas. Additionally, in urban areas, individuals from the north, northeast, and south have lower income IOp compared to individuals in the east, central, and western India. In rural areas, individuals from the northeast parts of India have lower income IOp compared to those from all other regions.

Conditional Inference Forests: To address the sensitivity or high variance inherent in the conditional inference trees approach, a more robust approach of conditional inference forests has been proposed by Hothorn et al. (2006) and Brunori et al. (2023). Conditional inference forests employ bootstrapping within the ML framework. In this approach, multiple conditional inference trees are generated, and the final prediction

Table 3.6 Conditional inference tree: ex-ante income IOp

	Types/IOp
Types	16
Overall Gini	0.392
Absolute Gini	0.208
Relative IOp	0.532

Source Authors' calculations from PLFS, 2022–23

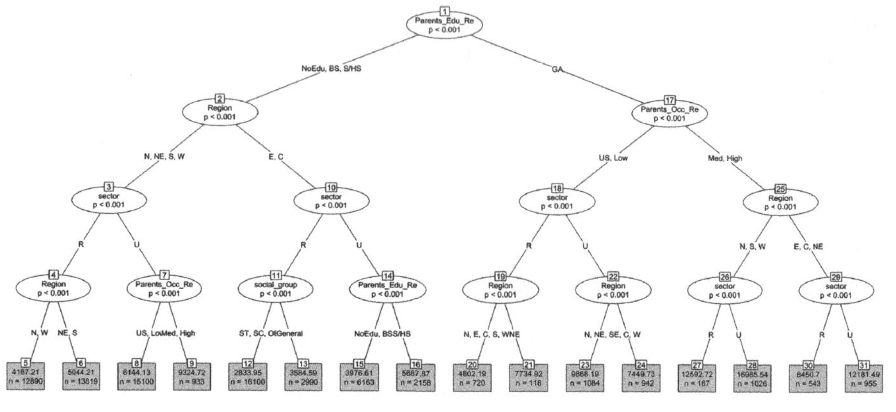

Fig. 3.1 Conditional inference tree for MPCI. *Note* R: Rural; U: Urban; N: North; NE: North East; S: South; W:West:E: East; C: Central; Sec/HS: Secondary/Higher Secondary; GradAbv: Graduate and Above; NoEdu: Illiterate or Nor Formal Schooling; BS: Below Secondary; US: Unskilled; Low: Low Skilled; Med: Medium Skill; High: High Skilled; M: Male; F: Female. *Source* Authors' calculations from PLFS, 2022–23

is obtained by averaging the predictions of all the trees. The use of subsamples ensures that each tree provides an independent estimate (Salas-Rojo & Rodríguez, 2022, p. 36). Similar to the conditional inference tree, an endogenous level of alpha has been obtained by Grid Search Cross-Validation method to determine the appropriate combination of the number of trees for the analysis. The level of alpha with the lowest RMSE is 0.06. The results obtained at 0.06% level are also compared with standard measures of alpha ranging from 1% to 5% (see Table 3.10 for detail).

Table 3.7 shows the results based on conditional inference forest using an endogenously chosen alpha level. The opportunity Gini coefficient for income IOp is estimated to be 0.190. This means that the difference in average income among the 16 subgroups of the sample population is significantly less than the overall income inequality, but slightly higher compared to the result obtained from the conditional inference tree. The relative IOp measured using the conditional inference forest approach is estimated to be 0.486. This suggests that around 48% of the overall income inequality is attributed to various circumstances such as sector, gender, caste, parents' occupations, parents' education, and regions. This relative IOp estimate obtained from the conditional inference forest method is marginally lower than those obtained from the conditional inference tree method. This difference can be credited to the bootstrapping within the ML algorithm used in the conditional inference forest method. This technique helps address the sensitivity or high variance inherent in the conditional inference tree. Consequently, this method provides a more robust measure of relative IOp compared to the conditional inference tree and parametric approach.

Ex-Ante Shapley Value Decomposition: The ex-ante decomposition exercise presented in Fig. 3.2 provides insights into the importance of different circumstance

Table 3.7 Conditional inference forest: ex-ante IOp Results

	Types/IOp
Types	16
Overall Gini	0.392
Absolute Gini	0.190
Relative IOp	0.486

Source Authors' calculations from PLFS, 2022–23

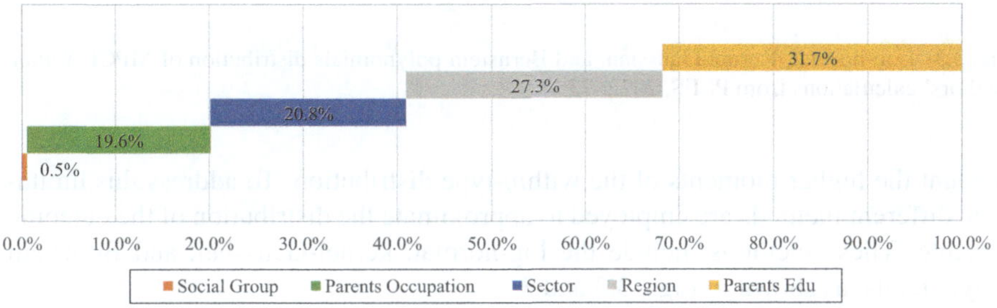

Fig. 3.2 Decomposition of factors contributing to ex-ante IOp (in %). *Source* Authors' calculations from PLFS, 2022–23

variables in contributing to income IOp. The analysis reveals the relative significance of each factor in explaining the observed variations in income IOp. Among the circumstance variables, the education of parents emerges as the most important factor, accounting for the largest share of income IOp at 31.7%. This suggests that the educational background and qualification of parents have a substantial impact on income IOp. The geographical location or region of individuals, with a contribution of 27.3%, is the second key factor, indicating that regional disparities in economic development and access to resources can significantly impact income levels. The sector (20.8%) and parents' occupation (19.6%) also play a vital role in shaping income IOp. This indicates that disparities in employment opportunities between rural and urban areas, as well as the occupation of parents, play an important role, reflecting the influence of employment opportunities and earnings across occupations based on skill level on income disparities. Social groups, although relatively less influential, also contribute to income IOp.

3.5.3 Ex-post Inequality of Opportunity

As previously discussed, the estimation of IOp using conventional parametric, non-parametric, and data-driven conditional inference tree ML techniques is primarily based on the mean difference between types. These methods do not take into

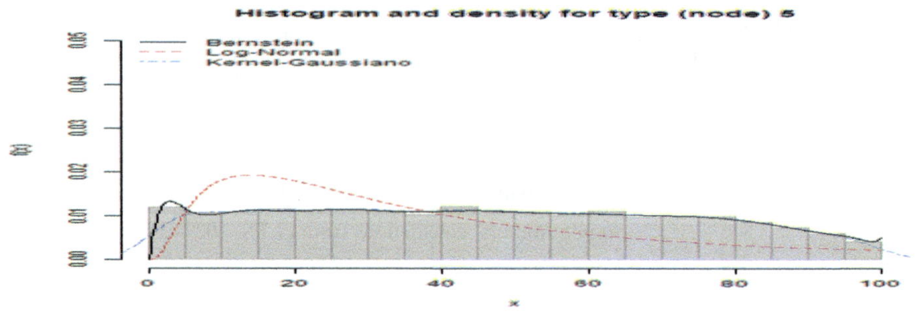

Fig. 3.3 Log-normal, Kernel-Gaussian, and Bernstein polynomials distribution of MPCI. *Source* Authors' calculations from PLFS, 2022–23

account the higher moments of the within-type distribution. To address this limitation, different methods are employed to approximate the distribution of the outcome variable. These methods include the log-normal, kernel-Gaussian, and Bernstein polynomials, as shown in Figs. 3.3 and 3.7.

Among these methods, the Bernstein polynomials are found to be more flexible in predicting the distribution of outcomes within each type. These polynomials enable a more accurate representation of the underlying distribution, capturing higher moments beyond the mean difference. By utilizing the Bernstein polynomials, the degree of effort or ex-post IOp can be measured following the approach proposed by Brunori and Neidhöfer (2021a, 2021b). The ex-ante approach focuses on the mean of each type, while the ex-post approach examines the distribution functions of each type. Instead of examining statistically significant differences between means, the ex-post approach identifies the most statistically significant differences between the full expected conditional distribution functions.

Transformation Tree: As previously mentioned, conditional inference trees and conditional inference forests select partitions based on differences in a single statistic of interest within each type, specifically the mean of the conditional outcome distribution (Brunori et al., 2023). In contrast, the transformation tree (TrT) approach utilizes splits or partitions based on differences across multiple functions of distribution, including variance, skewness, and kurtosis (Hothorn & Zeileis, 2021). In this paper, the TrT approach is employed to analyse the effects of different variables on the conditional outcome (MPCI or income) distribution. It reveals the configuration of variables that strongly influence the distribution and provides insights into specific conditional outcome distributions (Hothorn, 2018).

The TrT demonstrates the distributions obtained after applying the Bernstein polynomial transformation. For this study, the Bernstein polynomial of order 5 is used to transform the outcome variables, and a transformation tree model is employed to predict the types for each data point for ex-post income IOp analysis. The model predicts the income quantile position of each individual within each type to determine the 'degree of effort'. Based on these income quantile positions, the mean outcome value for each quantile, as well as the population mean, are determined.

Table 3.8 Transformation tree: ex-post IOp results

	Types/IOp
Types	16
Overall Gini	0.392
Absolute Gini	0.133
Relative IOp	0.339

Source Authors' calculations from PLFS, 2022–23

The individual's outcome value is adjusted using the ratio of the population mean to the quantile mean, enabling the measurement of ex-post IOp. As shown in Table 3.6, the number of types generated by the transformation trees is 16. The overall Gini inequality in the ex-post approach is 0.392, indicating a moderate level of inequality among the sample population. However, IOp measures for income in the ex-post approach yield relatively smaller values compared to the ex-ante approach. The estimated opportunity Gini coefficient is 0.133, and the relative IOp value is 0.339. This indicates that around 34% of the overall income inequality is attributed to differences in the degree of effort. These results suggest that the ex-post IOp measures, which consider the entire distribution functions obtained through the transformation trees or the contribution of efforts in explaining the IOp, are lower than the measures based on mean differences in the ex-ante approaches or the contribution of circumstances (Table 3.8).

The transformation tree, depicted in Fig. 3.4, highlights the significant factors influencing ex-post IOp. It reveals that parents' education emerges as the most important factor, exhibiting statistically significant variations in average income between the two groups. The first group consists of individuals whose parents are educated at the graduate level or above. The second group comprises individuals whose parents are educated below the graduate level, including up to secondary or higher secondary, below secondary, and no formal education. The first group, with graduate or above-educated parents, is further subdivided by parents' occupation, distinguishing those with parents in medium or high-skilled jobs from those with parents in low or unskilled jobs. For individuals with parents in medium and high-skilled jobs, a further split is made into two broad regions: North, Northeast, South, West (NNESW), and East and Central (EC), which are further subdivided into rural and urban areas.

The second group, comprising individuals whose parents have an education below the graduate level, is subdivided into two broad regions: North, Northeast, South, West (NNESW) and East and Central (EC). For those located in the NNESW regions, an additional division is made based on the sector (rural–urban). Urban individuals are further subdivided based on their parents' occupations into those whose parents have medium and high-skilled jobs and those whose parents have low and unskilled jobs. Rural areas in the NNESW regions are split again by region into two groups: one consisting of the Northeast and South, and the other consisting of the North and West. Similarly, individuals in the EC regions are divided based on rural and urban areas. In rural areas, there is an additional split based on social group: one group

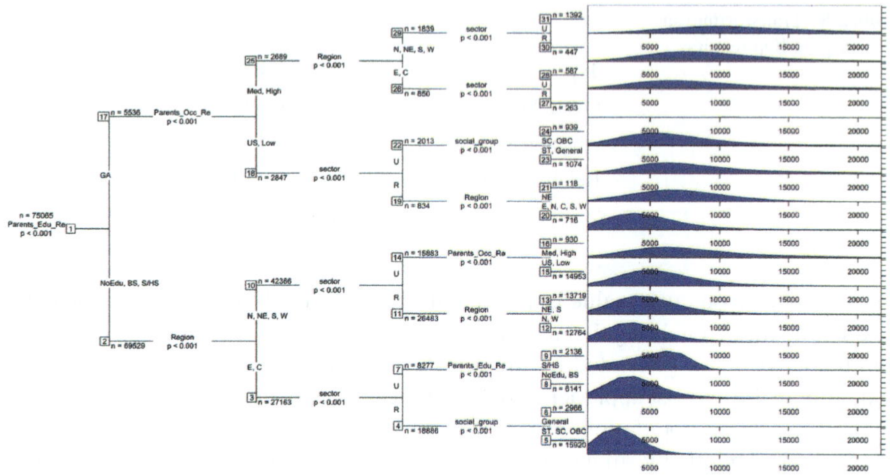

Fig. 3.4 Transformation tree for MPCI. *Note* R: Rural; U: Urban; N: North; NE: North East; S: South; W: West:E: East; C: Central; Sec/HS: Secondary/Higher Secondary; GradAbv: Graduate and Above; NoEdu: Illiterate or Nor Formal Schooling; BS: Below Secondary; US: Unskilled; Low: Low Skilled; Med: Medium Skill; High: High Skilled; M: Male; F: Female. *Source* Authors' calculations from PLFS, 2022–23

comprises individuals from the general caste, while the other consists of individuals from the ST, SC, and OBC categories. In urban areas, a further division is made based on parents' education, with one group comprising individuals whose parents have an education up to the secondary or higher secondary level and the other comprising individuals whose parents have an education below the secondary level or no formal schooling.

The final nodes of the transformation tree confirm the results of the conditional inference tree. These results indicate the lowest income distribution among individuals whose parents are educated below the graduate level, reside in rural areas of the central and eastern regions, and belong to the ST, SC, or OBC caste group. The highest income distribution is observed among individuals whose parents are educated to the graduate level or above, are involved in high and medium-skilled occupations, and reside in urban areas of the north, northeast, south, and western regions of India. Similar results can also be seen from the Expected Conditional Distribution Function (ECDF) as depicted in Fig. 3.5. The lowest average income (MPCI) is clearly seen at the leftmost node (Node 5), while the highest is at the rightmost part of the figure (Node 31), representing the two groups discussed above.

Ex-Post Shapley Value Decompositions: The final step in the ex-post analysis, similar to the ex-ante approach, is to assess the relative importance of individual circumstance variables using the Shapley value decomposition, as shown in Fig. 3.6. The results are quite similar to those obtained in the ex-ante analysis. Parents' education (46.3%) emerges as the most influential factor, indicating that different levels of parents' education significantly contribute to income IOp. This is closely followed

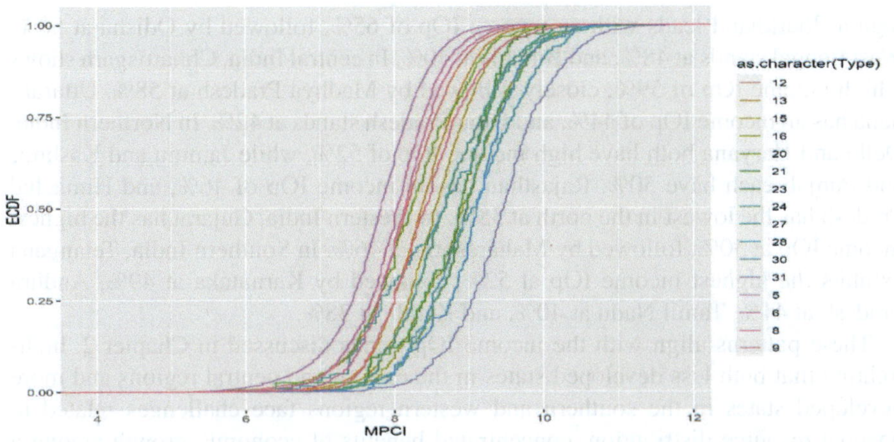

Fig. 3.5 Expected cumulative distribution functions for MPCI. *Source* Authors' calculations from PLFS, 2022–23

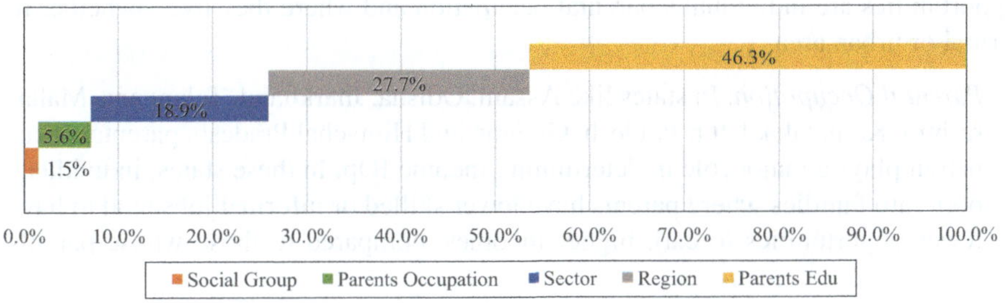

Fig. 3.6 Decomposition of factors contributing to ex-post IOp (in %). *Source* Authors' calculations from PLFS, 2022–23

by region (27.7%) and sector (18.9%), which also demonstrate considerable importance in explaining income IOp. However, parents' occupation and social groups have a minimal role in explaining income IOp, with their contributions being 5.6% and 1.5% respectively.

3.5.4 Regional Analysis

Labour Income IOp Analysis of labour income IOp, measured by the Gini, shows significant variations across Indian states. Jharkhand has the highest income inequality with an IOp of 65%, while Himachal Pradesh has the lowest at 35% (Fig. 3.2 and Table 3.11).

High-income inequality is particularly pronounced in the eastern (Jharkhand and Odisha) and central (Chhattisgarh and Madhya Pradesh) regions. In the eastern region, Jharkhand leads with an income IOp of 65%, followed by Odisha at 58%. West Bengal stands at 48%, and Bihar is at 40%. In central India, Chhattisgarh shows a high income IOp of 59%, closely followed by Madhya Pradesh at 58%. Uttarakhand has an income IOp of 44%, and Uttar Pradesh stands at 42%. In Northern India, Delhi and Haryana both have high income IOp of 52%, while Jammu and Kashmir and Punjab each have 50%. Rajasthan has an income IOp of 46%, and Himachal Pradesh has the lowest in the north at 35%. In Western India, Gujarat has the highest income IOp at 50%, followed by Maharashtra at 46%. In Southern India, Telangana exhibits the highest income IOp at 52%, followed by Karnataka at 49%, Andhra Pradesh at 41%, Tamil Nadu at 40%, and Kerala at 38%.

These patterns align with the income IOp trends discussed in Chapter 2, highlighting that both less developed states in the eastern and central regions and more developed states in the southern and western regions face challenges related to unequal resource distribution, concentrated benefits of economic growth among a few, and difficulties in implementing effective welfare programs (Map 3.1).

The factors contributing to income IOp vary significantly across different states in India (Table 3.12). Two of the most important factors driving unequal income opportunities are individual's parental occupation and where they live—whether in a rural or urban area.

- *Parental Occupation*: In states like Assam, Odisha, Jharkhand, Telangana, Maharashtra, Karnataka, Uttar Pradesh, Gujarat, and Himachal Pradesh, parental occupation plays a major role in determining income IOp. In these states, individuals born into families where parents have lower skilled or informal jobs tend to have fewer opportunities to earn higher incomes, compared to those whose parents

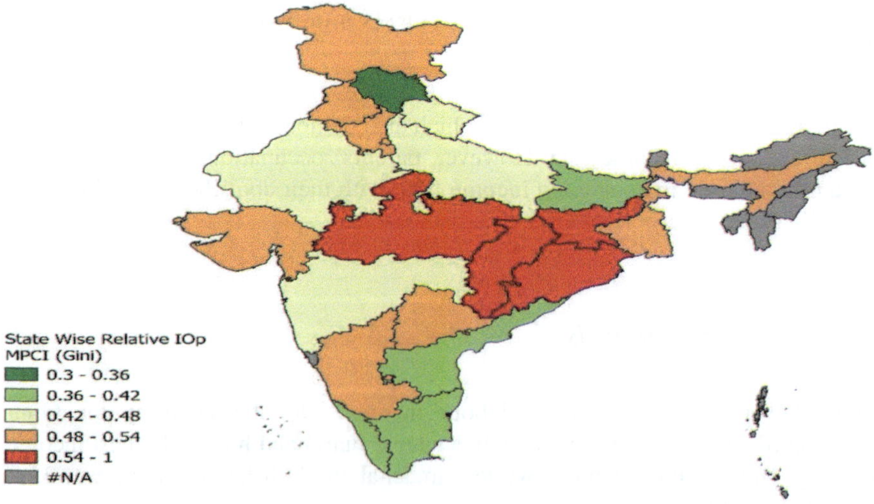

Map 3.1 Regional income IOp (Gini). *Source* Authors' calculations from PLFS, 2022–23

hold higher-status jobs. This creates a persistent cycle of inequal opportunity in earnings (well-paid occupations) that limits social mobility.

- *Location of Residence*: In other states, such as Rajasthan, Andhra Pradesh, Tamil Nadu, West Bengal, Haryana, Kerala, Bihar, Punjab, Uttarakhand, Jammu and Kashmir, and Chhattisgarh, whether a person is born in a rural or urban area is a key factor explaining income IOp. Rural areas often have fewer job opportunities, lower access to education, and weaker infrastructure, leading to unequal chances of improving one's income or well-paid occupations compared to people born in urban centres with better access to resources.
- *Gender*: In states like Delhi and Madhya Pradesh, gender is the leading factor contributing to income IOp. In these states, men often have more access to well-paying jobs, career advancement, and education compared to women, creating a significant gender gap in income IOp.

This variation in factors across states highlights the complex nature of income inequality in India and the need for targeted policy solutions that address these specific drivers. The findings emphasize the role of social background, location, and gender in shaping an individual's economic future.

3.6 Summary and Conclusion

This study provides both ex-ante and ex-post estimates of income inequality of opportunity (IOp) at the national level. It is also the first attempt to determine and represent the types and structure of opportunities in Indian society through the use of conditional inference trees, conditional inference forests, and transformation trees. These tree-based methodologies allow for graphical representations of the opportunities provided by society, making the results easily communicable to policymakers and other stakeholders. The ex-ante estimate of income IOp is relatively higher than the ex-post estimate, highlighting differences in interpretation and understanding of IOp within society. Using the ex-ante approach, approximately 48–63% of the total income-based inequality of opportunity can be attributed to differences in circumstances. In contrast, the ex-post method suggests that around 34% of the total income IOp is explained by differences within-tranche or efforts.

The tree-based analysis reveals that parents' occupation, areas of residence (rural or urban), and region (geographical location) are the most important variables in determining income IOp in Indian society, followed by parental education and social group. The ex-ante and ex-post Shapley decomposition exercises further confirm that parents' occupation, geographic location, sector (rural–urban areas), and parents' education are the most significant circumstances contributing to income IOp. In particular, individuals in the central and eastern regions, those residing in rural areas, those whose parents are employed in low-skilled and unskilled occupations, those with below secondary education or no formal education, and those belonging to marginalized social groups exhibit significantly lower average incomes. The regional analysis shows that income IOp varies widely across Indian states, with significant differences even within developed and underdeveloped regions.

This again highlights the urgent need for targeted regional-state level development policies that address the needs of marginalized groups to foster a more equitable society and reduce overall income inequality in India. The study's findings underscore the importance of targeted interventions to address income IOp and suggest that policies should prioritize improving educational opportunities, job prospects, and living conditions for disadvantaged groups. By doing so, India can make significant strides towards reducing income inequality and promoting social equity.

Appendices

Appendix 1: Grid Search Cross-Validation (CV) Process for Conditional Inference Tree and Conditional Inference Forest

The Grid Search Cross-Validation (CV) process involves splitting the dataset into training and test sets to evaluate model performance. This process tests various combinations of hyperparameters—specifically, the minimum number of observations required to perform a split (min-split) and alpha values. The goal is to identify the combination that results in the lowest root mean squared error (RMSE) on the test set, where RMSE measures the accuracy of the model's predictions.

Conditional Inference Tree Model: For the Conditional Inference Tree model with MPCI () as the dependent variable, the Grid Search CV was conducted to find optimal hyperparameters. After testing various combinations, it was found that an alpha value of 0.07 and a min-split value of 10,000 resulted in the lowest RMSE. To assess the robustness of the chosen alpha value, we compared the results with alpha values of 0.01 and 0.05, as detailed in Tables 3.9 and 3.10. This comparison follows the methodology outlined by Salas-Rojo and Rodríguez (2022).

Conditional Inference Forest Model: Similarly, for the Conditional Inference Forest model, the Grid Search CV process identified an alpha value of 0.06 and a tree count of 200 as yielding the lowest RMSE. To verify the robustness of this

Table 3.9 Ctree results for MPCI

Alpha	Types	Overall inequality (Gini)	Absolute Gini	IoP Gini
0.07	14	0.392	0.208	0.532
0.01	14	0.392	0.208	0.532
0.05	14	0.392	0.208	0.532

Source Authors calculations from PLFS, 2022–23

Table 3.10 Cforest results for MPCI

Alpha	Types	Overall inequality (Gini)	Absolute Gini	IoP Gini
0.06	16	0.392	0.190	0.486
0.01	16	0.392	0.190	0.486
0.05	16	0.392	0.190	0.486

Source Authors calculations from PLFS, 2022–23

alpha value, we compared the results with alpha values of 0.01 and 0.05, as shown in Tables 3.11 and 3.12.

These tables display the results for each combination of alpha values, showing the overall inequality, absolute Gini, and inequality of opportunity (IoP) Gini for the Conditional Inference Tree and Forest models. The consistency in results across different alpha values indicates the robustness of the chosen hyperparameters.

Regional IOp Tables

See Tables 3.11 and 3.12.

Density Plots for Terminal Nodes

See Fig. 3.7.

Table 3.11 Gini IOp measures for MPCI

State name	State code	Overall inequality Gini MPCI	Absolute IOp Gini MPCI	Gini MPCI relative IOp
Jharkhand	20	0.41	0.27	0.65
Chhattisgarh	22	0.44	0.26	0.59
Madhya Pradesh	23	0.38	0.22	0.58
Odisha	21	0.42	0.24	0.58
Delhi	7	0.41	0.21	0.52
Telangana	36	0.35	0.18	0.52
Haryana	6	0.36	0.18	0.51
Jammu & Kashmir	1	0.37	0.18	0.50
Gujarat	24	0.34	0.17	0.50
Punjab	3	0.38	0.19	0.50
Assam	18	0.31	0.16	0.50
Karnataka	29	0.36	0.17	0.49
West Bengal	19	0.34	0.16	0.48
Maharashtra	27	0.44	0.21	0.47
Rajasthan	8	0.42	0.19	0.46
Uttarakhand	5	0.35	0.15	0.44
Uttar Pradesh	9	0.41	0.17	0.42
Andhra Pradesh	28	0.37	0.15	0.41
Bihar	10	0.31	0.12	0.40
Tamil Nadu	33	0.35	0.14	0.40
Kerala	32	0.38	0.15	0.38
Himachal Pradesh	2	0.47	0.16	0.35

Source Authors calculations from PLFS, 2022–23

Table 3.12 Variable importance for each state

State	Region	Parents occupation	Sector	Gender	Social group	Parents education	Major var
Delhi	North	34.3	19.4	46.4	–	–	Gender
Madhya Pradesh	Central	7.5	11.1	42.5	31.6	7.3	Gender
Assam	North East	91.3	4.2	4.4	–	–	Parents occupation
Odisha	East	78.7	4.4	7.5	2.5	7	Parents occupation
Jharkhand	East	67.3	–	6.8	26.1	–	Parents occupations
Telangana	South	66.5	11.6	8.8	13.2	–	Parents occupation
Maharashtra	West	64	1.1	10.2	3.5	21.3	Parents occupations
Karnataka	South	55.2	32.1	4.5	8	0.3	Parents occupations
Uttar Pradesh	Central	54.8	6.5	12.7	22.4	3.6	Parents occupations
Gujarat	West	53.9	17.6	15.1	2.7	10.7	Parents occupations
Himachal Pradesh	North	47.8	16.8	21.8	12.7	0.9	Parents occupations
Rajasthan	North	27.4	41.8	11.9	11.8	7.1	Sector
Andhra Pradesh	South	19.4	35.2	6.9	30.2	8.3	Sector
Tamil Nadu	South	19.1	48.9	4	7	21	Sector
West Bengal	East	17.2	69.5	2.5	7.3	3.6	Sector
Haryana	North	16.7	61.6	6.6	3.3	11.8	Sector
Kerala	South	13.3	42.9	20.1	22.5	1.1	Sector
Bihar	East	9.7	61.4	15	4.7	9.2	Sector
Punjab	North	9.3	56.4	3.8	15.5	15	Sector
Uttarakhand	Central	9.2	61.3	5.2	8.9	15.3	Sector
Jammu & Kashmir	North	7.3	67	5.8	10.8	9.1	Sector
Chhattisgarh	Central	4.6	71	8.8	15.7	–	Sector

Source Authors calculations from PLFS, 2022–23

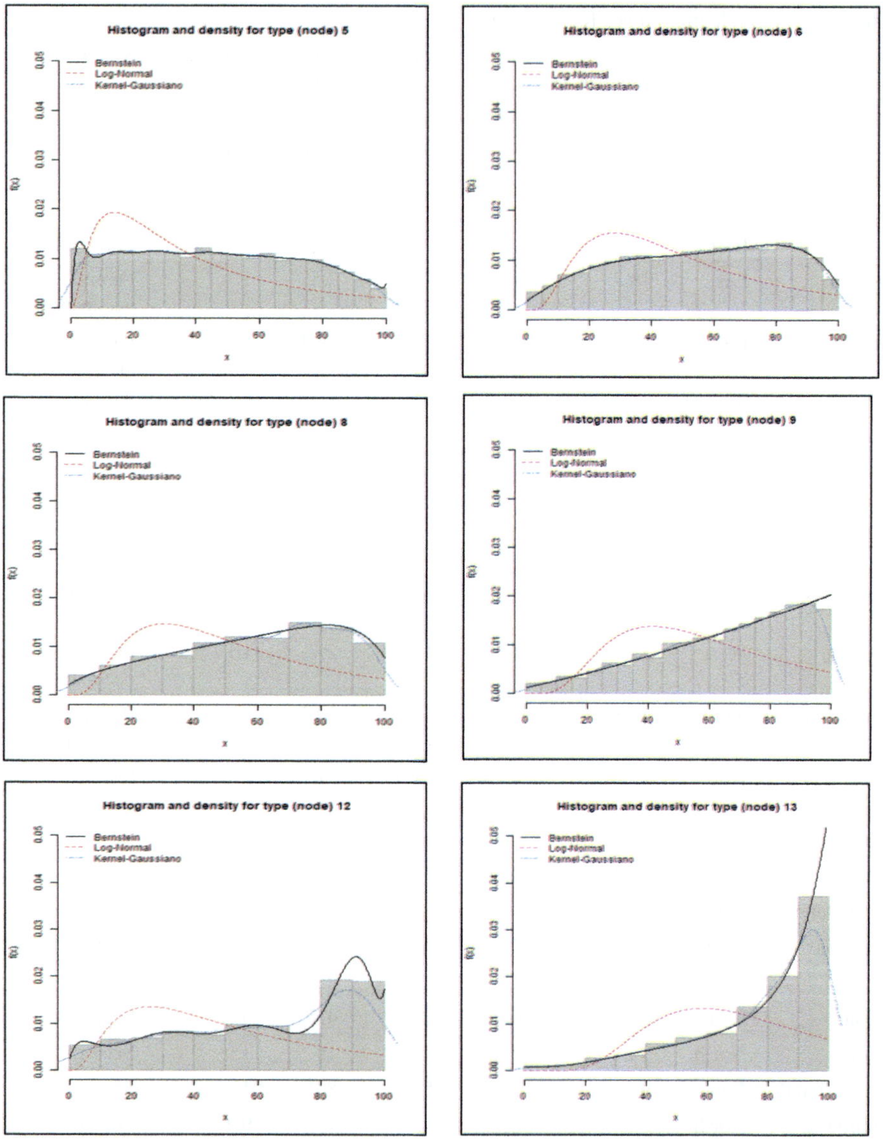

Fig. 3.7 Plots for MPCI. *Source* Authors calculations from PLFS, 2022–23

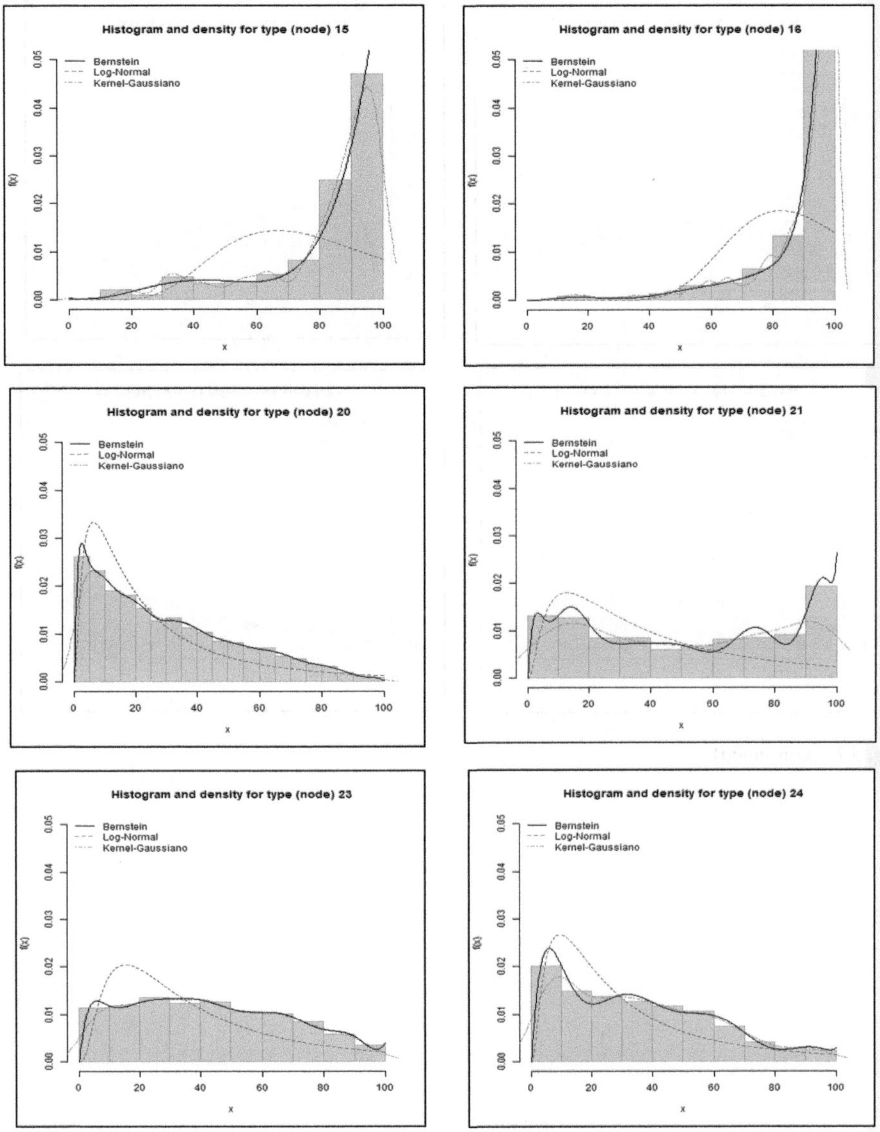

Fig. 3.7 (continued)

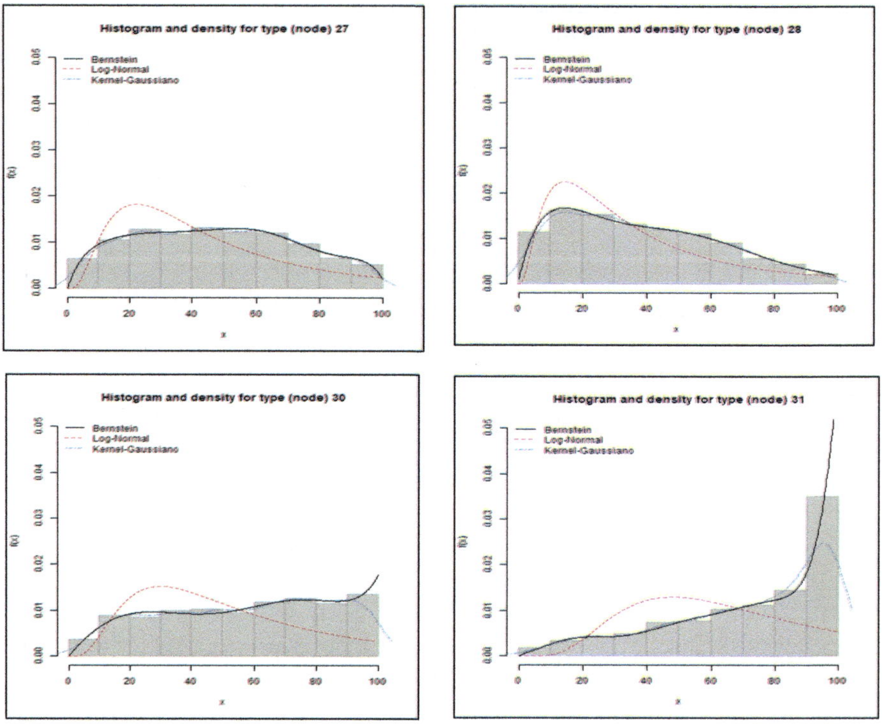

Fig. 3.7 (continued)

References

Anand, I., & Thampi, A. (2016). Recent trends in wealth inequality in India. *Economic and Political Weekly, 51*(50). https://www.epw.in/journal/2016/50/special-articles/recent-trends-wealth-inequality-india.html

Arneson, R. (1989). Equality and equal opportunity for welfare. *Philosophical Studies, 56*(1), 77–93.

Asadullah, M. N., & Yalonetzky, G. (2012). Inequality of educational opportunity in India: Changes over time and across states. *World Development, 40*(6), 1151–1163. https://doi.org/10.1016/j.worlddev.2011.11.008

Bourguignon, F. (2004). *The poverty-growth-inequality triangle* (Indian Council for Research on International Economic Relations Working Paper, 131, 35).

Brunori, P., Hufe, P., & Mahler, D. G. (2018, February). *The roots of inequality: Estimating inequality of opportunity from regression trees*. https://doi.org/10.1596/1813-9450-8349

Brunori, P., Ferreira, F. H. G., Neidhöfer, G., & UNU-WIDER. (2023). *Inequality of opportunity and intergenerational persistence in Latin America* (WIDER Working Paper 2023; Vol. 2023). UNU-WIDER. https://doi.org/10.35188/UNU-WIDER/2023/347-5

Brunori, P., & Neidhöfer, G. (2021a). Inequality of opportunity in comparative perspective: Recent advances and challenges. In *Handbook of income distribution* (Vol. 3B, pp. 1393–1479). Elsevier.

Brunori, P., & Neidhöfer, G. (2021b). The evolution of inequality of opportunity in Germany: A machine learning approach. *Review of Income and Wealth, 67*(4), 900–927. https://doi.org/10.1111/roiw.12502

Brunori, P., Palmisano, F., & Peragine, V. (2019). Inequality of opportunity in sub-Saharan Africa. *Applied Economics, 51*(60), 6428–6458. https://doi.org/10.1080/00036846.2019.1619018

Chancel, L., & Piketty, T. (2019). Indian income inequality, 1922–2015: From British Raj to Billionaire Raj? *Review of Income and Wealth, 65*(S1), S33–S62. https://doi.org/10.1111/roiw.12439

Chancel, L., Piketty, T., Saez, E., & Zucman, G. (2022). *World inequality report 2022*. UNDP, World Inequality Lab.

Checchi, D., & Peragine, V. (2010). Inequality of opportunity in Italy. *The Journal of Economic Inequality, 8*(4), 429–450. https://doi.org/10.1007/s10888-009-9118-3

Choudhary, A., Muthukkumaran, G. T., & Singh, A. (2019). Inequality of opportunity in Indian women. *Social Indicators Research, 145*(1), 389–413. https://doi.org/10.1007/s11205-019-02097-w

Cohen, G. A. (1989). On the currency of egalitarian justice. *Ethics, 99*(4), 906–944.

Das, P., & Biswas, S. (2022). Social identity, gender and unequal opportunity of earning in urban India: 2017–2018 to 2019–2020. *Indian Journal of Labour Economics, 65*(1), 39–57.

Deaton, A., & Stone, A. A. (2013). *Grandpa and the snapper: The wellbeing of the elderly who live with children* (Working Paper No. 19100). National Bureau of Economic Research. https://doi.org/10.3386/w19100

Deshpande, A., Goel, D., & Khanna, S. (2018). Bad karma or discrimination? Male-female wage gaps among salaried workers in India. *World Development, 102*, 331–344. https://doi.org/10.1016/j.worlddev.2017.07.012

Dworkin, R. (1981a). What is equality? Part 2: Equality of resources. *Philosophy & Public Affairs, 10*(4), 283–345.

Dworkin, R. (1981b). What is equality? Part 1: Equality of welfare. *Philosophy & Public Affairs, 10*(3), 185–246.

Farouki, R. T. (2012). The Bernstein polynomial basis: A centennial retrospective. *Computer Aided Geometric Design, 29*(6), 379–419.

Ferreira, F. H. G., & Gignoux, J. (2011). The measurement of inequality of opportunity: Theory and an application to Latin America. *Review of Income and Wealth, 57*(4), 622–657. https://doi.org/10.1111/j.1475-4991.2011.00467.x

Ferreira, F. H. G., & Gignoux, J. (2014). The measurement of educational inequality: Achievement and opportunity. *The World Bank Economic Review, 28*(2), 210–246. https://doi.org/10.1093/wber/lht004
Ferreira, F., & Peragine, V. (2015). *Equality of opportunity: Theory and evidence* (IZA Discussion Papers, No. 8994).
Fleurbaey, M. (1995). Equal opportunity or equal social outcome? *Economics and Philosophy, 11*(1), 25–55.
Fleurbaey, M. (2008). *Fairness, responsibility, and welfare.* Oxford University Press.
Fleurbaey, M., & Pergaine, V. (2013). Ex post inequalities and ex ante inequalities. In *Justice, political liberalism, and utilitarianism: Themes from Harsanyi and Rawls* (pp. 59–77). Cambridge University Press.
Ghose, A. K. (2021). Structural change and development in India. *Indian Journal of Human Development, 15*(1), 7–29. https://doi.org/10.1177/09737030211005496
Hothorn, T. (Director). (2018). *Video: Torsten Hothorn, "Transformation Forests."* http://www.birs.ca/events/2018/5-day-workshops/18w5054/videos/watch/201801161507-Hothorn.html
Hothorn, T., Hornik, K., & Zeileis, A. (2006). Unbiased recursive partitioning: A conditional inference framework. *Journal of Computational and Graphical Statistics, 15*(3), 651–674. https://doi.org/10.1198/106186006X133933
Hothorn, T., & Zeileis, A. (2021). Predictive distribution modeling using transformation forests. *Journal of Computational and Graphical Statistics, 30*(4), 1181–1196. https://doi.org/10.1080/10618600.2021.1872581
Hufe, P., Peichl, A., Roemer, J., & Ungerer, M. (2017). Inequality of income acquisition: the role of childhood circumstances. *Social Choice and Welfare*, 49, 499–544.
Institute for Human Development. (2014). *India Labour and Employment Report, 2014: Workers in the era of globalization.* Academic Foundation.
Kuznets, S. (1955). Economic growth and income inequality. *The American Economic Review, 45*(1), 1–28.
Leblanc, A. (2012). On estimating distribution functions using Bernstein polynomials. *Annals of the Institute of Statistical Mathematics*, 64, 919–943.
Lefranc, A., & Kundu, S. (2020). Machine learning approaches to inequality of opportunity measurement: A comparative study. *Applied Economics, 52*(16), 1723–1741.
Mehta, B. S., Dhote, S., & Srivastava, R. (2023). Decomposition of inequality of opportunity in India: An application of data-driven machine learning approach. *Indian Journal of Labour Economics, 66*(2), 439–469. https://doi.org/10.1007/s41027-023-00446-5
Motiram, S. (2018). Inequality of opportunity in India: Concepts, measurement and empirics. *Indian Journal of Human Development, 12*(2), 236–247.
Piketty, T. (2011). On the long-run evolution of inheritance: France 1820–2050. *The Quarterly Journal of Economics, 126*(3), 1071–1131.
Piketty, T., & Zucman, G. (2015). Wealth and inheritance in the long run. In A. B. Atkinson & F. Bourguignon (Eds.), *Handbook of income distribution* (Vol. 2B, pp. 1303–1368). Elsevier. https://doi.org/10.1016/B978-0-444-59429-7.00016-9
Plassot, M., Ramos, X., & Van de Gaer, D. (2022). The ex-ante and ex-post measurement of inequality of opportunity: A normative framework. *Review of Income and Wealth, 68*(1), 4–31.
Ramos, X., & Van de Gaer, D. (2016). Approaches to inequality of opportunity: Principles, measures and evidence. *Journal of Economic Surveys, 30*(5), 855–883.
Ramos, X., & Van de Gaer, D. (2021). Is inequality of opportunity robust to the measurement approach?. *Review of Income and Wealth, 67*(1), 18–36.
Ravallion, M., & Chen, S. (2003). Measuring pro-poor growth. *Economics Letters, 78*(1), 93–99. https://doi.org/10.1016/S0165-1765(02)00205-7
Rawls, J. (1958a). A theory of justice: Original edition. In *A theory of justice.* Harvard University Press. https://doi.org/10.4159/9780674042605
Rawls, J. (1958b). Justice as fairness. *The Philosophical Review, 67*(2), 164–194.

Rawls, J. (1971). *A theory of justice: Original edition.* Harvard University Press. https://doi.org/10.2307/j.ctvjf9z6v
Roemer, J. E. (1993). A pragmatic theory of responsibility for the egalitarian planner. *Philosophy & Public Affairs, 22*(2), 146–166.
Roemer, J. E. (1998). *Equality of opportunity.* Harvard University Press. https://link.springer.com/referenceworkentry/10.1057/978-1-349-95121-5_2223-1
Roemer, J. E. (2002). Equality of opportunity: A progress report. *Social Choice and Welfare, 19*(2), 455–471.
Roemer, J. E., & Trannoy, A. (2016). Equality of opportunity: Theory and measurement. *Journal of Economic Literature, 54*(4), 1288–1332. https://doi.org/10.1257/jel.20151206
Salas-Rojo, P., & Rodríguez, J. G. (2022). Inheritances and wealth inequality: A machine learning approach. *The Journal of Economic Inequality, 20*(1), 27–51.
Sen, A. (1980). Equality of what? In *Tanner Lectures on human values* (Vol. 1). Cambridge University Press.
Singh, A. (2012). Inequality of opportunity in earnings and consumption expenditure: The case of Indian men. *Review of Income and Wealth, 58*(1), 79–106.
Shapley, L. S. (1953). *A value for n-person games.*
Tagade, N., Naik, A. K., & Thorat, S. (2018). Wealth ownership and inequality in India: A socio-religious analysis. *Journal of Social Inclusion Studies, 4*(2), 196–213. https://doi.org/10.1177/2394481118808107
Van De Gaer, D. (1993). *Equality of opportunity and investment in human capital.* Katholieke Universiteit Leuven.
Weisskopf, T. E. (2011). Why worry about inequality in the booming Indian economy? *Economic and Political Weekly, 46*(47), 41–51.
Wendelspiess, F., & Soloaga, I. (2014). Iop: Estimating ex-ante inequality of opportunity. *The Stata Journal, 14*(4), 830–846.

References

Chapter 4
Predicting Poverty with Machine Learning and Geospatial Data

4.1 Introduction

Measurement of poverty is essential for comparing economic inequalities and designing effective policies. Ravallion (1994) notes that poverty can be measured in two main ways: ordinally, to track changes over time and between places, or cardinally, to measure its extent across different programs. There are two main approaches to measuring poverty: welfarist and non-welfarist. The welfarist approach, described by Sen (1981), focuses on individual well-being, highlighting the consumption of goods and services. In contrast, the non-welfarist approach prioritizes basic achievements like education and health. Understanding these approaches is important for accurately measuring poverty and designing effective strategies to reduce it, which is a key global goal outlined in Sustainable Development Goal 1 (SDG 1) to end all forms of poverty.

The World Bank global poverty update for March 2024 highlighted that global poverty rates have declined significantly in recent decades. However, progress has slowed recently due to economic disruptions from the COVID-19 pandemic and other conflicts. According to the update, about 8.9% of the world's population still lives in extreme poverty, which is defined as living on less than $2.15 (PPP) per day (Aguilar et al., 2024). This threshold aims to track progress towards reducing extreme poverty below 3% by 2030. Sub-Saharan Africa and South Asia have the highest poverty rates, with Sub-Saharan Africa accounting for over one-third (36.7%) and South Asia for one-fifth (10.6%) of the world's extremely poor. At the international poverty

Disclaimer: The presentation of material and details in maps used in this chapter does not imply the expression of any opinion whatsoever on the part of the Publisher or Author concerning the legal status of any country, area or territory or of its authorities, or concerning the delimitation of its borders. The depiction and use of boundaries, geographic names and related data shown on maps and included in lists, tables, documents, and databases in this chapter are not warranted to be error free nor do they necessarily imply official endorsement or acceptance by the Publisher or Author.

B. S. Mehta et al., *Predicting Inequality of Opportunity and Poverty in India Using Machine Learning*, India Studies in Business and Economics,
https://doi.org/10.1007/978-981-96-2544-4_4

line of \$3.65 (PPP), relevant for lower-middle-income countries (LMICs), the global poverty headcount ratio stands at 23.6%, with Sub-Saharan Africa at 62.3% and South Asia at 42.3%. These thresholds are used to gauge progress towards reducing extreme poverty to negligible levels in all its forms by 2030.

Monitoring poverty and identifying its determinants are essential for policymakers and researchers to understand living conditions and develop effective poverty alleviation strategies. Poverty is measured using various indicators: income-based, consumption-based, nutrition-based, anthropological, and multidimensional poverty index (MPI) (Alkire et al., 2017). Each method has its advantages and limitations. The global commitment to eradicating extreme poverty, as outlined in SDG 1 as mentioned above, also emphasizes the need for timely and accurate poverty data (Jean et al., 2016). However, the traditional methods of evaluating poverty through household surveys are costly, time-consuming, and often delayed. Standard methods like census enumeration and household surveys are often delayed. For example, censuses are conducted every 10 years in most countries, and household sample surveys are conducted every 3–5 years (Blumenstock, 2016). These time lags hinder accurate monitoring of progress (Devarajan, 2013; Njuguna & McSharry, 2017), leading to calls for a data revolution by the UN (IEAG, 2014). This revolution requires more frequent data collection, which traditional methods often cannot support due to high costs (Demombynes & Sandefur, 2014; Jerven, 2017). This is especially challenging in developing countries like India, where poverty is a pressing issue (Blumenstock, 2016).

In India, poverty is primarily measured using a consumption-based approach, which calculates the poverty headcount ratio by comparing consumption expenditure to a defined poverty line. Despite its criticisms, this method remains fundamental due to its simplicity and long-standing use. Traditionally, poverty data in India is obtained from household consumption surveys conducted by the National Statistics Office (NSO). Additionally, the Multidimensional poverty data has more recently been calculated by India's policy think tank, NITI Aayog using the National Family Health Survey (NFHS). The NFHS surveys are conducted by the International Institute for Population Studies (IIPS) with support from the Ministry of Health and Family Welfare of the Government of India. However, issues such as outdated methods, infrequent estimates, lack of regional granularity, cost, and timeliness impact the reliability of these surveys (Deaton & Kozel, 2005; Devarajan, 2013).

To address these challenges globally, researchers and policymakers are increasingly using advanced methods like machine learning (ML) algorithms and high-resolution satellite imagery to predict and analyse poverty levels (Jean et al., 2016). These techniques help identify poverty hotspots, track changes over time, and evaluate the impact of policy interventions. By applying ML to satellite images, mobile phone data, and geospatial information, researchers gain valuable insights into how poverty is distributed. These methods offer a cost-effective, timely, and detailed alternative to traditional data collection methods, especially in areas where conventional surveys are hard to carry out. Using these technologies, policymakers can create targeted poverty reduction programs, allocate resources more effectively, and make progress towards ending poverty by 2030. Recent studies also show that ML algorithms can accurately predict poverty using geospatial data. In India, where reliable, high-frequency data are limited, researchers and policymakers are proposing the use of geospatial data as an alternative for development indicators (Duan et al., 2017; Dugoua et al., 2018; Ghosh et al., 2013; Nischal et al., 2015; Suraj et al., 2018). This underscores the need for comprehensive India-specific studies that use various geospatial data using ML techniques to enhance poverty predictions.

This chapter is organized into seven sections. After the introduction, the second section reviews related work on the topic. The third section outlines the study's objectives and research questions. The fourth section describes the study framework and data sources, providing detailed descriptions of the data and machine learning techniques used, as well as limitations of the study. The fifth section presents the results and discussions. The sixth section forecasts poverty levels. The final, seventh section concludes with key findings and policy recommendations.

4.2 Related Work

Over the past two decades, the use of geospatial data combined with machine learning (ML) techniques has significantly advanced methods for predicting poverty. Researchers have utilized satellite data to study various socio-economic aspects, including poverty and economic activity (Asher et al., 2021; Donaldson & Storeygard, 2016; Hodler et al., 2023). Nightlight data, in particular, has proven useful for assessing the impact of natural disasters, policy actions, and conflicts on the economy and poverty (Beyer et al., 2018; Chodorow-Reich et al., 2018; Bundervoet et al., 2015).

Jean et al. (2016) used satellite nightlight data to estimate poverty levels in African countries with high accuracy. In Nepal, Bilton et al. (2017) combined geospatial data with survey data using ML techniques such as random forests and decision trees, achieving a 67% accuracy in predicting cluster-level poverty. Tingzon et al. (2019) further advanced this by integrating data from OpenStreetMap and regional indicators, reaching 63% accuracy in poverty predictions. A key study by Henderson et al. (2012) demonstrated that nightlights could effectively augment economic growth for 188 countries, showing a significant correlation between nightlights and GDP. This 'Henderson elasticity' has been validated across various contexts. Nightlight data is especially valuable in countries facing challenges in collecting timely data (Chen & Nordhaus, 2011; Hu & Yao, 2018). For example, in China, nightlight-adjusted GDP growth was found to be lower than official estimates (Zhou & Zeng, 2018). Similarly, in India and Angola, national accounts data were more accurate than household survey-based income estimates (Pinkovskiy & Sala-i-Martin, 2016). Advancements in short-term economic growth applications have emerged with the availability of monthly nightlight data. For instance, Bhadury et al. (2018) used nightlight data to improve the accuracy of nowcasts for India's gross value-added estimates. Machine learning, particularly deep learning, has also been applied to satellite imagery for tasks such as image segmentation and object identification, which aids in predicting poverty-related parameters (Bruzzone & Demir, 2014; Huang et al., 2015; Xie et al., 2016; Abelson et al., 2014).

In India, nightlight data has been employed to estimate economic activity at the district level, where reliable estimates are often lacking. Studies by Bhandari and Roychowdhury (2011) demonstrated that nightlights could capture GDP differences at the district level using multinomial regression techniques. Non-linear models yielded better results, as linear models often underestimated urban GDP and overestimated GDP in agriculture-dominated areas. Regional studies using nightlight data have highlighted intra-state divergence, with significant differences observed across districts (Chakravarty & Dehejia, 2017). Chanda and Kabiraj (2018) found evidence of both absolute and conditional convergence in rural areas, but not in urban areas. The nightlight data for about 600,000 villages from 1993 to 2013 (University of Michigan, n.d.) used by researchers shows that rural economic activity and poverty using ML regression algorithms and neural networks shows that higher nightlight intensity often corresponds to lower poverty rates (Ghosh et al., 2013).

However, studies in India have faced several limitations, such as variations in data quality and resolution, which can impact the accuracy of poverty predictions (Chen & Nordhaus, 2011). Factors like power outages and regional economic differences can distort the relationship between nightlight intensity and income levels (Gibson et al., 2019). Additionally, the use of nightlight data in India has revealed gaps in understanding long-term economic trends and state-specific effects. There is a need for further research to explore other geospatial data and to consider sectoral and regional variations in poverty levels with the application of more sophisticated ML algorithms. While satellite nightlight data combined with ML techniques offers valuable insights, integrating these with other data sources and refining predictive models is crucial for improving accuracy. This study aims to address these gaps by exploring advanced ML techniques and alternative data sources to enhance poverty prediction and policy interventions in India.

4.3 Objectives and Questions

The primary objective of this study is to assess the effectiveness of novel machine learning (ML) techniques in predicting poverty levels using geospatial data in India. By integrating various datasets, the study aims to enhance the accuracy of poverty estimates, providing more timely and precise information essential for effective policymaking and resource allocation.

This study explores several important questions:

- How can integration of geospatial and survey data using ML techniques predict poverty more effectively? This involves examining methods and approaches for combining these data types to enhance prediction models.

- How can geospatial data contribute to accurate and cost-effective poverty predictions? This question focuses on the value of geospatial data in improving the precision and efficiency of poverty estimates.
- How are ML methods used for poverty prediction? This involves reviewing various ML techniques applied to predict poverty and assessing their performance. The ML methods generate a functional relationship between dependent variables like poverty and its determinants.
- What are the advantages of using ML techniques in poverty measurement, and what are their potential future uses? This includes evaluating the benefits of ML methods over traditional approaches and exploring their future applications in poverty analysis.

Overall, this study seeks to advance the understanding of how innovative data and ML techniques can refine poverty measurement. The insights gained will be crucial for developing more effective poverty alleviation strategies and policies for developing countries like India.

4.4 Study Framework and Data Sources

The study involves a detailed process of data collection, pre-processing, and integration of data, followed by using the various predictive machine learning (ML) models.

4.4.1 Data Sources

This study employed various geospatial data, including nightlight intensity, the Normalized Difference Vegetation Index (NDVI), Land Surface Temperature (LST), rainfall, and Point of Interest (POI) density. These variables serve as proxies for economic activity, urbanization, climate risk, and accessibility to basic services. Additionally, indicators such as Monthly Per Capita Consumption and the Multidimensional Poverty Index are used as proxies for poverty or outcome variables. Table 4.1 and Fig. 4.1 provide an overview of these data sources.

4.4.2 Description of Data Sources

The data, their sources and importance are briefly discussed below.

- *Point of Interest (POI) Density:* POI density data from OpenStreetMap provides information on the accessibility of basic services and economic activities. It reveals the distribution of facilities such as schools, hospitals, and markets, which

Table 4.1 Data sources and variables

Variable	Dataset	Source	Proxy
POI density	Open street map	Open source	Accessibility to services and economic activities
NightLight	VNP46A2: VIIRS Lunar Gap-Filled BRDF Nighttime Lights Daily L3 Global 500 m	NASA LP DAAC at USGS EROS Center	Economic activities
Land Surface Temperature (LST)	MOD11A1.061 Terra Land Surface Temperature and Emissivity Daily Global 1 km	NASA LP DAAC at USGS EROS Center	Urbanization and climate risk
NDVI	MOD13A1.061 Terra Vegetation Indices 16-Day Global 500 m	NASA LP DAAC at USGS EROS Center	Economic activities and urbanization
Rainfall	CHIRPS Pentad: Climate Hazards Group InfraRed Precipitation with Station Data (Version 2.0 Final)	University of California, Santa Barbara	Climate risk
Multidimensional Poverty Index (MPI)	National Family and Health Surveys (NFHS)	IIPS	Poverty
Monthly Per Capita Expenditure	Periodic Labour Force Survey (PLFS)	NSO	Poverty

are crucial for understanding the availability of essential services (Hu et al., 2016; Ye et al., 2019; Nattapong et al., 2022).

- *NightLight Data:* Nightlight data, specifically the VIIRS Lunar Gap-Filled BRDF Nighttime Lights Daily L3 Global 500 m dataset, is used as a proxy for economic activities. The intensity of nighttime lights is indicative of economic development and has been utilized in various studies to estimate poverty levels (Head et al., 2017; Jean et al., 2016).
- *Land Surface Temperature* (*LST*): The MOD11A1.061 Terra LST dataset provides insights into urbanization and climate risk by measuring the surface temperature of the land. This data is essential for understanding the impact of urban heat islands and climate-related factors on poverty (Weng, 2001; Ruthirako et al., 2015).
- *Normalized Difference Vegetation Index* (*NDVI*): NDVI data from the MOD13A1.061 Terra Vegetation Indices dataset reflects vegetation health and land use changes. This measure helps in analysing economic activities and urbanization (Leroux et al., 2017; Sruthi et al., 2015).

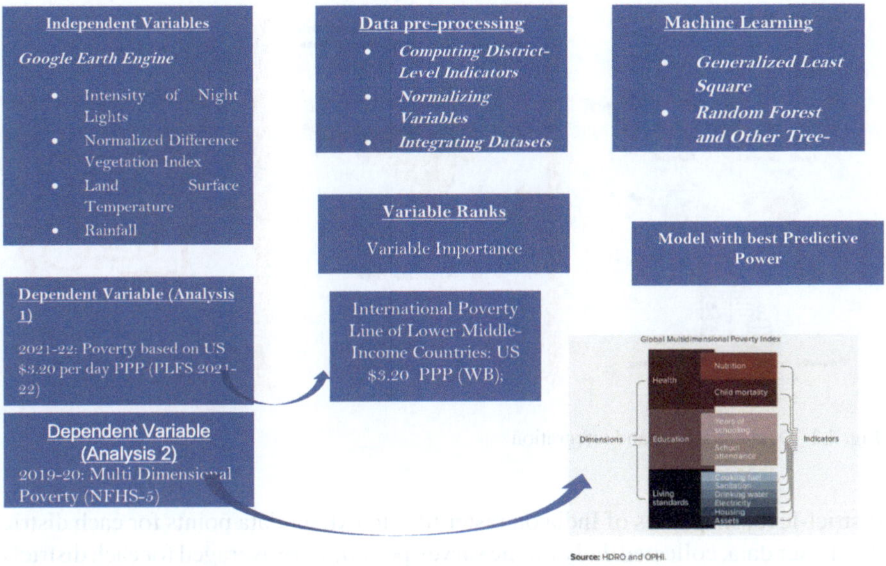

Fig. 4.1 Study framework

- *Rainfall Data*: Rainfall data from the CHIRPS Pentad dataset captures climate factors affecting poverty levels. Rainfall can impact economic activities and amplify climate risks (Richardson, 2007; Arzeki & Brückner, 2012).
- *Monthly Per Capita Consumption* (*MPCE*): The MPCE data is sourced from the Periodic Labour Force Survey conducted by the National Sample Survey Organisation, Government of India. This international poverty lines for Low- and Middle-Income Countries (LMICs) was at $3.20 PPP upto 2022. This international poverty line for LMICs have been used on household MPCE after converting into US dollar PPP from NSS survey to calculate poverty rate.
- *Multidimensional Poverty Index* (*MPI*): The MPI assesses poverty across three dimensions: Health, Education, and Living Standards. It uses ten indicators to measure deprivations and provides a comprehensive view of poverty beyond mere income metrics (Alkire & Santos, 2010; Alkire et al., 2011). The MPI approach highlights disparities in well-being and aids in designing targeted poverty interventions. The data for calculating the MPI is sourced from the National Family Health Survey (NFHS) conducted by IIPS, Mumbai, India.

4.4.3 Data Extraction and Integration

Data Pre-processing: Geospatial data, including nightlights, NDVI (Normalized Difference Vegetation Index), LST (Land Surface Temperature), and rainfall, were extracted using the geemap package in Python. This package allows for overlaying

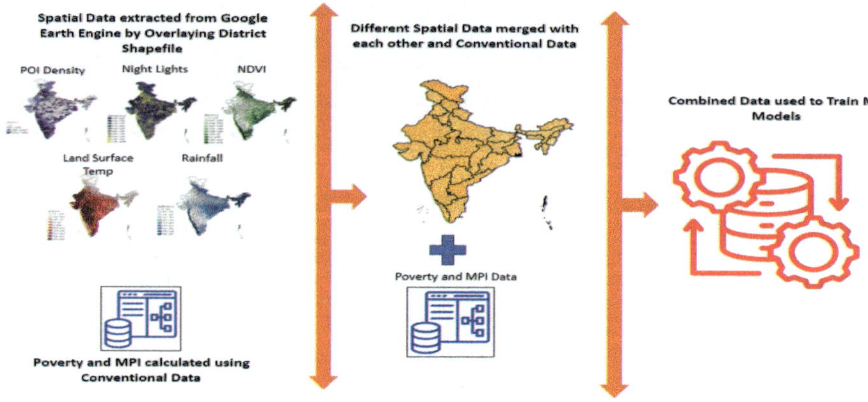

Fig. 4.2 Data extraction and integration

district-level shapefiles of India on raster files to extract data points for each district. The raster data, collected daily for the survey period, were averaged for each district to create vector data. Normalization was performed according to Google Earth Engine's dataset instructions before averaging. For Points of Interest (POI) data from OpenStreetMap, district shapefiles were used to intersect geographical points, calculating POI density by dividing the number of points within a district's boundary by the district's total area (Figs. 4.1 and 4.2).

Data Integration or Merging: The geospatial data were merged with the PLFS (Periodic Labour Force Survey) and NFHS (National Family Health Survey) data, as well as district-level poverty headcount data. Poverty headcount data were derived using the international poverty line for PLFS data and the Multidimensional Poverty Index (MPI) for NFHS data. The combined data were used to predict poverty, with PLFS data predicting based on the international poverty line and NFHS data predicting MPI-based poverty (Figs. 4.1 and 4.2).

4.4.4 Analytical Tools

The predictive power of geospatial variables was assessed using various methods: Generalized Least Squares (GLS), Random Forest (RF), and other tree-based algorithms such as Decision Trees, Bagging, Gradient Boosting, and Adaboost. Neural Networks (NN) were also employed. The model with the highest accuracy was selected to determine variable importance, revealing each variable's contribution to poverty prediction and identifying the most influential geographical variables.

- *Generalized Least Squares* (*GLS*): GLS is a statistical technique for modelling relationships between variables when error terms may be correlated or have varying variances. It adjusts for these issues, offering more reliable estimates than Ordinary Least Squares (OLS), especially in complex socio-economic data.

- *Random Forest* (*RF*): RF is an ensemble learning method using multiple decision trees built from random subsets of data. It averages predictions (for regression) or takes a majority vote (for classification) from all trees. RF handles large datasets with many features and is robust to overfitting, making it effective for predicting poverty with diverse geospatial and socio-economic data.
- *Decision Trees*: This technique splits data into subsets based on feature values. Each node represents a decision rule, and branches indicate the outcomes. Decision Trees are easy to interpret and visualize, useful for understanding how variables impact poverty.
- *Gradient Boosting*: An ensemble method that builds models sequentially, correcting errors of previous models. It combines predictions of several weak learners to form a strong model. Gradient Boosting is known for its high accuracy and ability to capture complex patterns, aiding in precise poverty prediction.
- *Neural Networks* (*NN*): Inspired by the human brain, NN consists of interconnected nodes organized in layers. NN models complex, non-linear relationships and are effective for handling large datasets with intricate patterns, helping to identify subtle interactions affecting poverty.

The data were split into 80% for training and 20% for testing. Performance metrics compared different algorithms (Hu et al., 2022; McBride & Nichols, 2018). Combining survey and geospatial data helped determine the predictive power of geospatial variables and their contribution to poverty prediction.

4.4.5 Limitations

Geospatial Data: While useful for economic activity measurement, the relationship between nightlight intensity and economic activity is inconsistent in some geographical areas. Variations in electricity generation, sectoral output, and other factors can influence the intensity differently across regions and times. Additionally, nightlight data are better for cross-sectional rather than longitudinal predictions. On the other hand, the point of interest data is continuously updated, which sometimes may not fully give the current status of available facilities.

Data Variability: The heterogeneity in data sources and their resolutions can introduce inconsistencies. The normalization and integration process attempts to mitigate these issues but may not completely eliminate them.

Model Dependency: The accuracy of predictions heavily depends on the chosen ML techniques and their implementation. Different algorithms might yield varying results, which can affect the robustness of poverty estimates.

Survey Data Limitations: Survey data, while comprehensive, may have inherent biases and limitations in capturing the full scope of socio-economic conditions, especially in remote or underrepresented areas. In the NSS survey data for some districts in India, the sample size is too small (less than 30) to estimate a robust value. In these cases, the missing values for those districts have been imputed using the K-Nearest Neighbours (KNN) method.

4.5 Results and Discussions

This section provides an overview of poverty in India and regional level using two distinct approaches: the monetary approach, which employs the international poverty line, and the non-monetary approach, which utilizes the Multidimensional Poverty Index (MPI).

4.5.1 Poverty in India: Status and Trends

Poverty in India is a complex and multifaceted issue, measured using various metrics to capture its different dimensions. Over the past few decades, India has made significant progress in reducing poverty, a trend that is evident through both income-based and multidimensional measures. As discussed earlier, the international poverty line, set at $3.20 per day for lower-middle-income countries (LMICs), is a key benchmark for tracking poverty. This threshold helps identify individuals who struggle to meet basic needs such as food, shelter, and clothing. India has shown remarkable progress in reducing poverty during the last two decades. In 2004–05, approximately 37% of the population lived in poverty, which declined to 22% in 2011–12 and further to 17% in 2021–22. This reduction underscores India's progress, especially compared to other LMICs, where the average poverty headcount was 46.1% in 2021–22, according to the World Bank. Additionally, the Poverty Clock data indicates that India's extreme poverty dropped to below 3% (2.4%) in 2022, suggesting the country is on track to achieve the SDG 2030 target of eliminating extreme poverty. The poverty headcount as measured using PLFS data, is estimated at 41.3% in 2021–22 (Appendix Table 4.4).

Beyond income or consumption-based measures, India also estimates poverty through multidimensional poverty index. As discussed earlier, this method considers deprivations in health, education, and living standards. According to Oxford Poverty and Human Development Initiative (OPHI), the multidimensional poverty in India decreased from 55.1% in 2005–06 to 27.9% in 2015–16, and further to 16.4% in 2019–21[1](see Appendix Table 4.5 for MPI headcounts for 2019–21). In 2005–06, approximately 645 million people were classified as multidimensionally poor, but this number dropped to about 370 million in 2015–16, and further to 230 million in 2019–21. This indicates that around 415 million individuals escaped multidimensional poverty over a span of thirteen years.

---

[1] CB_IND_2023.pdf (ophi.org.uk).

In addition, the recent poverty estimates based on the Household Consumption Survey 2022–23 by the National Statistics Office (NSO) and the India Human Development Survey (IHDS) by the National Council of Applied Economic Research (NCAER) also reveal a substantial reduction in poverty over the last decade. According to Rangarajan and Mahendra Dev (2022), India's poverty rate decreased from 21.9% in 2011–12 to 10.8% in 2022–23, using updated poverty lines recommended by the Rangarajan committee. Similarly, SBI Research found a lower poverty rate of around 4.5–5% for 2022–23, based on NSO data but using the updated Tendulkar committee poverty line (Gera, 2024). The IHDS survey indicates that poverty in India, according to the updated Tendulkar committee poverty line, declined from 21.2% in 2011–12 to 8.5% in 2023–24 (Desai et al., 2024). However, these estimates have reignited debates on the methodology of poverty measurement in India, given the long gap between surveys and varying poverty lines.

4.5.2 Regional Level Poverty

District-level poverty headcount calculated using the international poverty line ($3.20 PPP) and data from the Periodic Labour Force Survey (PLFS) reveal significant regional differences. A higher concentration of poverty is evident in the districts of eastern and central India. Specifically, districts in Bihar, Jharkhand, and Odisha in the east, as well as Chhattisgarh, Madhya Pradesh, and Uttar Pradesh in the central region, exhibit notably higher poverty rates (Map 4.1).

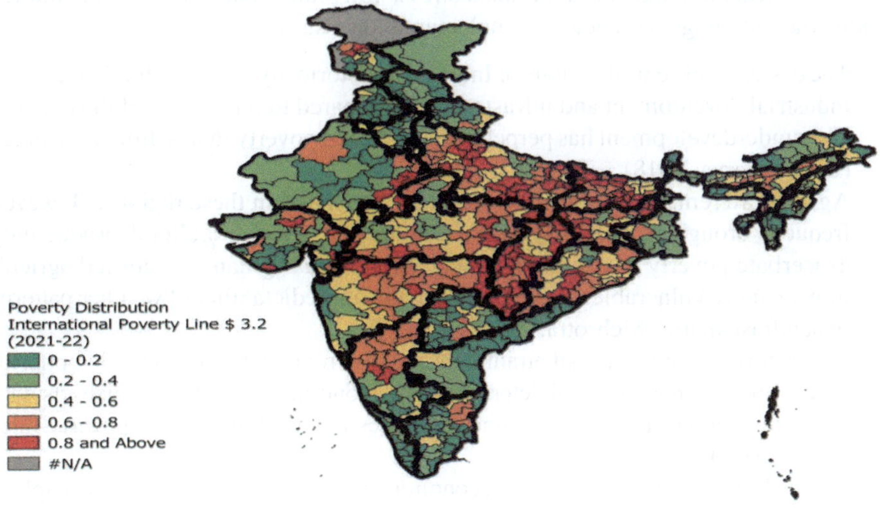

Map 4.1 Spatial distribution of poverty in India at district level using poverty head count. *Source* Authors' calculations from PLFS, 2021–22

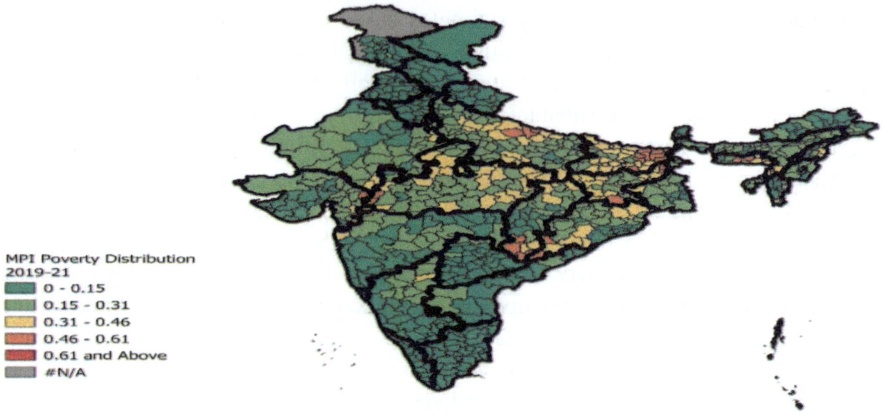

Map 4.2 Spatial distribution of poverty in India at district level using MPI approach. *Source* Authors' calculations from NFHS, 2019–21

The MPI approach, also reveals that poverty remains notably high in specific districts of eastern and central India. In the eastern states of Bihar, Jharkhand, and Odisha, the MPI indicates elevated levels of multidimensional poverty, reflecting persistent deprivations beyond income (Map 4.2). Similarly, central Indian states including Madhya Pradesh, Uttar Pradesh, and Chhattisgarh exhibit significant MPI-based poverty, highlighting widespread challenges in accessing essential services and improving living conditions.

Several factors contribute to these regional disparities in poverty such as historical and structural factors, agrarian distress, low educational attainment, limited industrialization, governance and implementation issues.

- The eastern and central regions of India have historically lagged behind in terms of industrial development and infrastructure compared to other parts of the country. This underdevelopment has perpetuated a cycle of poverty that is difficult to break (Bhattacharya, 2018).
- Agriculture remains the primary source of livelihood in these regions. However, frequent droughts, poor irrigation facilities, and low agricultural productivity exacerbate poverty levels. Studies indicate that areas reliant on rain-fed agriculture are more vulnerable to poverty due to the unpredictability of weather patterns (Chandrasekhar & Mehrotra, 2016).
- Lower levels of educational attainment in these regions limit economic opportunities. Education is a critical determinant of economic mobility, and districts with poor educational infrastructure and outcomes tend to have higher poverty rates (Tilak, 2015).
- The lack of industrialization and economic diversification means fewer employment opportunities outside of agriculture. Industrial hubs in western and southern India have attracted more investment and job creation, leaving eastern and central regions behind (Saxena, 2018).

– Inefficiencies in governance and the implementation of poverty alleviation programs can hinder progress. Effective delivery of social welfare schemes is often weaker in these regions, contributing to persistent poverty (Jha, 2019).

The above analysis of the data on poverty reveals that India has achieved significant progress in poverty reduction through both income and multidimensional measures. The decline in poverty rates, even amidst global challenges such as the COVID-19 pandemic, underscores the effectiveness of the country's economic and social policies.

4.5.3 Poverty Prediction: Poverty Head Count

(i) Correlation Analysis of Poverty Predictors: A correlation heatmap was employed to analyse the relationships among various variables used in predicting poverty. The results of this analysis offer valuable insights into how these factors interact and influence poverty levels (Fig. 4.3).

– *Nightlight Intensity*: Nightlight intensity measures the brightness of nighttime illumination in an area. The analysis revealed a negative correlation between nightlight intensity and poverty, suggesting that regions with higher levels of nightlight generally experience lower poverty. This correlation is attributed to the fact that greater nightlight intensity often indicates higher economic activity and better infrastructure, which are associated with improved living conditions and economic opportunities (Elvidge et al., 2017).

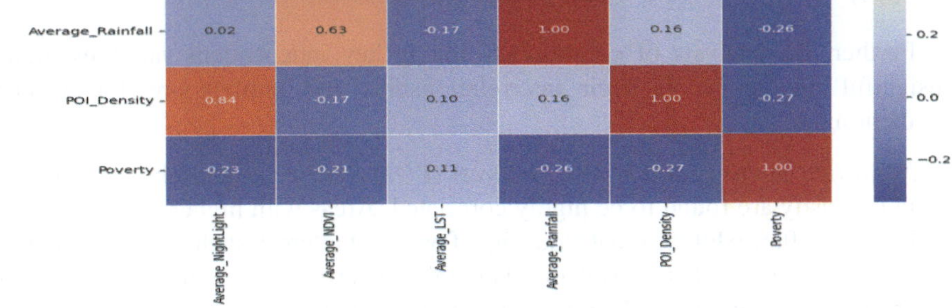

Fig. 4.3 Correlation heat map: poverty head count. *Source* Authors' calculations

- *Normalized Difference Vegetation Index (NDVI)*: The NDVI assesses the health and density of vegetation. A negative correlation with poverty was observed, indicating that higher NDVI values—reflecting lush, healthy vegetation—are often linked to reduced poverty. This relationship suggests that robust vegetation correlates with better agricultural productivity and environmental conditions, which can alleviate poverty (Pettorelli et al., 2014). However, this correlation is not uniform across regions. The states in eastern India like Odisha and West Bengal have high green cover due to favourable rainfall conditions but still face economic disadvantages. This discrepancy highlights the need to integrate NDVI with other socio-economic indicators for a more comprehensive understanding of poverty dynamics (Kumar & Patel, 2021).
- *Rainfall*: Rainfall is a crucial factor for agriculture, a primary livelihood source for many rural inhabitants in India. The analysis shows a negative correlation between rainfall and poverty, indicating that higher rainfall generally correlates with lower poverty levels due to improved agricultural yields (Dube et al., 2021). However, this correlation is nuanced. In regions such as Punjab and Haryana, where extensive irrigation systems and advanced agricultural practices mitigate the impact of lower natural rainfall, poverty rates are lower despite less rainfall. Conversely, eastern regions with higher rainfall often encounter issues like flooding and underdeveloped agricultural infrastructure, which can constrain productivity and limit poverty reduction (Kumar & Verma, 2023).
- *Point of Interest (POI) Density*: POI density, which measures the concentration of essential services like schools, hospitals, and markets, shows a negative correlation with poverty. This suggests that higher POI density provides better access to essential services and economic opportunities, contributing to lower poverty levels. Areas with more POIs typically offer enhanced services and infrastructure, which support economic growth and improve quality of life (Henderson et al., 2018).
- *Land Surface Temperature (LST)*: LST, in contrast to other variables, exhibits a positive correlation with poverty. Higher land surface temperatures can signify harsher living conditions and lower agricultural productivity due to heat stress, leading to increased poverty levels. Elevated temperatures can exacerbate climate risks, affecting both economic activities and overall living standards (Zhao et al., 2014).

Further, the analysis of correlations among key independent variables yields insightful findings about their interrelationships and implications for poverty prediction.

- *Nightlight Intensity and Point of Interest (POI) Density*: Nightlight intensity and POI density are found to be highly correlated. Areas with higher nighttime light intensity often exhibit a greater density of points of interest, such as schools, hospitals, and markets. This correlation is logical, as urban and economically vibrant areas, which tend to be better illuminated at night, are likely to host a greater number of essential services and facilities. This relationship underscores how economic activity and infrastructure development, reflected in higher nightlight intensity, are closely associated with the availability of essential services, which can support poverty reduction (Elvidge et al., 2017; Henderson et al., 2018).

- *Rainfall and Normalized Difference Vegetation Index (NDVI)*: Rainfall and NDVI are also strongly correlated. Regions with adequate rainfall typically support healthier and denser vegetation, which is captured in higher NDVI values. Higher NDVI often reflects better environmental conditions and robust agricultural productivity, which are critical for reducing poverty. This relationship indicates that regions benefiting from sufficient rainfall are likely to experience improved vegetation health, contributing to better agricultural yields and, consequently, lower poverty levels (Kumar & Verma, 2023; Pettorelli et al., 2014).

This correlation analysis highlights the significance of various geospatial and environmental factors in understanding and predicting poverty levels. Nightlight Intensity, NDVI, Rainfall, and POI Density show a negative correlation with poverty, suggesting that improvements in these areas are associated with reduced poverty. Enhanced nightlight intensity and higher POI density indicate better infrastructure and access to essential services, while higher NDVI and adequate rainfall contribute to better environmental conditions and agricultural productivity. These factors collectively support poverty alleviation efforts by improving living conditions and economic opportunities. In contrast, LST is positively correlated with poverty. Higher land surface temperatures often indicate harsher living conditions and lower agricultural productivity due to heat stress. This correlation emphasizes the need for targeted climate mitigation and adaptation strategies to address the adverse effects of elevated temperatures and support poverty reduction in vulnerable regions (Zhao et al., 2014).

(ii) Goodness of Fit: When predicting poverty using machine learning and deep learning techniques, evaluating the goodness of fit is crucial for determining how well a model's predictions align with actual observed values. In this analysis, various methods were tested, and their performance was assessed using metrics such as Root Mean Squared Error (RMSE) and R-Squared (R^2). The Random Forest algorithm emerged as the most effective model, demonstrating superior performance compared to other methods (Figs. 4.4, 4.5 and Table 4.2).

- *Random Forest (RF) and Other Tree-Based Models*: The Random Forest model exhibited the best performance among the tested methods. It achieved the lowest RMSE of 0.074 and the highest R-Squared value of 0.91. This indicates that Random Forest predictions were closest to the actual values, and the model accounted for a significant proportion of the variance in the data. The low RMSE suggests minimal prediction error, while the high R-Squared indicates strong explanatory power. Other tree-based models, including Adaboost, Bagging, and Gradient Boosting, also performed well but had slightly higher RMSE values compared to Random Forest, though their R-Squared values were similarly high (Breiman, 2001; Chen & Guestrin, 2016).

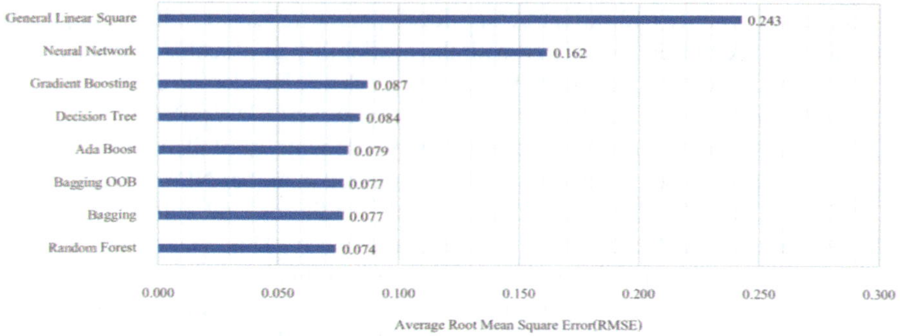

Fig. 4.4 Root mean squared error for different models: poverty head count. *Source* Authors' calculations

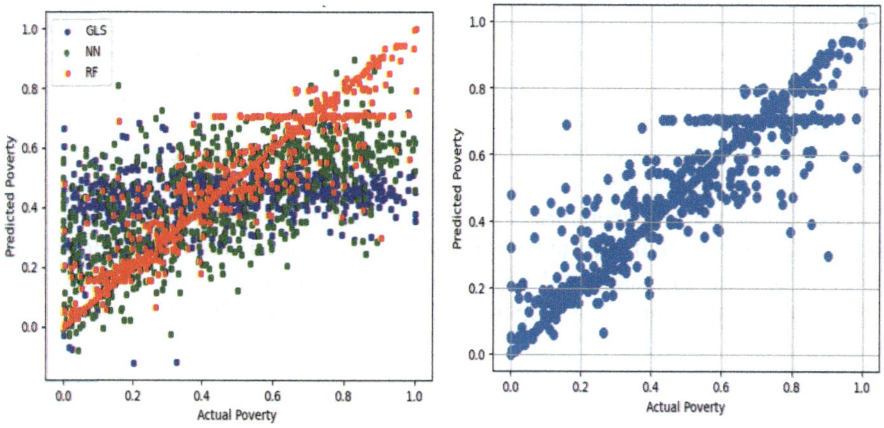

Fig. 4.5 Goodness of fit of GLS, NN, RF and RF only: poverty head count. *Source* Authors' calculations

Table 4.2 R-squared value of major models (least squares, neural network, and random forest): poverty head count

Model	R-square
Generalize Least Squares (GLS)	0.243
Neural Network (NN)	0.630
Random Forest (RF)	0.919

Source Authors' calculations

- *Generalized Least Squares (GLS)*: The Generalized Least Squares method showed the poorest performance. It recorded the highest RMSE of 0.243 and the lowest R-Squared value of 0.15. This suggests that GLS predictions were the least accurate, with substantial discrepancies between predicted and actual values. The high RMSE and low R-Squared indicate that GLS was unable to effectively capture the variance in the data and provided a less reliable fit compared to other methods (Greene, 2018).

- *Neural Networks:* Neural Networks outperformed GLS but were less effective compared to Random Forest. The RMSE for neural networks was 0.162, and the R-Squared value was 0.63. While these results were an improvement over GLS, they still fell short of the accuracy achieved by Random Forest. Neural networks, despite their complexity and potential for capturing non-linear relationships, did not match the performance of tree-based models in this context (Goodfellow et al., 2016).

This analysis clearly demonstrates that the Random Forest model is the most effective technique for poverty prediction among those tested. Its superior performance, evidenced by the lowest RMSE and highest R-Squared value, makes it the most reliable method for generating accurate predictions. In contrast, GLS exhibited the least accuracy, with significant discrepancies in predictions, while neural networks performed moderately but did not surpass the efficacy of tree-based models. This evaluation highlights the importance of selecting appropriate machine learning techniques for predictive tasks. The Random Forest model's robustness and precision make it a preferred choice for poverty prediction, while other methods may offer value but with varying degrees of accuracy.

(iii) Regional Poverty Predication Using Random Forest: The Random Forest (RF) model, noted for its superior accuracy and minimal Root Mean Squared Error (RMSE), has been utilized to predict poverty levels across districts. The process began by establishing a benchmark with district-level poverty headcount data from the Periodic Labour Force Survey (PLFS). This data served as the foundation for the RF model, which then generated poverty predictions for each district.

To validate the RF model's predictions, a comparative analysis was performed between the actual poverty headcounts from the PLFS and the predicted values from the RF model. This comparison is visually represented in Map 4.3. Both maps illustrate a similar spatial pattern, confirming that the RF model's predictions closely align with real-world data. This correspondence highlights the model's accuracy and reliability in forecasting poverty levels at the district level.

Further analysis shows that the distribution of poverty across districts predicted by the RF model is almost identical to the actual distribution, with only minor discrepancies in the 40–60% range of poverty headcounts. This close alignment underscores the effectiveness of the RF model in capturing the spatial distribution of poverty. For policymakers and social scientists, this capability is invaluable as it provides a precise tool for identifying regions in need of targeted interventions and resource allocation (Fig. 4.6).

This indicates that Machine learning techniques like Random Forest offer significant advantages over traditional methods by enabling granular, district-level predictions that are otherwise challenging to achieve. The consistency between the actual and predicted poverty headcounts not only demonstrates the RF model's accuracy but also its practical utility in guiding effective poverty alleviation strategies.

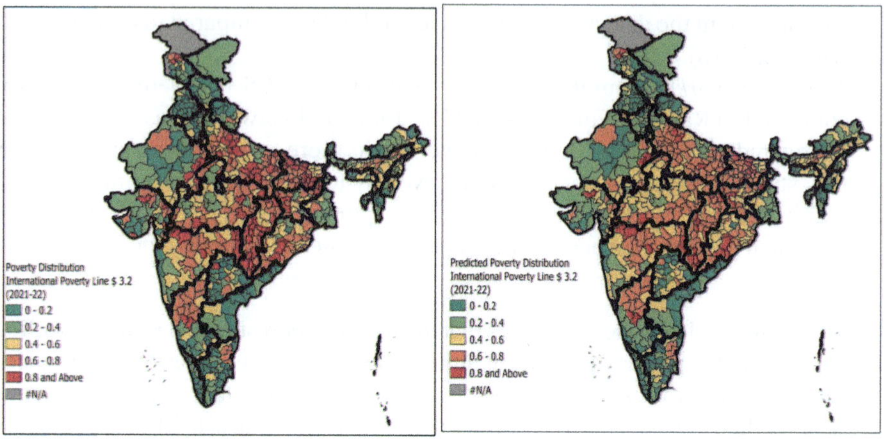

Map 4.3 Actual and predicted spatial distribution of poverty: poverty head count. *Source* Authors' calculations

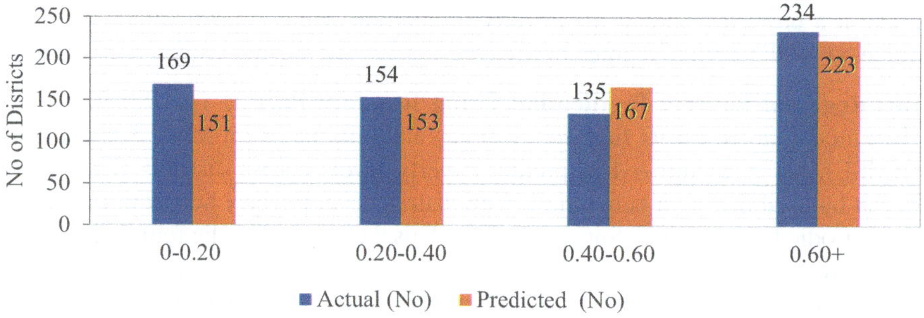

Fig. 4.6 Districts falling in similar poverty range: poverty head count. *Source* Authors' calculations

(iv) Variable Importance: To improve the accuracy of poverty prediction, a Variable Importance Analysis was conducted to determine which spatial variables are most influential. This analysis utilized three different models to assess the impact of various spatial variables on poverty predictions: Model 1: All Variables Included—This model includes all spatial variables employed in the analysis. Model 2: Excludes Point of Interest (POI) Density—This model evaluates the impact of excluding POI density on predictive performance. Model 3: Excludes Average Nightlight—This model assesses the effect of removing average nightlight data (Fig. 4.7).

- *Model 1*: All Variables Included: In Model 1, where all variables were considered, POI density emerged as the most influential predictor, whereas nightlight intensity as the least. However, the high correlation between these two variables affected their individual importance. Specifically, POI density accounted for 40% of the variability in poverty, while average nightlight explained 9%. The overlap

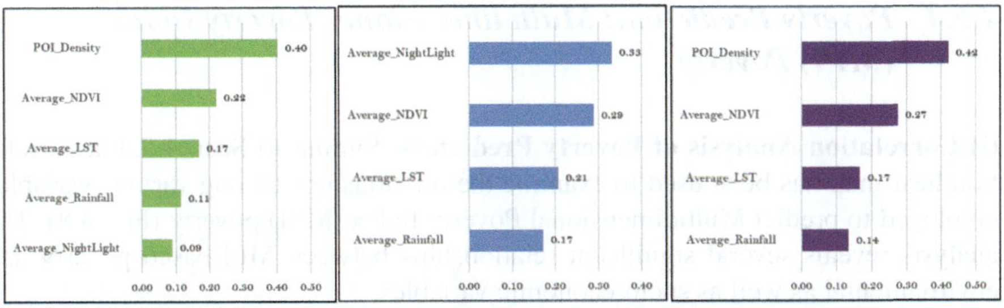

Random Forest with All Variables Random Forest with Nightlight data Random Forest with POI Density

Fig. 4.7 Variable importance from RF: poverty head count. *Source* Authors' calculations

between POI density and nightlight data suggests that much of the information captured by nightlight is also reflected in POI density, which may reduce the distinct contribution of nightlight to the model (Fig. 4.7, Panel 1) (Chen et al., 2020).

- *Model 2*: Excluding POI Density: When POI density was excluded from Model 2, average nightlight became the most significant variable, explaining 33% of the variability in poverty (Fig. 4.7, Panel 2). This shift highlights the substantial role of nightlight data in capturing poverty variation when POI density is not considered. Nightlight data, often associated with economic activity and infrastructure, provides valuable insights into poverty levels (Doll et al., 2008).

- *Model 3*: Excluding Average Nightlight: In Model 3, where average nightlight was excluded, POI density emerged as the predominant predictor, explaining 42% of the variability in poverty (Fig. 4.7, Panel 3). This finding underscores the substantial role of POI density in predicting poverty when nightlight data is not available. POI density reflects the accessibility of essential services and infrastructure, which are critical factors in poverty alleviation (Yao et al., 2023).

This analysis reveals the crucial roles of both nightlight and POI density in predicting poverty. The combined use of these variables enhances model stability and prediction accuracy. For instance, Model 1, incorporating both variables, achieved a lower Root Mean Squared Error (RMSE) of 0.075 compared to 0.089 in models using only one variable. This demonstrates that integrating both nightlight and POI density improves the reliability and comprehensiveness of poverty predictions (Gao et al., 2017). Although POI density is a significant predictor, its limitations, such as periodic updates and potential errors, can affect its reliability. On the other hand, nightlight data provides a more stable and consistent measure of economic activity and infrastructure. Therefore, combining both variables offers a more robust approach to predicting poverty, leveraging the strengths of each data source to achieve more accurate and reliable predictions.

4.5.4 Poverty Prediction: Multidimensional Poverty Index (MPI) Poverty

(i) Correlation Analysis of Poverty Predictors: Similar to Sect. 4.5.3, a correlation heat map has been used to examine the relationships among various variables employed to predict Multidimensional Poverty Index (MPI) poverty (Fig. 4.8). The analysis reveals several significant relationships between MPI-based poverty and environmental as well as socio-economic variables.

- *Nightlight Intensity, NDVI, Rainfall, and POI Density*: There is negative correlation with Nightlight Intensity, NDVI, Rainfall, and POI Density. The brightness of nighttime lights in an area is inversely related to MPI poverty levels. Areas with higher nightlight intensity typically have lower levels of MPI poverty. This correlation suggests that increased economic activity and infrastructure, often reflected in brighter nightlights, are associated with improved living conditions and reduced poverty.
- *Normalized Difference Vegetation Index (NDVI)*: The NDVI shows a negative correlation with MPI poverty. Higher NDVI values, indicating lush and healthy vegetation, are linked to better agricultural productivity and environmental conditions, which contribute to lower poverty levels. Adequate and consistent rainfall is crucial for agriculture, a primary livelihood source for many in rural areas. The analysis shows that regions with higher rainfall tend to have lower MPI poverty. This is because sufficient rainfall improves agricultural yields, boosting income levels and reducing poverty.

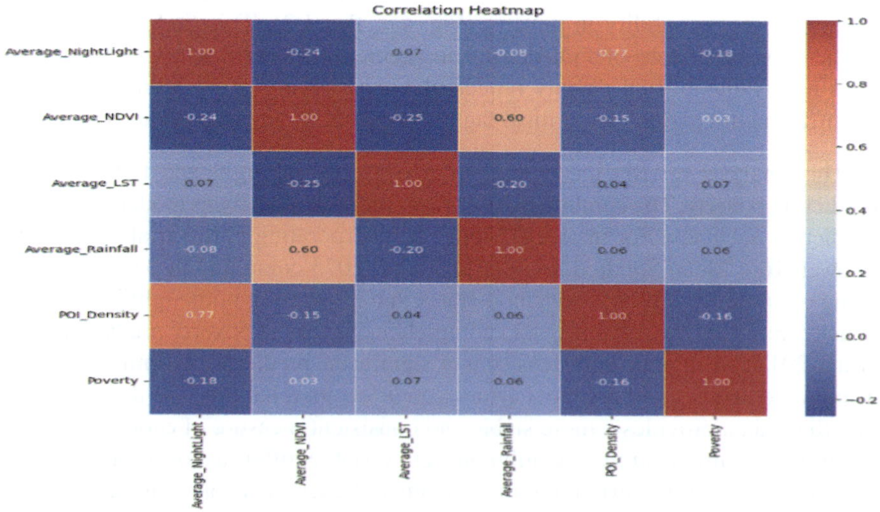

Fig. 4.8 Correlation heat map: MPI approach. *Source* Authors' calculations

- *Point of Interest (PoI) Density*: The PoI density, is negatively correlated with MPI poverty. Higher PoI density indicates better access to crucial services and economic activities, thereby reducing MPI poverty levels.
- *Land Surface Temperature (LST)*: Unlike the other variables, LST is positively correlated with MPI poverty. Higher land surface temperatures often indicate harsher living conditions, reduced agricultural productivity due to heat stress, and increased vulnerability to climate risks. These factors contribute to higher levels of MPI poverty.

These correlations observed in the analysis have significant implications for poverty alleviation strategies. The negative correlations with nightlight intensity, NDVI, rainfall, and PoI density suggest that improving infrastructure, adequate rainfall, enhancing vegetation health, and increasing access to essential services can effectively reduce MPI poverty. Conversely, the positive correlation with LST underscores the need for climate adaptation strategies to mitigate the adverse impacts of higher temperatures on vulnerable populations. Studies have also shown that nighttime light intensity is a strong indicator of economic activity and development. It reflects infrastructure development and economic prosperity, which are crucial for reducing poverty (Henderson et al., 2012).

The health of vegetation, as measured by NDVI, is closely linked to agricultural productivity. Higher NDVI values indicate better crop yields, which are essential for the livelihoods of rural populations (Tucker, 1979). Consistent and adequate rainfall is vital for agricultural productivity, especially in regions dependent on rain-fed agriculture. Improved rainfall patterns can significantly enhance crop yields and reduce poverty (Grove, 1996). Access to essential services such as education, health care, and markets is critical for improving living standards and reducing poverty. Higher PoI density facilitates better access to these services, contributing to poverty reduction (Baker & Grosh, 1994). Higher land surface temperatures can exacerbate living conditions and reduce agricultural productivity, making populations more vulnerable to poverty. Climate adaptation measures are essential to address these challenges (Sivakumar et al., 2005). However, there are limitations of these high correlation across the regions in the country as discussed in the earlier section.

(ii) Goodness of Fit: The results of the goodness of fit of different ML models are presented in Figs. 4.9, 4.10, and Table 4.3. Among all the ML techniques, the Random Forest method exhibited the best performance. It had the lowest RMSE of 0.054 and the highest R-Square value of 0.85. These metrics indicate that: The predictions made by the Random Forest model were very close to the actual values, demonstrating high accuracy. The model explained a significant portion of the variance in the data, highlighting its robustness in capturing the underlying patterns. Other tree-based models, such as AdaBoost, Bagging, and Gradient Boosting, also demonstrated low RMSE and high R-Square values but were not as effective as Random Forest. These models had slightly higher RMSE values, indicating that while they were accurate, they did not perform as well as Random Forest in predicting poverty.

On the other hand, the Generalized Least Squares method showed the poorest performance among the methods tested with high RMSE (0.140) suggests a larger

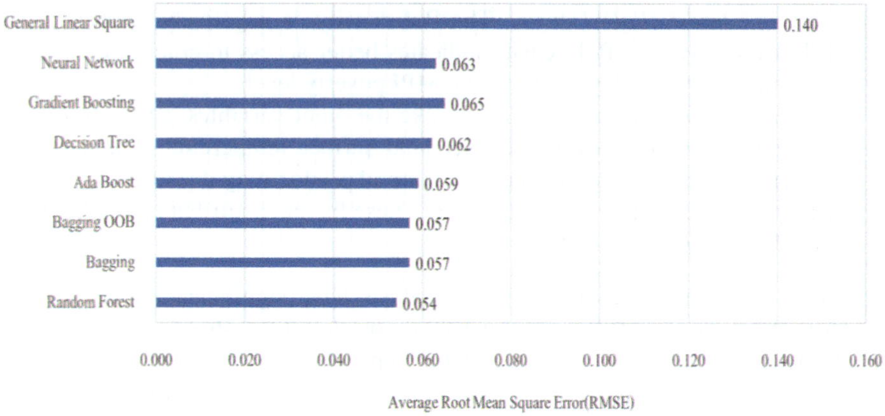

Fig. 4.9 Root mean squared error for different models: MPI poverty. *Source* Authors' calculations

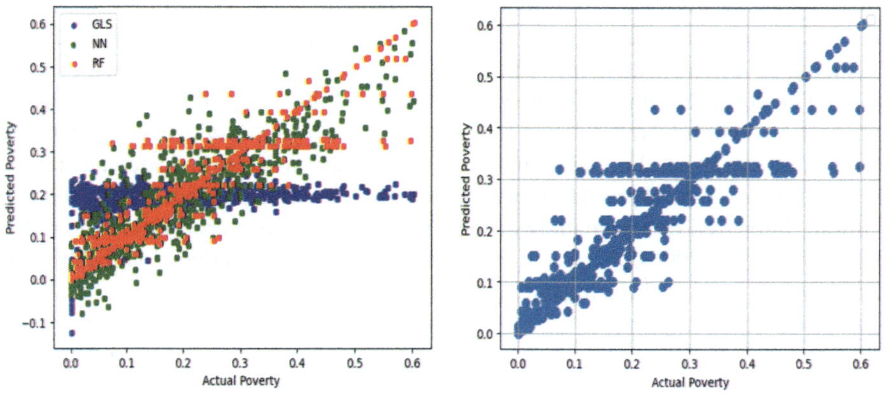

Fig. 4.10 Goodness of fit of GLS, NN, RF and RF only: MPI poverty. *Source* Authors' calculations

Table 4.3 R-squared of major models (leas squares, neural network, and random forest): MPI poverty

Model	R-square
Generalize Least Squares (GLS)	0.04
Neural Network (NN)	0.79
Random Forest (RF)	0.85

Source Authors' calculations

discrepancy between the predicted and actual values, indicating poor predictive accuracy. Also, low R-Square (0.04) indicate that the model failed to capture much of the variance in the data, making it ineffective in predicting poverty. The high RMSE and low R-Square values suggest that GLS is not suitable for generating accurate poverty predictions.

Similarly, the Neural Networks performed better than GLS but were still not as effective as other machine learning models. The RMSE (0.063) value is lower than that of GLS, indicating improved predictive accuracy. Although R-Square (0.79) is higher than GLS, this value is still lower than that of Random Forest, suggesting that Neural Networks were less effective in capturing the variance in the data compared to tree-based models. The performance of Neural Networks, while better than GLS, lagged behind Random Forest and other tree-based models in predicting poverty.

Random Forest is the most effective method for predicting MPI poverty among the ML techniques tested. Its superior performance, evidenced by the lowest RMSE and highest R-Square, makes it the best choice for generating accurate poverty predictions. On the contrary, GLS showed the least accuracy, while Neural Networks performed moderately but still lagged behind other machine learning models.

(iii) Regional Poverty Predication Using Random Forest: The Random Forest (RF) model, which demonstrated the highest accuracy and lowest Root Mean Squared Error (RMSE), has been used to predict MPI poverty levels for each district. To conduct the regional poverty prediction, district-wise MPI poverty headcount data from the National Family Health Survey 5 (NFHS-5) was used as a benchmark. The RF model was then applied to these headcount figures to generate predicted poverty levels for each district. The actual poverty headcounts from the NFHS-5 data and the predicted headcounts from the RF model were compared in Map 4.4. Both maps exhibit a similar pattern, demonstrating that the RF model's predictions closely align with the real-world data.

This alignment further validates the accuracy and reliability of the RF model in predicting district-level poverty levels (Fig. 4.11). The almost identical number of districts (99%, 705 districts out of total of 709 districts) falling within different poverty ranges, except for the 31–46% range, for the actual and predicted poverty headcounts, highlights the effectiveness of the RF model in capturing the spatial distribution of MPI poverty. This capability is crucial for policymakers and social

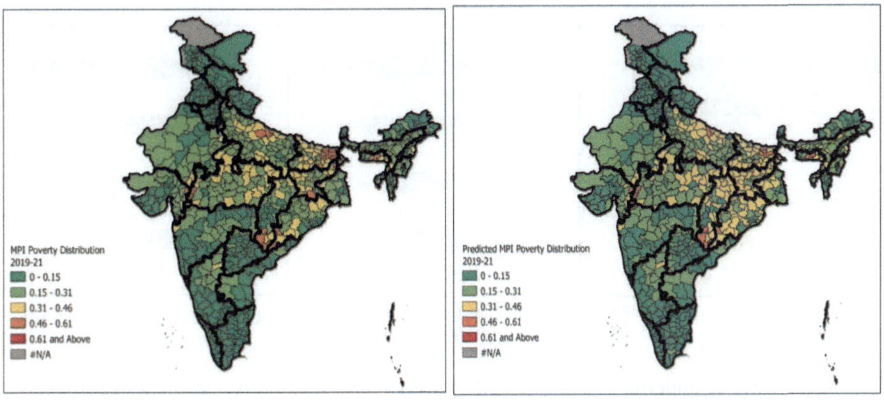

Map 4.4 Actual and predicted spatial distribution of poverty: MPI poverty. *Source* Authors' calculations

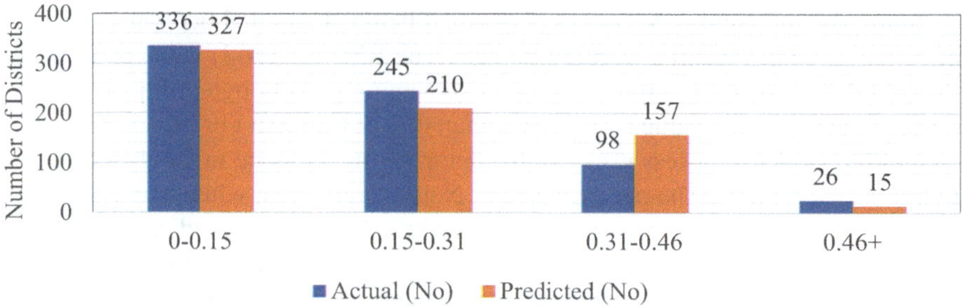

Fig. 4.11 Districts falling in similar MPI poverty range. *Source* Authors' calculations

scientists as it provides a robust tool for identifying regions that require more focused interventions and resources.

This analysis reveals that RF model is the invaluable tools for predicting MPI poverty at granular levels, which is not feasible with traditional methods. The consistency between the actual and predicted poverty headcounts not only underscores the model's accuracy but also its practical utility in guiding poverty alleviation efforts.

(iv) Variable Importance: A Variable Importance Analysis was conducted to determine which spatial variables most significantly contribute to predicting MPI poverty levels. Three models were evaluated to assess the impact of various spatial variables (Fig. 4.11):

- *Model 1—All Variables Included*: With all variables included, POI density and average nightlight emerged as the most influential. However, due to their high correlation, their individual contributions were affected. POI density explained 42% of the variability in MPI poverty, while nightlight explained 11%. The overlap in information provided by these variables reduced the apparent importance of nightlight (Fig. 4.12, Panel 1) (Liaw & Wiener, 2002).

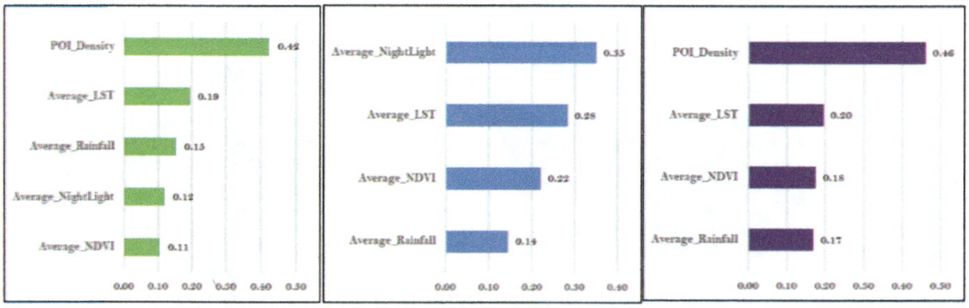

Random Forest with All Variables | Random Forest with Nightlight data | Random Forest with POI Density

Fig. 4.12 Variable importance from RF: MPI poverty. *Source* Authors' calculations

- *Model 2—Excluding POI Density*: When POI density was excluded, average nightlight became the most significant variable, accounting for 35% of the variability in MPI poverty (Fig. 4.12, Panel 2). This highlights that nightlight data alone can capture a substantial portion of poverty variation when POI density is not considered.
- *Model 3—Excluding Average Nightlight*: In the absence of average nightlight data, POI density emerged as the primary contributor, explaining 46% of the variability in MPI poverty (Fig. 4.12, Panel 3). This underscores the significant role of POI density in poverty prediction when nightlight data is not available.

4.6 Poverty Projection for 2023–24

The poverty projections for the years 2023–24 using ML techniques and geospatial data using monetary based international poverty line and non-monetary based MPI poverty has been estimated to explore that how in absence of survey data, the poverty can be estimated using the integration of geospatial data and survey trend past poverty trends in India.

4.6.1 Poverty Projection Based on Poverty Head Count

The poverty projections of poverty head count using the international poverty line for 2023–24 indicate that India as a whole is expected to see a decrease in poverty from 41.3% in 2021–22 to 34.7% in 2023–24, reflecting overall progress, yet state-level trends show a mix of increases and decreases (Fig. 4.13).

States with Decrease in Poverty: Delhi's poverty rate is projected to decrease from 3.0 to 2.3%, likely due to effective urban poverty alleviation strategies and robust economic activity. Haryana and Karnataka are also expected to see reductions from 26.6% to 25.2% and 39.1% to 33.0%, respectively, possibly due to economic growth and improved social programs. Maharashtra shows a decrease from 42.0 to 38.8%, while Assam is projected to reduce poverty from 49.2 to 42.9%, indicating successful state-level interventions and growth. Madhya Pradesh and Odisha are expected to see slight decreases from 50.2% to 49.0% and 53.1% to 51.3%, respectively. Uttar Pradesh shows a significant reduction from 58.1 to 32.5%, reflecting major improvements in poverty reduction programs and economic development. Jharkhand and Bihar, among the poorest states, are projected to reduce their poverty rates from 59.9% to 57.5% and 72.1% to 62.5%, respectively, indicating progress in targeted poverty alleviation efforts. Chhattisgarh is also expected to decrease from 74.2 to 63.1%, showing substantial improvements.

States with Increase in Poverty: Kerala is projected to see an increase in poverty from 7.9 to 10.2%, which may be attributed to economic challenges or shifts in poverty measurement criteria. Punjab shows a rise from 13.1 to 17.2%, potentially

Fig. 4.13 Poverty projection for major states in India: poverty head count (2023–24). *Note* The 2021–22 figure represents the actual poverty headcount based on the World Bank's international poverty line for Lower-Middle-Income Countries (LMICs). The 2023–24 figure is a projected poverty headcount, estimated using machine learning techniques. *Source* Authors' calculations

due to economic disruptions or inefficacies in poverty alleviation measures. Andhra Pradesh and Tamil Nadu are expected to see significant increases from 16.0% to 25.6% and 17.8% to 27.8%, respectively, possibly due to socio-economic disruptions or policy challenges. Telangana and Himachal Pradesh are also expected to experience increases from 18.3% to 21.2% and 19.6% to 23.0%, respectively. West Bengal shows a marginal increase from 26.4 to 27.4%, and Uttarakhand sees a slight rise from 26.7 to 27.5%. Jammu & Kashmir and Gujarat are projected to see increases from 29.8% to 30.2% and 32.0% to 35.3%, respectively, while Rajasthan shows a significant increase from 34.6 to 38.5%, indicating potential challenges in poverty reduction strategies.

The mixed trends across states highlight the complex interplay of economic, social, and policy factors influencing poverty. States with decreasing poverty rates often benefit from effective poverty alleviation programs, robust economic growth, and improved social services, while those with increasing rates may face economic disruptions, policy challenges, or measurement changes.

4.6.2 Poverty Projection Based on MPI Poverty

The MPI poverty projections for 2023–24 reveal substantial differences across Indian states compared to the all-India rate, which is expected to decline from 17.1% in 2019–21 to 10.2% in 2023–24 (Fig. 4.14).

Among the states in India, Kerala is expected to further reduce its poverty rate from 0.9 to 0.3%, highlighting its continued focus on high education and healthcare standards. Punjab and Telangana are also set to see significant reductions, with

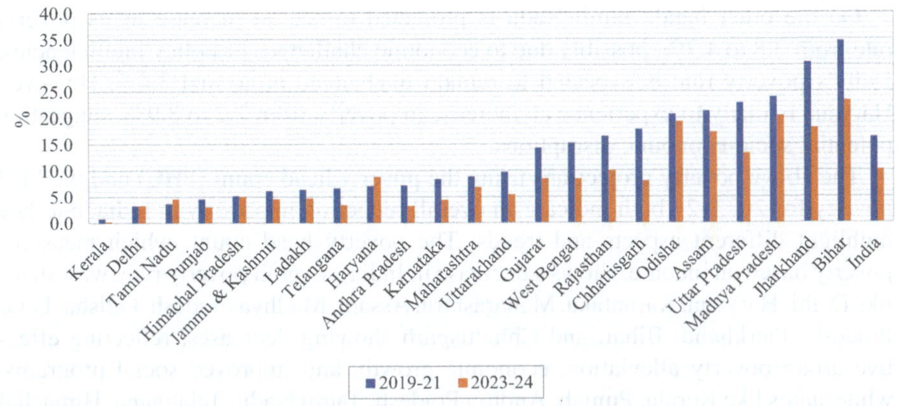

Fig. 4.14 Poverty projection for major states in India: MPI (2023–24). *Note* The 2019–21 figure represents the actual poverty based on the MPI. The 2023-24 figure is a projected MPI poverty, estimated using machine learning techniques. *Source* Authors' calculations

Punjab's rate dropping from 4.7 to 3.1% and Telangana's from 6.8 to 3.5%, showing the success of their poverty alleviation measures and economic policies.

Andhra Pradesh and Karnataka are projected to make notable progress, with poverty rates declining from 7.3% to 3.3% and from 8.5% to 4.5%, respectively. Maharashtra's rate is expected to decrease from 9 to 6.9%, Uttarakhand's from 9.8 to 5.5%, Gujarat's from 14.4 to 8.5%, and West Bengal's from 15.3 to 8.5%. These reductions reflect the successful implementation of targeted social and economic interventions.

Despite high poverty levels, Jharkhand and Bihar are projected to achieve considerable reductions, with Jharkhand's rate falling from 30.6 to 18.1% and Bihar's from 34.7 to 23.3%, indicating effective poverty reduction strategies. Himachal Pradesh is expected to see a slight decrease from 5.3 to 5.2%.

Ladakh and Jammu & Kashmir show modest improvements, with Ladakh's rate decreasing from 6.5 to 4.8% and Jammu & Kashmir's from 6.3 to 4.7%. Odisha's poverty rate is projected to slightly decrease from 20.8 to 19.4%, while Assam's is expected to drop from 21.4 to 17.4%. Madhya Pradesh's rate is likely to fall from 24 to 20.5%, and Uttar Pradesh's from 22.9 to 13.4%, reflecting effective poverty alleviation programs.

On the other hand, Tamil Nadu is projected to see an increase in its poverty rate from 3.8 to 4.7%, possibly due to economic challenges or policy inefficiencies. Delhi's poverty rate is expected to remain unchanged at around 3.4%. However, Haryana is likely to experience an increase in poverty from 7.2 to 8.9%, suggesting potential socio-economic disruptions.

The above poverty projections using the poverty head count (PHC) and the MPI poverty for 2023–24 both indicate an overall reduction in poverty in India, but they highlight different aspects and trends. The poverty head count, which measures poverty based on income, shows a decrease in India's overall poverty rate, with states like Delhi, Haryana, Karnataka, Maharashtra, Assam, Madhya Pradesh, Odisha, Uttar Pradesh, Jharkhand, Bihar, and Chhattisgarh showing decreases, reflecting effective urban poverty alleviation, economic growth, and improved social programs, while states like Kerala, Punjab, Andhra Pradesh, Tamil Nadu, Telangana, Himachal Pradesh, West Bengal, Uttarakhand, Jammu & Kashmir, Gujarat, and Rajasthan. In contrast, the MPI poverty, which considers multiple dimensions of poverty such as education, health, and living standards, also shows a decrease in the all-India poverty rate, with states like Kerala, Punjab, Telangana, Andhra Pradesh, Karnataka, Maharashtra, Uttarakhand, Gujarat, West Bengal, Jharkhand, and Bihar showing significant reductions, while states like Tamil Nadu, Delhi, Himachal Pradesh, Haryana, Jammu & Kashmir, Odisha, and Assam show either slight increases or minor improvements. The difference in poverty rate for PHC and MPI can be attributed to several factors, including the methods of measurement, variable used, the socio-economic factors, and implementation of variations in social welfare schemes, and other policy implementations. This highlights the importance of considering both income and multiple dimensions of poverty reduction policies to address poverty in different regions of the country.

4.7 Summary and Conclusion

This chapter explores the use of machine learning techniques combined with geospatial and survey data to improve poverty prediction in India. The goal is to determine if integrating multiple data sources can provide more accurate and timely poverty estimates compared to traditional, expensive survey methods, and also predict poverty. The analysis shows significant declines in poverty using both income-based and multidimensional methods, though regional disparities persist, especially in states like Bihar and Uttar Pradesh. Geospatial variables like nightlight intensity and NDVI (Normalized Difference Vegetation Index) are negatively correlated with poverty, while higher land surface temperatures are positively correlated.

Among the various machine learning techniques tested, the Random Forest Model proved to be the most accurate in predicting poverty levels, particularly when using variables such as nightlight intensity and Point of Interest (POI) density. This indicates that integrating machine learning techniques with geospatial data offers a highly effective, timely, and cost-efficient method for obtaining detailed poverty estimates. This approach provides valuable insights for policymakers to target poverty alleviation efforts more effectively. Compared to traditional survey methods, which are costly and infrequent, this method offers more immediate and detailed insights into poverty distribution. The relevance of these ML methods and use of geospatial data include, strengthening the ability of national statistical systems, producing better and more timely data to inform policies and monitor progress, contributing to existing literature and leveraging data innovations, and also potential to improve integration of geospatial and other statistical data.

This analysis highlights the effectiveness of machine learning techniques, particularly Random Forest, in predicting poverty at granular levels. This integrated approach improves the accuracy of poverty predictions and supports more effective policymaking, contributing to better-targeted interventions and resource allocation in the fight against poverty. The contribution of this study is introduction of the integration of conventional household survey data with non-conventional data like geospatial information and satellite imagery. Demonstrates the potential of applying ML algorithms on integrated data for timely analysis of the spatial distribution of poverty. This can be extended in the future to other non-conventional data sources, enabling a multidimensional examination of spatial associations. Expanding analysis with enhanced spatial resolution will provide better insights into poverty and inequality.

Appendix

See Tables 4.4 and 4.5.

Table 4.4 Poverty Head Count: 2021–22 (actual) and 2023–24 (projected)

	2021–22	2023–24
Delhi	3.0	2.3
Kerala	7.9	10.2
Punjab	13.1	17.2
Andhra Pradesh	16.0	25.6
Tamil Nadu	17.8	27.8
Telangana	18.3	21.2
Himachal Pradesh	19.6	23.0
West Bengal	26.4	27.4
Haryana	26.6	25.2
Uttarakhand	26.7	27.5
Jammu & Kashmir	29.8	30.2
Gujarat	32.0	35.3
Rajasthan	34.6	38.5
Karnataka	39.1	33.0
Maharashtra	42.0	38.8
Assam	49.2	42.9
Madhya Pradesh	50.2	49.0
Odisha	53.1	51.3
Uttar Pradesh	58.1	32.5
Jharkhand	59.9	57.5
Bihar	72.1	62.5
Chhattisgarh	74.2	63.1
India	41.3	34.7

Source Authors calculations from PLFS, 2021–22, and various other geospatial sources

Table 4.5 MPI poverty: 2019–21 (actual) and 2023–24 (projected)

	2019–21	2023–24
Kerala	0.9	0.3
Tamil Nadu	3.8	4.7
Delhi	3.4	3.4
Punjab	4.7	3.1
Himachal Pradesh	5.3	5.2
Ladakh	6.5	4.8
Jammu & Kashmir	6.3	4.7
Haryana	7.2	8.9
Telangana	6.8	3.5
Andhra Pradesh	7.3	3.3
Maharashtra	9.0	6.9
Karnataka	8.5	4.5
Uttarakhand	9.8	5.5
Gujarat	14.4	8.5
West Bengal	15.3	8.5
Rajasthan	16.6	10.1
Chhattisgarh	17.9	8.1
Odisha	20.8	19.4
Assam	21.4	17.4
Madhya Pradesh	24.0	20.5
Uttar Pradesh	22.9	13.4
Jharkhand	30.6	18.1
Bihar	34.7	23.3
India	16.4	10.2

Source Authors calculations from NFHS, 2019–21, and various other geospatial sources

References

Aguilar, R. A. C., Bonilla, C. D., Fujs, T., Lanker, C., Nguyen, M. C., Viveros, M., & Baah, S. K. T. (2024). March 2024 global poverty update from the World Bank: First estimates of global poverty until 2022 from survey data. World Bank Blogs. https://blogs.worldbank.org/en/opendata/march-2024-global-poverty-update-from-the-world-bank--first-esti

Alkire, S., & Santos, M. E. (2010). Acute multidimensional poverty: A new index for developing countries. United Nations Development Programme Human Development Reports Research Paper.

Alkire, S., Roche, J. M., & Santos, M. E. (2011). *Multidimensional poverty index 2011: Brief methodological note.*

Alkire, S., Roche, J. M., & Vaz, A. (2017). Changes over time in multidimensional poverty: Methodology and results for 34 countries. *World Development, 94*, 232–249. https://doi.org/10.1016/j.worlddev.2017.01.011

Arezki, R., & Brückner, M. (2012). Rainfall, financial development, and remittances: Evidence from Sub-Saharan Africa. *Journal of International Economics, 87*(2), 377–385. https://doi.org/10.1016/j.jinteco.2011.12.010

Asher, S., Lunt, T., Matsuura, R., & Novosad, P. (2021). Development research at high geographic resolution: An Analysis of night-lights, firms, and poverty in India using the SHRUG open data platform. *The World Bank Economic Review, 35*(4), 845–871. https://doi.org/10.1093/wber/lhab003

Baker, J., & Grosh, M. (1994). Poverty reduction through geographic targeting: How well does it work? *World Development, 22*(7), 983–995.

Bhadury, J., Jain, K., & Saxena, A. (2018). Nowcasting Indian gross value-added using night-time lights. *Economic and Political Weekly, 53*(48), 55–64.

Bhattacharya, S. (2018). *Industrial development and infrastructure in India: The challenge of balancing regional development*. Oxford University Press.

Beyer, R. C. M., Chhabra, E., Galdo, V., & Rama, M. (2018). Night-time lights as a proxy for economic activity in developing countries: A cross-country analysis.

Bilton, C., Chohan, B., & Smith, R. (2017). Predicting poverty with remote sensing and machine learning: A case study of Nepal.

Blumenstock, J. (2016). Fighting poverty with data: Machine learning algorithms measure and target poverty. *Science, 353*(6301), 753–754.

Breiman, L. (2001). Random forests. *Machine Learning, 45*(1), 5–32. https://doi.org/10.1023/A:1010933404324

Bruzzone, L., & Demir, B. (2014). A Review of Modern Approaches to Classification of Remote Sensing Data. In I. Manakos & M. Braun (Eds.), *Land Use and Land Cover Mapping in Europe: Practices & Trends* (pp. 127–143). Springer Netherlands. https://doi.org/10.1007/978-94-007-7969-3_9

Bhandari, L., & Roychowdhury, K. (2011). Night lights and economic activity in India.

Bundervoet, T., Maiyo, L., & Sanghi, A. (2015). Bright lights, big cities: Measuring national and sub-national economic growth in Africa from outer space.

Chanda, A., & Kabiraj, S. (2018). Economic convergence in Indian districts: What role do night-time lights play?

Chandrasekhar, S., & Mehrotra, N. (2016). Doubling farmers' incomes by 2022: What would it take? *Economic and Political Weekly, 51*(18), 10–13.

Chakravarty, S., & Dehejia, R. (2017). India's districts and the divergence within.

Chen, T., & Guestrin, C. (2016). XGBoost: A scalable tree boosting system. In *Proceedings of the 22nd ACM SIGKDD International Conference on Knowledge Discovery and Data Mining* (pp. 785–794).

Chen, X., & Nordhaus, W. D. (2011). Using luminosity data as a proxy for economic statistics. *Proceedings of the National Academy of Sciences, 108*(21), 8589–8594. https://doi.org/10.1073/pnas.1017031108

Chen, X., Zhuang, L., & Zhang, Y. (2020). Variable importance analysis for poverty prediction using random forests. *Journal of Computational Statistics, 25*(4), 523–539.

Chodorow-Reich, G., Gopinath, G., Mishra, P., & Narayan, A. (2018). Cash and the economy: Evidence from India's demonetization. *Quarterly Journal of Economics, 133*(1), 239–311.

Deaton, A., & Kozel, V. (2005). Data and dogma: The great Indian poverty debate. *The World Bank Research Observer, 20*(2), 177–199. https://doi.org/10.1093/wbro/lki009

Demombynes, G., & Sandefur, J. (2014). *Costing a data revolution* (SSRN Scholarly Paper 2622756). https://doi.org/10.2139/ssrn.2622756

Desai, S., Barik, D., Choudhuri, P., Chouhan, B., Sharma, O. P., Sharma, S., & Tiwari, D. K. (2024). Rethinking social safety nets in a changing society. *NCAER Working Paper, 171.*

Devarajan, S. (2013). Africa's statistical tragedy. *Review of Income and Wealth, 59*(S1), S9–S15. https://doi.org/10.1111/roiw.12013

Doll, C. N. H., Muller, J. P., & Morley, J. (2008). Assessing the impact of night-time light data on poverty measurement. *Remote Sensing of Environment, 112*(12), 4026–4037. https://doi.org/10.1016/j.rse.2008.07.003

Donaldson, D., & Storeygard, A. (2016). The view from above: Applications of satellite data in economics. *Journal of Economic Perspectives, 30*(4), 171–198.

Duan, T., Chartock, E., Ishfaq, H., Burke, M., Lobell, D., & Ermon, S. (2017). *Predicting poverty with satellite imagery in Bangladesh and India.* https://web.stanford.edu/~hmishfaq/cs325b.pdf

Dube, O. P., Jha, S., & Singh, A. (2021). Impact of climate variability on agricultural productivity and poverty in rural India. *Agricultural Economics Review.*

Dugoua, E., Kennedy, R., & Urpelainen, J. (2018). Satellite data for the social sciences: Measuring rural electrification with night-time lights. *International Journal of Remote Sensing, 39*(9), 2690–2701. https://doi.org/10.1080/01431161.2017.1420936

Elvidge, C. D., Baugh, K. E., & Kihn, E. A. (2017). The night-time light data for poverty mapping: Insights from satellite observations. *Remote Sensing.*

Gao, J., Wang, Y., & Zhang, Z. (2017). Integration of geospatial and socioeconomic data for improved poverty prediction. *International Journal of Applied Earth Observation and Geoinformation, 62*, 127–138.

Gera, I. (2024, February 27). India's poverty rate declined to 4.5–5% in 2022–23: SBI Research. *The Economic Times.* https://economictimes.indiatimes.com/news/economy/indicators/indias-poverty-rate-declined-to-4-5-5-in-2022-23-sbi-research/articleshow/108029519.cms?from=mdr

Gibson, J., Olper, A., & Rapsomanikis, G. (2019). Data limitations in poverty research: The case of India. *Economic Development and Cultural Change, 67*(4), 891–912. https://doi.org/10.1086/702105

Goodfellow, I., Bengio, Y., & Courville, A. (2016). *Deep learning.* MIT Press.

Greene, W. H. (2018). *Econometric analysis* (8th ed.). Pearson.

Ghosh, T., Powell, R. L., Elvidge, C. D., Baugh, K. E., Sutton, P. C., & Anderson, S. (2013). Shedding light on the global distribution of economic activity. *The Open Geography Journal, 6*, 13–21. https://doi.org/10.2174/1874913501306010013

Grove, A. T. (1996). *The changing geography of Africa.* Oxford University Press.

Head, A., Manguin, M., Tran, N., & Blumenstock, J. E. (2017). Can human development be measured with satellite imagery? *Ictd, 17*, 16–19.

Henderson, J. V., Storeygard, A., & Weil, D. N. (2012). Measuring economic growth from outer space. *American Economic Review, 102*(2), 994–1028.

Henderson, J. V., Squires, T., Storeygard, A., & Weil, D. (2018). The global distribution of economic activity: Nature, history, and the role of trade1. *The Quarterly Journal of Economics, 133*(1), 357–406. https://doi.org/10.1093/qje/qjx030

Hodler, R., Lechner, M., & Raschky, P. A. (2023). Institutions and the resource curse: New insights from causal machine learning. *PLoS ONE, 18*(6), e0284968.

Hu, S., Ge, Y., Liu, M., Ren, Z., & Zhang, X. (2022). Village-level poverty identification using machine learning, high-resolution images, and geospatial data. *International Journal of Applied Earth Observation and Geoinformation, 107*, 102694. https://doi.org/10.1016/j.jag.2022.102694

Hu, T., Yang, J., Li, X., & Gong, P. (2016). Mapping urban land use by using landsat images and open social data. *Remote sensing, 8*(2), 151.

Huang, X., Xie, C., Fang, X., & Zhang, L. (2015). Combining Pixel- and Object-Based Machine Learning for Identification of Water-Body Types From Urban High-Resolution Remote-Sensing Imagery. *IEEE Journal of Selected Topics in Applied Earth Observations and Remote Sensing, 8*(5), 2097–2110. https://doi.org/10.1109/JSTARS.2015.2420713

IEAG. (2014). *A world that counts: Mobilizing the data revolution for sustainable development.* Independent Expert Advisory Group. https://www.undatarevolution.org/wp-content/uploads/2014/11/A-World-That-Counts.pdf

Jean, N., Burke, M., Xie, M., Davis, W. M., Lobell, D. B., & Ermon, S. (2016). Combining satellite imagery and machine learning to predict poverty. *Science, 353*(6301), 790–794. https://doi.org/10.1126/science.aaf7895

Jha, P. (2019). Governance and poverty in India. *Indian Journal of Public Administration, 65*(4), 763–776.

Jerven, M. (2017). How much will a data revolution in development cost? *Forum for Development Studies, 44*(1), 31–50. https://doi.org/10.1080/08039410.2016.1260050

Kumar, A., & Patel, R. (2021). The role of vegetation and environmental factors in poverty alleviation. *Environmental Research Letters, 16*(4), 044023.

Kumar, R., & Verma, N. (2023). Rainfall, agricultural productivity, and poverty in India: A regional analysis. *Agricultural Systems, 222*, 103556.

Sivakumar, M. V., Das, H. P., & Brunini, O. (2005). Impacts of present and future climate variability and change on agriculture and forestry in the arid and semi-arid tropics. *Climatic change*, 70, 31–72.

Leroux, L., Bégué, A., Lo Seen, D., Jolivot, A., & Kayitakire, F. (2017). Driving forces of recent vegetation changes in the Sahel: Lessons learned from regional and local level analyses. *Remote Sensing of Environment, 191*, 38–54. https://doi.org/10.1016/j.rse.2017.01.014

Liaw, A., & Wiener, M. (2002). Classification and regression by random Forest. *R news, 2*(3), 18–22.

McBride, L., & Nichols, A. (2018). Retooling poverty targeting using out-of-sample validation and machine learning. *The World Bank Economic Review, 32*(3), 531–550. https://doi.org/10.1093/wber/lhw056

Nattapong, P., Martinez, A. J., Addawe, M., & Bulan, J. A. N. (2022). Predicting Poverty Using Geospatial Data in Thailand | Request PDF. ResearchGate. https://doi.org/10.2139/ssrn.3785116

Nischal, K. N., Radhakrishnan, R., Mehta, S. & Chandani, S. (2015). Correlating night-time satellite images with poverty and other census data of India and estimating future trends. In *Proceedings of the Second ACM IKDD Conference on Data Sciences—CoDS, 15 (March 2015)*, pp. 75–79.

Njuguna, C., & McSharry, P. (2017). Constructing spatiotemporal poverty indices from big data. *Journal of Business Research, 70*(C), 318–327.

Pettorelli, N., Laurance, W. F., O'Brien, T. G., Wegmann, M., Nagendra, H., & Turner, W. (2014). Satellite remote sensing for applied ecologists: Opportunities and challenges. *Journal of Applied Ecology, 51*(4), 839–848. https://doi.org/10.1111/1365-2664.12261

Pinkovskiy, M., & Sala-i-Martin, X. (2016). Lights, Camera … Income! Illuminating the National Accounts- Household Surveys Debate *. *The Quarterly Journal of Economics, 131*(2), 579–631. https://doi.org/10.1093/qje/qjw003

Rangarajan, C., & Mahendra Dev, S. (2022). Poverty in India: Measurement, trends and other issues. In S. R. Hashim, R. Mukherji, & B. Mishra (Eds.), *Perspectives on inclusive policies for development in India: In Honour of Prof. R. Radhakrishna* (pp. 255–284). Springer Nature. https://doi.org/10.1007/978-981-19-0185-0_13

Ravallion, M. (1994). Measuring social welfare with and without poverty lines. *The American Economic Review, 84*(2), 359–364.

Richardson, C. J. (2007). How much did droughts matter? Linking rainfall and GDP growth in Zimbabwe. *African Affairs, 106*(424), 463–478. https://doi.org/10.1093/afraf/adm013

Ruthirako, P., Darnsawasdi, R., & Chatupote, W. (2015). Intensity and pattern of land surface temperature in Hat Yai city, Thailand. *Walailak Journal of Science and Technology (WJST), 12*(1), Article 1.

Saxena, R. (2018). *Regional disparities in industrialization and economic diversification in India.* Sage Publications.

Sen, A. (1981). *Poverty and famines: An essay on entitlement and deprivation.* Clarendon Press.

Sruthi, S., & Aslam, M. A. M. (2015). Agricultural Drought Analysis Using the NDVI and Land Surface Temperature Data; a Case Study of Raichur District. *Aquatic Procedia*, 4, 1258–1264. https://doi.org/10.1016/j.aqpro.2015.02.164

Suraj, P. K., Gupta, A., Sharma, M., Paul, S., & Banerjee, S. (2018). *On monitoring development indicators using high resolution satellite images* [Paper]. arXiv.org. https://econpapers.repec.org/paper/arxpapers/1712.02282.htm

Tilak, J. B. G. (2015). How inclusive is higher education in India? *Social Change, 45*(2), 185–223. https://doi.org/10.1177/0049085715574178

Tingzon, J., Kundu, S., & Yeo, H. (2019). Combining geospatial data with machine learning to predict poverty in developing regions. *Geospatial Research Letters, 10*(2), 145–159. https://doi.org/10.1016/j.grsl.2019.03.002

Weng, Q. (2001). A remote sensing? GIS evaluation of urban expansion and its impact on surface temperature in the Zhujiang Delta, China. *International Journal of Remote Sensing, 22*(10), 1999–2014. https://doi.org/10.1080/713860788

Xie, M., Jean, N., Burke, M., Lobell, D., & Ermon, S. (2016). Transfer Learning from Deep Features for Remote Sensing and Poverty Mapping. *Proceedings of the AAAI Conference on Artificial Intelligence, 30*(1), Article 1. https://doi.org/10.1609/aaai.v30i1.9906

Yao, Y., Zhou, J., Sun, Z., Guan, Q., Guo, Z., Xu, Y., Zhang, J., Hong, Y., Cai, Y., & Wang, R. (2023). Estimating China's poverty reduction efficiency by integrating multi-source geospatial data and deep learning techniques. *Geo-Spatial Information Science, 0*(0), 1–17. https://doi.org/10.1080/10095020.2023.2165975

Ye, T., Zhao, N., Yang, X., Ouyang, Z., Liu, X., Chen, Q., Hu, K., Yue, W., Qi, J., Li, Z., & Jia, P. (2019). Improved population mapping for China using remotely sensed and points-of-interest data within a random forests model. *Science of The Total Environment*, 658, 936–946. https://doi.org/10.1016/j.scitotenv.2018.12.276

Zhao, E., Qian, Y., Gao, C., Huo, H., Jiang, X., & Kong, X. (2014). Land surface temperature retrieval using airborne hyperspectral scanner daytime mid-infrared data. *Remote Sensing, 6*(12), Article 12. https://doi.org/10.3390/rs61212667

References

Chapter 5
Inequality of Opportunity in Education

5.1 Introduction

Education stands as a cornerstone for achieving the United Nation's Sustainable Development Goals (SDGs), particularly Goal 4, which aims to 'ensure inclusive and equitable quality education and promote lifelong learning opportunities for all'. The significance of education transcends individual benefits, extending to societal progress and economic development. However, educational inequality poses a significant obstacle in achieving not only SDG 4 but also other interconnected SDGs such as reduced inequalities (Goal 10) and poverty alleviation (Goal 1). The educational inequalities and their resultant socio-economic consequences are more pronounced in the developing countries compared to the developed countries. Post-1980s, with the advent of globalization, education systems in developing countries faced further challenges. Structural adjustment policies imposed by the World Bank and other international financial institutions constrained national budgets, leading to cuts in education spending and weakening secondary and higher education systems.

The Global Education Monitoring Report 2023 by UNESCO highlights significant disparities in educational access across different regions. Globally, 9% of children of primary school age are out of school. This figure varies significantly across regions. In Europe and North America, only 1% of primary school-aged children are out of school, while in Sub-Saharan Africa, the rate is much higher at 20%. Other regions with high out-of-school rates include North and West Africa (9%), Oceania (7%), and South Asia (7%). Among all the regions, the situation is more challenging

Disclaimer: The presentation of material and details in maps used in this chapter does not imply the expression of any opinion whatsoever on the part of the Publisher or Author concerning the legal status of any country, area or territory or of its authorities, or concerning the delimitation of its borders. The depiction and use of boundaries, geographic names and related data shown on maps and included in lists, tables, documents, and databases in this chapter are not warranted to be error free nor do they necessarily imply official endorsement or acceptance by the Publisher or Author.

B. S. Mehta et al., *Predicting Inequality of Opportunity and Poverty in India Using Machine Learning*, India Studies in Business and Economics,
https://doi.org/10.1007/978-981-96-2544-4_5

for older children in Sub-Saharan Africa and South Asia: 33% of lower secondary and 48% of upper secondary school-aged children are out of school in Sub-Saharan Africa, while 13% of lower secondary and 39% of upper secondary school-aged children out of school in South Asia. This shows that the proportion of children out of school is relatively low at primary level schooling in South Asia compared to other regions, whereas, the rate increases significantly for older age groups. Among South Asian countries, the rates of out-of-school children are relatively high in India (13%), Bangladesh (10%), and Bhutan (10%) for lower secondary school-aged children. However, the situation is even more critical for upper secondary school-aged children, with Afghanistan (56%), the Maldives (50%), and India (44%) exhibiting significantly high out-of-school rates. These disparities highlight the urgent need for targeted educational interventions and policies to ensure that all children in South Asia have access to quality education. This high rate of out-of-school children at both lower and upper secondary levels in India underscores the need for urgent attention.

Further, the level of education among the labour force aged 15 and older in India shows significant disparities compared to developed countries like the USA and Germany, as well as developing countries such as Brazil and South Africa (Fig. 5.1). A large portion of India's labour force has less than a basic education, meaning many people do not even finish primary school. Additionally, a significant number of workers in India only have basic education. This uneven educational distribution is further highlighted by the relatively low percentage of individuals achieving intermediate and advanced education levels, which are crucial for developing a skilled and competitive workforce. In contrast, higher rates of intermediate and advanced education are seen in developed nations like the USA and Germany, as well as in developing countries such as South Africa and Brazil. This situation reflects persistent educational inequality in India, manifesting in various forms, including unequal access based on socio-economic background, gender, and geography (Tilak, 2007; Kingdon, 2010; IER, 2024).

This educational disparity has deep-rooted causes. Economic barriers, such as poverty, prevent many families from sending their children to school or keeping them in school long enough to complete higher levels of education. Social inequalities, including caste and gender discrimination, further limit educational opportunities for many individuals. Additionally, inadequate infrastructure, such as poorly equipped schools and a shortage of qualified teachers, exacerbates the problem, particularly in rural and underserved areas. Despite significant policy efforts, such as the Right to Education Act in 2009, which aims to provide free and compulsory education to children, these initiatives have not fully addressed the underlying issues. In 2020, the Government of India also introduced a new education policy aimed at enhancing early childhood education and improving overall educational quality. Despite its promise, the policy has yet to be fully implemented across many states in the country. Studies suggest that improving educational outcomes in India necessitates targeted policies that tackle specific challenges, including the quality of education, investment in educational infrastructure, and support for disadvantaged groups. Addressing these issues is crucial for reducing educational inequality. Understanding and addressing the inequality of educational opportunities—an essential

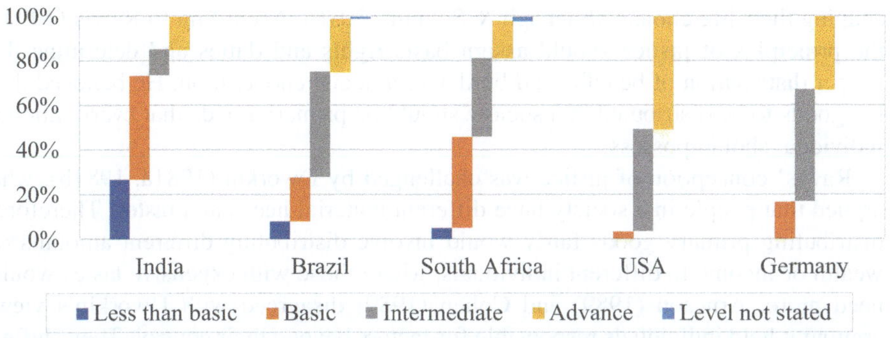

Fig. 5.1 Education level of labour force (15+ years) in India and major countries: 2023. 2024*Note* Less than basic: Not completed primary education may also include no formal education; Basic: Completed primary education and some case first stage of secondary education; Intermediate: Completed lower secondary education and upper secondary education; Advance: Post-secondary education including both tertiary education and advance vocational training *Source* International Labour Organisation (ILO)

aspect of educational disparity—requires recognizing and overcoming barriers that hinder equitable access to quality education for individuals across different socio-economic background, gender, and geographical locations (Das, 2022; Kundu, 2023). By tackling these root causes, India can work towards building a more equitable and skilled workforce. In this context, this chapter examines the inequality of educational opportunities (IOp) in India and investigates the factors contributing to these disparities.

This chapter is organized into five sections. Following the introduction, the second section outlines the study's framework, detailing the theoretical and conceptual foundations underpinning the research. The third section delves into the methodology and data sources, explaining the approach and data used to analyse educational IOp. The fourth section presents the results and discussion, offering an in-depth analysis of the findings and their implications. The final section summarizes the key findings and provides concluding remarks, highlighting the main insights and their relevance to understanding and addressing educational IOp in India.

5.2 Study Framework

As discussed in detail in Chapters 2 and 3 earlier, the concept of equality of opportunity stems from the idea of distributive justice. This idea pertains to the principles and rules governing the distribution of resources and evaluates outcomes against expectations (Sabbagh & Schmitt, 2016). John Rawls (1971) pioneered the theory of justice by proposing a normative framework for creating a just society through social, political, and economic institutions. These institutions play a significant role in regulating the distribution of goods and social burdens among individuals, thereby shaping their life choices (Sabbagh & Schmitt, 2016). According to Rawls (1999), the principles of justice should assign basic rights and duties and determine the proper distribution of benefits and burdens for social cooperation. He believed that the goods to be distributed in a society should be primary goods that every rational individual should possess.

Rawls' conception of justice was challenged by Dworkin (1981a, 1981b), who argued that people in a society have different material needs and tastes. Therefore, distributing primary goods fairly would involve distributing different amounts of wealth or income to different individuals, where those with expensive tastes would need more. Arneson (1989) and Cohen (1989) disagreed with Dworkin's view, arguing it held individuals responsible for factors beyond their control. They shifted the focus from resource distribution to the availability of opportunities. Arneson (1989) advocated for 'equal opportunity for welfare', suggesting that every individual should face the same set of possibilities for fulfilling their preferences. Cohen (1989) proposed the idea of 'equality of advantage,' extending beyond welfare to include broader aspects of advantage. Despite their different views, Rawls, Dworkin, Arneson, and Cohen all emphasized that an equitable society is one where everyone has an equal opportunity to achieve their desired outcomes (Mehta & Dhote, 2022).

Roemer (1998) further refined this idea by distinguishing between effort and circumstances. Effort refers to factors within an individual's control, such as hours dedicated to work or study, occupational choices, and quality of work. Circumstances, on the other hand, are factors beyond an individual's control, such as family background, ethnicity, gender, and socio-economic status. This relationship can be mathematically represented for a population of individuals from 1, ..., N, where each individual's outcome (y_i), is determined by their circumstance (C_i) and effort (e_i):

$$y_i = g(C_i, e_i)\forall_i = 1, \ldots, N \tag{5.1}$$

Roemer (2002) proposed a framework for achieving equality of opportunity by categorizing individuals based on circumstances (types) and effort levels (tranches). The literature on inequality of opportunity (IOp) includes the ex-ante and ex-post approaches. The ex-ante approach focuses on inequalities between individuals with different circumstances or types, while the ex-post approach assesses inequality among people with the same effort level (Fleurbaey & Peragine, 2013; Ramos & Van de Gaer, 2016). The ex-ante approach considers the type-specific outcome distribution as the opportunity set for individuals, with the value of this set determined by the mean outcome of each type (Ferreira & Gignoux, 2011).

The counterfactual distribution ($\acute{Y}_{EA}$): $\acute{\text{Y}}_{\text{EA}}$ is constructed by replacing the actual outcomes of individuals with the mean outcome of their respective types. This is done to isolate the effect of circumstances (types) on the outcomes, removing the influence of individual effort. The type-specific outcome distribution is considered the opportunity set, with its value determined by the mean outcome of each type:

$$\acute{y}_i^k(\pi) = \mu^k, \ \forall i = 1, \ldots, N; \ \forall k = 1, \ldots, K; \ \forall i, \ \pi \in [0, 1] \tag{5.2}$$

where

- $\acute{y}_i^k(\pi)$: This represents the counterfactual outcome for individual i of type k when considering the distribution of opportunities (π).
- μ^k: This is the mean (average) outcome for type k.
- $\forall$: This symbol means "for all" and is used to indicate that the statement applies to all specified elements.
- $i = 1, \ldots,$ N: This specifies that i ranges from 1 to N, where N is the total number of individuals.
- $k = 1, \ldots, K$: This specifies that k ranges from 1 to K, where K is the total number of types.
- $\pi \in [0,1]$: This specifies that π (the distribution of opportunities) is a value between 0 and 1.

By replacing each individual's outcome y_i with the mean outcome of their type μ^k, a new distribution $\acute{Y}_{EA}$ is constructed. This new distribution reflects only the differences between types, ignoring within-type variation due to effort or other factors.

Calculating Ex-Ante Inequality of Opportunity (IOp_{EA}): The ex-ante inequality of opportunity $\mathrm{IOp_{EA}}$ is then measured by applying an inequality index I (such as the Gini coefficient or another inequality measure) to the counterfactual distribution $\acute{Y}_{EA}$.

$$\mathrm{Ex-ante\ IO}p_{EA} = I\left(\acute{Y}_{EA}\right) \tag{5.3}$$

The transformation from the individual outcomes to the counterfactual distribution $\acute{Y}_{EA}$ and the subsequent calculation of $\mathrm{IOp_{EA}}$ allows us to measure the inequality that arises solely from differences in circumstances, abstracting away the influence of individual effort. This provides a clearer picture of inequality of opportunity in the given context.

Education is a crucial factor for distributive justice because educational institutions distribute a variety of resources that play a significant role in shaping individuals' futures. These resources include not just academic knowledge, but also attention, support, care, and respect (Resh & Sabbagh, 2016). By distributing these resources, schools create different learning opportunities and social experiences that influence individuals' motivation, academic achievements, and ultimately their life chances (Bills & Wacker, 2003; Hurn, 1985; Oakes et al., 1992). In the context of education, the concept of Equality of Educational Opportunity (EEO) asserts that every child has the right to education, regardless of their family background, nationality, ethnicity, socio-economic status, religion, or gender (Resh & Sabbagh, 2016). The idea behind EEO is that a common schooling system can act as a great equalizer, allowing individuals effort and ability to overcome differences in their initial circumstances and educational outcomes (Resh & Sabbagh, 2016).

The interpretation of EEO has evolved over time, reflecting a shift in understanding from 'equality of input' to 'equality of output' (Resh & Sabbagh, 2016). 'Equality of input' focuses on distributing resources equally among all individuals.

In contrast, 'equality of output' emphasizes addressing the different starting points of individuals. This means compensating for disadvantages faced by weaker and marginalized groups to provide them with equal opportunities to achieve similar outcomes (Coleman, 1968; Kellough, 2005). The participation in the labour market is significantly influenced by level of education, as it plays crucial role in ensuring a smooth transition from school to decent work.

This analysis indicates that education as a part of distributive justice means making sure all individuals get fair resources and support, helping them reach their full potential no matter their background. The evolving idea of Equality of Educational Opportunity (EEO) emphasizes not only distributing resources equally but also addressing the different starting points of children to achieve true educational fairness. This approach helps to ensure their smooth transition from school to work after completing the education and contributes to building a skilled labour force.

5.3 Methodology and Data Sources

This chapter uses machine learning techniques to calculate ex-ante educational Inequality of Opportunity (IOp) in India. As discussed in the earlier chapter, ML algorithms are preferred over conventional methods, such as Ordinary Least Squares (OLS), because conventional methods often suffer from researchers' discretion in selecting circumstance variables. Arbitrary selection can lead to the exclusion of important variables or the inclusion of too many variables. Excluding important variables reduces the model's explanatory power, leading to downward biases, while including excessive variables results in upward biased estimates (Brunori et al., 2019; Hufe et al., 2017; Ferreira & Gignoux, 2011). ML algorithms help overcome these limitations by minimizing the risks of ad-hoc and arbitrary data selection, balancing upward and downward biases (Hothorn et al., 2006; Brunori et al., 2019; Brunori & Neidhofer, 2021; Hothorn & Zeileis, 2021; Salas-Rojo & Rodriguez, 2022). The ML algorithms used in this study to measure ex-ante educational IOp are called conditional inference trees and conditional inference forests. These algorithms serve a dual purpose: they create circumstance-based types and predict the outcome variable. They have been used in several studies predicting income-based IOp (Brunori et al., 2018, 2019; Brunori & Neidhofer, 2021; Lefranc & Kundu, 2020; Mehta & Dhote, 2022; Mehta et al., 2023).

Conditional inference trees provide a visual representation of the opportunity structure for a particular outcome variable by recursively splitting the range of circumstances, enabling the identification of sub-groups with similar circumstances. Conditional inference forests, a variant of conditional inference trees, generate multiple trees and combine their results by averaging. The repetitive extraction of subsamples by the algorithm ensures the independence of each tree, enhancing the reliability of IOp estimates. An additional feature of conditional forests is their ability to provide the relative importance of factors used in creating the trees. Furthermore, a significant advantage of machine learning methods is that when a large

Table 5.1 Circumstance variables

S. no	Variable	Categories
1	Sector	1. Rural, 2. Urban
2	Gender	1. Male, 2. Female
3	Social group	1. Scheduled Tribe (ST), 2. Scheduled Castes (SC), 3. Other Backward Classes (OBC), 4. General (Gen)
4	Region	1. Central, 2. East, 3. North, 4. Northeast, 5. South, 6. West
5	Parents' education	1. No Education, 2. Below Secondary, 3. Secondary/Higher Secondary, 4. Graduate or Above
6	Parents' occupation	1. Unskilled, 2. Low, 3. Medium, 4. High

set of circumstances is present, only those circumstances that have a statistically meaningful relationship with the outcome variable are considered.

This study uses data from the Periodic Labour Force Survey (PLFS) of 2022–23 conducted by the National Statistics Office (NSO), which is representative at the national and state levels. The outcome variable used to assess educational IOp is years of education, given in number of years. The circumstance variables used to measure educational IOp (Table 5.1) are as follows:

The sample used for measuring educational IOp includes 30,087 individuals. This sample consists of individuals who have completed their education or dropped out, are above the age of 15, and have information on their parents' education and occupation. The choice of machine learning methods over conventional approaches in this chapter aims to provide more accurate and unbiased estimates of educational IOp by effectively handling the selection of circumstance variables and ensuring robust results.

5.4 Results and Discussion

5.4.1 Sample Characteristics

The sample characteristics in Table 5.2 provide a snapshot of the individuals included in the study. Understanding these characteristics helps to contextualize the findings and the extent to which they might reflect broader trends in India. Most of the sample individuals are from rural areas (65%), reflecting India's population distribution according to the Census of India. The sample is predominantly male, with 71% males and 29% females. In terms of social groups, the majority belong to the Other Backward Classes (OBC), making up 42% of the sample. About 20% of the sample is from the Scheduled Castes (SC), and another 20% belong to the general category. Individuals from the Scheduled Tribes (ST) have the smallest representation in the

Table 5.2 Characters of sample individuals (%)

Variable	Category	(%)
Sector	Rural	64.6
	Urban	35.4
Gender	Male	70.8
	Female	29.2
Social Group	ST	15.9
	SC	20.3
	OBC	42.3
	General	21.5
Region	Central	24.0
	East	16.6
	North	17.4
	North East	12.3
	South	16.9
	West	12.9

Source Authors calculation from PLFS, 2022–23

sample at 16%. Geographically, the largest portion of the sample, around one-fourth, resides in Central India, while the Northeastern region has the smallest representation.

The characteristics of the parents in the sample provide an important context for understanding educational outcomes, as parental education and occupation significantly influence children's educational attainment and opportunities. Table 5.3 details the educational and occupational qualifications of the parents of the sampled individuals. Among the sampled individuals, approximately half have parents educated below the secondary level, followed by 34% whose parents have no formal education. About 13% have parents educated up to the secondary or higher secondary level. The smallest group, 4%, consists of individuals whose parents are educated up to the graduate level or above. Regarding occupational composition, approximately three-fourths of the sampled individuals have parents in low-skill occupations, and about one-fourth have parents in unskilled occupations. The proportion of individuals with parents in medium- and high-skilled jobs is low, at 2% each.

Average Years of Schooling of Individuals: This section explores the average years of educational attainment among individuals, across sector (rural or urban), gender, social group, and region. Understanding these characteristics helps reveal disparities and patterns in educational attainment across different demographics (Table 5.4).

Sector: In rural areas, the average years of education is 10.11 years, with a median of 10 years and a standard deviation of 3.58 years. This indicates that most individuals in rural areas have completed just about 10 years of schooling, with some variation. Urban areas show a higher average of 11.48 years of education, with a median of 12 years and a standard deviation of 3.89 years. This suggests that urban residents

Table 5.3 Characteristics of parents of sample individuals (%)

		%
Parents education	No education	34.3
	Below secondary	48.8
	Secondary/higher secondary	13.1
	graduate and above	3.7
Parents occupation	Unskilled	23.3
	Low skill	72.5
	Medium skill	1.8
	High skill	2.3

Source Authors Calculation from, PLFS, 2022–23

Table 5.4 Average, median, and standard deviation of years of education by sector, gender, social group and region

Variable	Category	Mean	Median	SD
Sector	Rural	10.11	10.00	3.58
	Urban	11.48	12.00	3.89
Gender	Male	10.55	10.00	3.64
	Female	10.71	10.00	4.01
Social Group	ST	9.67	9.00	3.48
	SC	10.15	10.00	3.79
	OBC	10.74	10.00	3.76
	General	11.44	12.00	3.68
Region	Central	9.88	10.00	3.82
	East	10.20	10.00	3.73
	North	10.46	10.00	3.97
	North East	10.30	10.00	3.36
	South	12.13	12.00	3.53
	West	10.92	10.00	3.34

Source Authors calculation from PLFS, 2022–23

generally have access to more educational resources, leading to a higher average level of schooling compared to their rural counterparts (Desai & Kulkarni, 2020).

Gender: The average years of education for males is 10.55 years, with a median of 10 years and a standard deviation of 3.64 years. For females, the average is slightly higher at 10.71 years, with a median of 10 years and a standard deviation of 4.01 years. Although women in India, on average, have slightly more years of education than men, the difference is not substantial. The higher standard deviation for females indicates more variability in educational attainment among women compared to men (Bhat & Zavier, 2021).

Social Group: Individuals from Scheduled Tribes (ST) have the lowest average years of education at 9.67 years, with a median of 9 years and a standard deviation of 3.48 years. Scheduled Castes (SC) have an average of 10.15 years, with a median of 10 years and a standard deviation of 3.79 years. Other Backward Classes (OBC) average 10.74 years, with a median of 10 years and a standard deviation of 3.76 years. The General category, which includes those not classified under the reserved categories, has the highest average at 11.44 years, with a median of 12 years and a standard deviation of 3.68 years. This distribution shows a clear gradient where educational attainment increases with the social status of the group, reflecting historical and ongoing socio-economic disparities (Kumar & Rao, 2022).

Region: Educational attainment varies significantly across regions. The South region shows the highest average of 12.13 years of education, with a median of 12 years and a standard deviation of 3.53 years. This suggests better access to education and higher levels of educational attainment in Southern India compared to other regions. The Central region has the lowest average at 9.88 years, with a median of 10 years and a standard deviation of 3.82 years. Other regions like the East, North, North East, and West have averages ranging from 10.20 to 10.92 years. The variation across regions reflects the impact of regional disparities in educational infrastructure, economic development, and access to resources (Sharma & Gupta, 2021).

Average Years of Schooling: Table 5.5 the average, median, and variability in years of education of children based on educational and occupational backgrounds of their parents.

Average years of Schooling of Individual by their Parents' Education: The educational background of parents significantly influences their children's educational attainment. Individuals whose parents with no formal education have an average of 9.20 years of schooling, with a median of 9 years and a standard deviation of 3.81 years. This lower level of education for the individual reflects the limited educational opportunities and resources available when parents themselves have not pursued education (Chaudhury et al., 2020). For individuals whose parents

Table 5.5 Average, median, and standard deviation of years of education based on parent's characteristics

Variable	Category	Mean	Median	SD
Parents education	No education	9.20	9.00	3.81
	Below secondary	10.78	10.00	3.33
	Secondary/higher secondary	12.55	12.00	3.44
	Graduate and above	14.31	15.00	3.28
Parents occupation	Unskilled	9.62	10.00	3.70
	Low skill	10.76	10.00	3.68
	Medium skill	13.17	15.00	3.43
	High skill	13.38	15.00	3.64

Source Authors Calculation from PLFS, 2022–23

have education below secondary level, the average years of education is 10.78, with a median of 10 years and a standard deviation of 3.33 years. This shows a moderate improvement in educational attainment compared to individual of uneducated parents, indicating some positive impact of having at least some formal education among parents (Kumar et al., 2021).

Individuals whose parents have completed secondary or higher secondary education average 12.55 years of schooling, with a median of 12 years and a standard deviation of 3.44 years. This reflects a significant increase in educational attainment, demonstrating the critical role that higher parental education levels play in encouraging and supporting their individuals' educational achievements (Singh & Gupta, 2019). Individuals with parents having graduate or higher education have the highest average of 14.31 years of schooling, with a median of 15 years and a standard deviation of 3.28 years. This substantial difference highlights the strong correlation between greater educational levels among individuals and parental education. Educated parents often have more resources, better knowledge about educational pathways, and higher expectations, which contribute to their children's performance (Yadav & Sharma, 2022).

Average years of Schooling of Individual by their Parents' Occupation: Individual with parents involved in unskilled occupations have an average of 9.62 years of education, with a median of 10 years and a standard deviation of 3.70 years. This lower average reflects the economic challenges and limited access to quality educational resources associated with lower-skilled jobs (Reddy & Sinha, 2018). Individuals whose parents are engaged in low-skilled occupations, the average years of education is 10.76, with a median of 10 years and a standard deviation of 3.68 years. This indicates a slight improvement compared to those with unskilled parents but still falls short compared to children whose parents hold medium to high-skilled jobs (Mohan & Kumar, 2021).

Individuals with parents in medium-skilled occupations have an average of 13.17 years of education, with a median of 15 years and a standard deviation of 3.43 years. This significant increase reflects better access to educational resources and support, as medium-skilled occupations often provide more stable and higher incomes, allowing for greater investment in education (Patel & Sharma, 2020). Finally, individuals with parents in high-skilled occupations average 13.38 years of schooling, with a median of 15 years and a standard deviation of 3.64 years. This high level of education is indicative of the advantages associated with high-skilled occupations, including better job security, higher income, and greater emphasis on education, which collectively contribute to higher educational attainment for their children (Jain & Singh, 2022).

Table 5.6 IOp in education by different approaches (Gini)

Method	Types	Overall inequality	Absolute IOp	Relative IOp
Regression	1536	0.22	0.09	0.39
Conditional inference tree	16	0.22	0.08	0.35
Conditional inference forest	–	0.22	0.06	0.31

Source Authors calculation from PLFS, 2022–23

5.4.2 *Educational IOp: Results from Different Approaches*

The IOp in Education metrics provide insights into how disparities in educational outcomes are influenced by factors beyond individual control. Table 5.6 presents the IOp results using different methodological approaches based on Gini coefficient.

Regression Approach: This method involves using conventional regression techniques to assess IOp. The regression analysis revealed an overall inequality of 0.22 in 2022–23, which reflects the general level of inequality in educational attainment within the sample. The absolute IOp, which measures the extent of inequality that can be attributed to factors beyond individual control, was found to be 0.09. This indicates a moderate level of absolute inequality. The relative IOp, which compares the inequality in educational outcomes attributable to different circumstances relative to the overall inequality, was 0.39. This higher relative IOp suggests that a significant portion of the educational inequality observed can be explained by circumstances beyond individual effort, such as socio-economic status or family background (Bourguignon et al., 2007; Ferreira & Gignoux, 2011).

Conditional Inference Tree Approach: Conditional inference tree is a ML approach that splits the data into groups based on various circumstances to estimate IOp. This approach provided an overall inequality measure of 0.22 in 2022–23,[1] similar to the regression method, indicating consistent levels of general educational inequality. The absolute IOp using conditional inference trees was slightly lower at 0.08, suggesting that this method might capture more nuanced differences in circumstances affecting educational outcomes. The relative IOp was 0.35, indicating that while the contribution of circumstances to educational inequality is significant, it is somewhat less pronounced compared to the regression approach. This result highlights the effectiveness of conditional inference trees in isolating and understanding the influence of different factors on educational inequality (Brunori et al., 2019; Hothorn et al., 2006).

Conditional Inference Forest Approach: This method uses an ensemble of conditional inference trees to estimate IOp. The overall inequality measure remained consistent at 0.22 in 2022–23, reinforcing the findings from the previous methods. The absolute IOp was the lowest at 0.06, which suggests that this approach might

[1] The Gini coefficient for education inequality is considerably higher at 0.40 when the entire population is considered. However, it is significantly lower when the analysis is restricted to sample individuals with parental information. This is one of the limitations of the study.

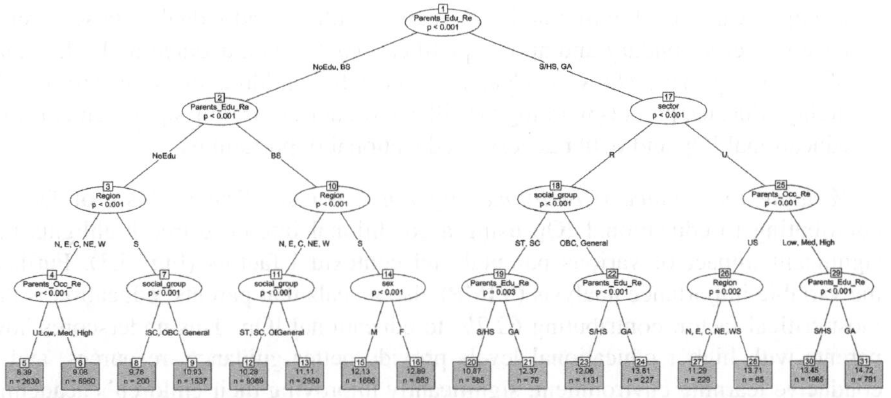

Fig. 5.2 Conditional inference tree for educational IOp. *Note* R: Rural; U: Urban; N: North; NE: North East; S: South; W: West:E: East; C: Central; Sec/HS: Secondary/Higher Secondary; GradAbv: Graduate and Above; NoEdu: Illiterate or Nor Formal Schooling; BS: Below Secondary; US: Unskilled; Low: Low Skilled; Med: Medium Skill; High: High Skilled; M: Male F: Female *Source* Authors Calculation from PLFS. 2022–23

be more effective in accounting for various circumstances that contribute to educational disparities. The relative IOp was 0.31, showing a reduction in the proportion of inequality attributable to circumstances beyond individual control. The use of multiple trees in the forest helps in averaging out biases and improving the robustness of the estimates, which might explain the lower relative IOp (Breiman, 2001; Hothorn & Zeileis, 2021).

Factors contributing to IOp (*Conditional Inference Tree*): The conditional inference tree using ML algorithms reveals that parental education is the most critical factor in determining educational IOp (Fig. 5.2). For individuals whose parents have below secondary or no education (Group 1), the second most important factor is the parents' education. For those whose parents have higher secondary or graduate-level education (Group 2), the second most important factor is the location (rural or urban).

- Group 1: Parents with Below-Secondary or No Education: In Group 1, individuals with uneducated parents, especially those from the northern, eastern, central, north-eastern, and western regions of India, whose parents are involved in unskilled and low-skilled jobs, have the lowest average years of schooling at 8.29 years. In the southern region, those from the Scheduled Caste (SC) category also have relatively lower average years of schooling at 9.76 years. This indicates that children from these regions, with parents lacking education and working in unskilled or low-skilled jobs, face significant educational disadvantages. These groups experience the highest levels of educational IOp and require urgent policy interventions to improve their access to education.
- Group 2: Parents with Higher Secondary or Graduate-Level Education: For Group 2 individuals, those living in urban areas and whose parents are engaged in skilled jobs, and additionally have graduate and above qualifications, have the highest

average years of schooling at 14.72 years. Similarly, individuals whose parents have higher secondary and above qualifications have an average of 13.45 years of schooling. This shows a clear advantage for children in urban areas with highly educated parents working in skilled jobs, demonstrating significantly lower educational IOp and better access to educational opportunities.

Variable Importance (Conditional Inference Forest): The analysis of factors contributing to educational IOp using a conditional inference tree highlights the significant impact of various parental and contextual factors (Fig. 5.3). Further, the variable importance analysis (VIMP) also reveals that parents' education is the most critical factor, contributing 62.7% to educational IOp. This underscores how parents with higher educational levels provide better guidance, resources, and a conducive learning environment, significantly improving their children's academic success (Azam & Bhatt, 2015; Desai & Kulkarni, 2008). The region where a child resides accounts for 20.6% of educational IOp, indicating substantial regional disparities in development, infrastructure, and access to quality education. For example, states like Kerala often outperform less developed regions in the north and east due to better educational policies and investments (Kingdon, 2007). Parents' occupation contributes 7.2%, with higher income and higher-status occupations enabling better educational opportunities for children through better schooling and resources (Borooah & Iyer, 2005). The sector, distinguishing between rural and urban areas, explains 5.8% of educational inequality, with urban areas generally offering superior educational infrastructure and resources (Tilak, 2002). Social group or caste accounts for 3.0%, with historically disadvantaged groups such as Scheduled Castes (SC) and Scheduled Tribes (ST) facing systemic barriers to education (Jayaraman & Murthy, 2009). Finally, gender contributes the least at 0.7%, though gender disparities persist due to societal norms and biases, particularly affecting female education (UNESCO, 2012).

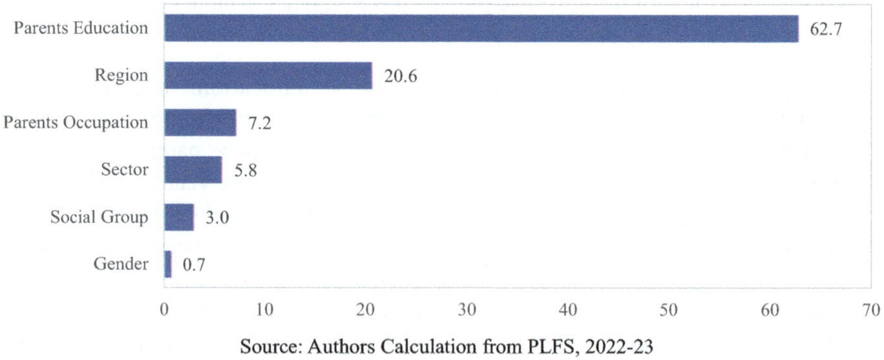

Fig. 5.3 Variable importance analysis (in %). *Source* Authors calculation from PLFS, 2022–23

5.4.3 Regional Analysis of Education Inequality and IOp

Educational inequality in India varies significantly across states, with some regions experiencing high levels of inequality while others show moderate or low levels (Map 5.1 and Appendix A5.1). States with high educational inequality, such as Bihar (Gini coefficient: 0.31) and Rajasthan (Gini coefficient: 0.27), face considerable challenges in ensuring equitable access to education. Bihar, in particular, exhibits high values for MLD (0.07) and GE2 (0.23), reflecting severe disparities in educational attainment. Rajasthan also shows significant inequality, with a high Gini coefficient (0.27) and moderate values for other inequality metrics, indicating pronounced disparities in educational outcomes. Literature highlights that such high inequality often results from socio-economic factors, inadequate infrastructure, and limited access to quality education (Desai et al., 2019; Muralidharan & Prakash, 2017).

Moderate educational inequality is observed in states like Uttar Pradesh (Gini coefficient: 0.24) and West Bengal (Gini coefficient: 0.21). Uttar Pradesh's inequality is characterized by moderate MLD (0.07) and GE1 (0.06) values, suggesting a noticeable but not extreme disparity in educational access. West Bengal, while showing moderate inequality (Gini coefficient: 0.21), has relatively stable metrics across MLD, GE1, and GE2, indicating less severe but still notable disparities (Chaudhuri &

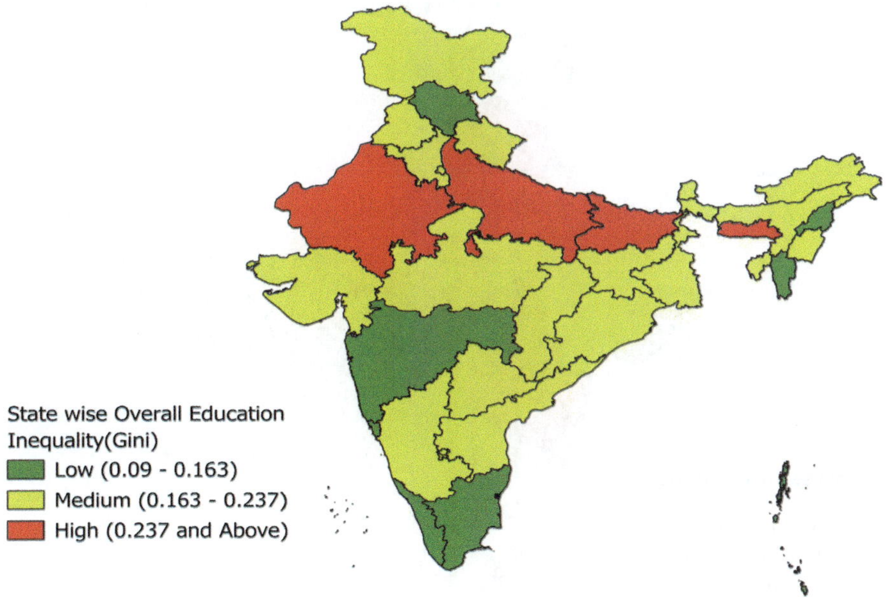

Map 5.1 Overall educational inequality in Indian states (Gini). *Source* Authors calculation from 2022–23

Banerjee, 2021). Low educational inequality is seen in states like Kerala (Gini coefficient: 0.1), which exhibit very low values across all indicators, reflecting a more equitable distribution of educational resources and outcomes (Kumar & Bhattacharya, 2022). These states benefit from effective educational policies, better infrastructure, and more inclusive access to education.

Further, Map 5.2 and Appendix A5.2 illustrate the inequality of opportunity (IOp) in education, highlighting the factors (circumstances) such as parental education, occupation, place of birth, gender, and social groups that contribute to inequality across different states. The results show distinct patterns:

- *States with Low Educational Inequality but High IOp*: Himachal Pradesh, Maharashtra, and Kerala have low overall educational inequality but high IOp. This suggests that circumstances significantly influence educational opportunities in these states.
- *States with Medium Educational Inequality and High IOp*: Punjab, Haryana, Uttarakhand, and Delhi exhibit medium levels of educational inequality and high IOp. In these states, circumstances play a crucial role in creating educational disparities.
- *States with High Educational Inequality and Medium IOp*: Bihar, Uttar Pradesh, and Rajasthan show high educational inequality and medium levels of IOp. This

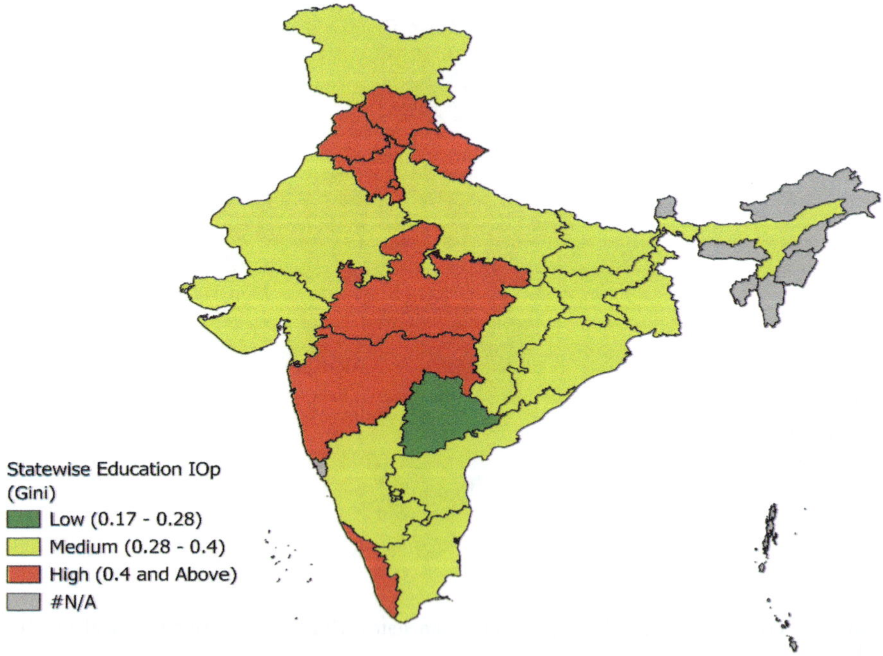

Map 5.2 Educational IOp in Indian states (Gini). *Source* Authors calculation from PLFS, 2022–23

indicates that circumstances also contribute to educational inequality in these states.

– *States with Medium Educational Inequality and Low IOp*: Telangana has a medium level of educational inequality but low IOp, suggesting that circumstances have a smaller impact on overall inequality.

These findings highlight the varying influence of circumstances on educational inequality across different states and emphasize the need for tailored policy interventions to address these disparities.

5.5 Summary and Conclusion

There are significant differences in educational access between rural and urban areas, with rural areas generally having lower average years of schooling compared to urban areas. Gender disparities, while present, are less severe, but there is still variation in educational attainment among women. Social group disparities are noticeable, with Scheduled Tribes (ST) and Scheduled Castes (SC) having lower average education levels compared to Other Backward Classes (OBC) and the General category. Regional differences also play a role, with states like Central India falling behind more developed regions like the South.

The Gini coefficient is 0.22, which indicate significant disparities in education. However, the factors beyond individual control or circumstance or IOp account for about one-third (35%) of the total education inequality. Machine learning methods like conditional inference trees and forests also confirm the same, and highlight that parental education is the most important factor affecting educational inequality, with regional disparities also playing a significant role. The most influential factors contributing to educational inequality are: parental education (62.7%), region (20.6%), occupation (7.2%), sector (5.8%), social group/caste (3.0%), and gender (0.7%). Among states, educational inequality is highest in Bihar and Rajasthan, moderate in Uttar Pradesh and West Bengal, and lowest in Kerala.

The conditional tree classification analysis reveals that the most disadvantaged group in terms of educational opportunities includes individuals with uneducated parents and those whose parents are in low-skilled or unskilled jobs, especially in the northern, eastern, central, northeastern, and western regions of India. These individuals have the lowest average schooling of 8.3 years. In contrast, the most advantaged group includes those living in urban areas with parents who have skilled jobs and graduate level or higher qualifications, achieving the highest average schooling of 14.7 years.

The regional analysis indicates that less developed states like Uttar Pradesh and Rajasthan show high educational inequality, where factors such as parental background, social groups, and gender contribute significantly to this inequality. On the other hand, states like Himachal Pradesh, Maharashtra, Kerala, Punjab, Haryana,

Uttarakhand, and Delhi have lower levels of educational inequality, but circumstances still play a significant role in contributing to the inequality in these states.

To address these challenges, targeted policies should focus on enhancing educational infrastructure in underserved areas and implementing programs specifically designed to support disadvantaged groups. Investing in quality education, particularly in rural and less developed regions, is crucial. Policies should also aim to improve access to education for marginalized social groups and ensure gender equity in educational opportunities. States like Kerala, which exhibit low educational inequality due to effective policies and better infrastructure, can serve as models for other regions. By adopting and adapting successful strategies from these states, India can work towards reducing educational disparities nationwide.

Appendix

See Tables A5.1 and A5.2.

Table A5.1 Educational inequality

State	GE0 (MLD)	GE1	GE2	Gini
Jammu & Kashmir	0.05	0.04	0.18	0.2
Himachal Pradesh	0.03	0.03	0.15	0.14
Punjab	0.04	0.04	0.18	0.18
Chandigarh	0.03	0.03	0.14	0.13
Uttarakhand	0.06	0.05	0.18	0.19
Haryana	0.05	0.05	0.18	0.2
Delhi	0.05	0.04	0.18	0.2
Rajasthan	0.08	0.07	0.22	0.27
Uttar Pradesh	0.07	0.06	0.2	0.24
Bihar	0.07	0.06	0.23	0.31
Sikkim	0.07	0.06	0.15	0.19
Arunachal Pradesh	0.06	0.06	0.17	0.21
Nagaland	0.03	0.03	0.14	0.14
Manipur	0.05	0.05	0.16	0.18
Mizoram	0.03	0.03	0.13	0.14
Tripura	0.07	0.06	0.15	0.19
Meghalaya	0.15	0.12	0.21	0.3
Assam	0.05	0.05	0.16	0.19
West Bengal	0.07	0.06	0.17	0.21
Jharkhand	0.05	0.05	0.17	0.21
Odisha	0.05	0.05	0.16	0.18
Chhattisgarh	0.06	0.05	0.17	0.19
Madhya Pradesh	0.06	0.06	0.19	0.23
Gujarat	0.06	0.05	0.16	0.2
D & N. Haveli & Daman & Diu	0.02	0.02	0.12	0.13
Maharashtra	0.04	0.04	0.15	0.16
Andhra Pradesh	0.06	0.05	0.16	0.21
Karnataka	0.04	0.03	0.17	0.18
Goa	0.05	0.04	0.13	0.16
Lakshadweep	0.01	0.01	0.13	0.09
Kerala	0.01	0.01	0.1	0.1
Tamil Nadu	0.03	0.03	0.13	0.14
Puducherry	0.03	0.02	0.12	0.12
Andaman & N. Island	0.03	0.02	0.12	0.13
Telangana	0.07	0.05	0.16	0.19
India	0.06	0.05	0.18	0.22

Source Authors calculation from PLFS, 2022–23,

Table A5.2 Educational IOp by state (Gini)

State	State code	Overall	Absolute IOp	Relative IOp
Punjab	3	0.1794	0.0917	0.511
Himachal Pradesh	2	0.1437	0.0733	0.510
Uttarakhand	5	0.1927	0.0852	0.442
Madhya Pradesh	23	0.2293	0.0977	0.426
Haryana	6	0.2009	0.0851	0.424
Maharashtra	27	0.1625	0.0688	0.424
Kerala	32	0.1011	0.0428	0.423
Delhi	7	0.2011	0.0831	0.413
Odisha	21	0.1832	0.0669	0.365
Rajasthan	8	0.2731	0.0938	0.343
West Bengal	19	0.2091	0.0692	0.331
Tamilnadu	33	0.1416	0.0459	0.324
Karnataka	29	0.1822	0.0585	0.321
Jammu & Kashmir	1	0.1975	0.0625	0.317
Bihar	10	0.3069	0.0949	0.309
Jharkhand	20	0.2089	0.0643	0.308
Andhra Pradesh	28	0.2081	0.0618	0.297
Uttar Pradesh	9	0.2424	0.0709	0.293
Gujarat	24	0.1972	0.0575	0.292
Assam	18	0.1949	0.0561	0.288
Chhattisgarh	22	0.1944	0.0558	0.287
Telangana	36	0.1902	0.0318	0.167

Source Authors calculation from PLFS, 2022–23

References

Arneson, R. J. (1989). Equality and equality of opportunity for welfare. *Philosophical Studies, 56*(1), 77–93.

Azam, M., & Bhatt, V. (2015). Like father, like son? Intergenerational education mobility in India. *Demography, 52*(6), 2091–2112.

Bhat, M., & Zavier, A. (2021). Gender disparities in education in India: Trends and implications. *Journal of Gender Studies.*

Bills, D. B., & Wacker, M. E. (2003). Acquiring credentials when signals don't matter: Employers' support of employees who pursue postsecondary vocational degrees. *Sociology of Education*, 170–187.

Borooah, V. K., & Iyer, S. (2005). Vidya, Veda, and Varna: The influence of religion and caste on education in rural India. *Journal of Development Studies, 41*(8), 1369–1404.

Bourguignon, F., Ferreira, F. H. G., & Menéndez, M. (2007). Inequality of opportunity in Brazil. *World Bank Policy Research Working Paper Series.*

Breiman, L. (2001). Random forests. *Machine Learning, 45*(1), 5–32.

Brunori, P., Hufe, P., & Mahler, D. G. (2018), The roots of inequality: Estimating inequality of opportunity from regression trees. *World Bank Policy Research Working Paper* (8349).

Brunori, P., Ferreira, F. H. G., & Peragine, V. (2019). Inequality of opportunity and equality of outcome: A review of the literature. *Journal of Economic Surveys.*

Brunori, P., & Neidhöfer, G. (2021). The evolution of inequality of opportunity in Germany: A machine learning approach. *Review of Income and Wealth, 67*(4), 900–927. https://doi.org/10.1111/roiw.12502

Chaudhury, N., Hammer, J., Kremer, M., Muralidharan, K., & Rogers, H. (2020). Missing in action: Teacher and health worker absence in developing countries. *Journal of Economic Perspectives.*

Chaudhuri, S., & Banerjee, A. (2021). Assessing inequality in West Bengal: A study of Gini coefficient and generalized entropy measures. *Economic and Political Weekly, 56*(8), 55–65.

Cohen, G. A. (1989). On the currency of egalitarian justice. *Ethics, 99*(4), 906–944.

Coleman, J. (1968). The concept of equality of educational opportunity. *Harvard Educational Review, 38*(1), 7–22.

Desai, S., & Kulkarni, V. (2008). Changing educational inequalities in India in the context of affirmative action. *Demography, 45*(2), 245–270.

Desai, S., & Kulkarni, V. (2020). Urban-rural differences in educational attainment in India. *Indian Economic Review.*

Desai, S., Adams, C. D., Dubey, A., & Vanneman, R. (2019). India human development survey: Growing socio-economic inequality and its impact on education. *World Development, 117*, 213–224.

Dworkin, R. (1981a). What is equality? Part 1: Equality of welfare. *Philosophy & Public Affairs, 10*(3), 185–246.

Dworkin, R. (1981b). What is equality? Part 2: Equality of resources. *Philosophy & Public Affairs, 10*(4), 283–345.

Ferreira, F. H. G., & Gignoux, J. (2011). The measurement of educational inequality: Achievement and opportunity. *World Bank Policy Research Working Paper Series.*

Fleurbaey, M., & Pergaine, V. (2013). Ex post inequalities and ex ante inequalities. In *Justice, political liberalism, and utilitarianism: Themes from Harsanyi and Rawls* (pp. 59–77). Cambridge University Press.

Hothorn, T., & Zeileis, A. (2021). *A tour of the conditional inference forest*. Springer.

Hothorn, T., Hornik, K., & Zeileis, A. (2006). Unbiased recursive partitioning: A conditional inference framework. *Journal of Computational and Graphical Statistics, 15*(3), 651–674.

Hurn, C. (1985). Changes in authority relationships in schools: 1960–1980. *Research in Sociology of Education and Socialization, 5*(1), 31–57.

International Labour Organization. (2024). *India Employment Report 2024: Youth employment, education and skills.* International Labour Office. http://www.indiaenvironmentportal.org.in/files/file/India%20Employment%20Report%202024.pdf

Jayaraman, R., & Murthy, S. (2009). Village and household characteristics: From the census to the NSS. *Economic and Political Weekly, 44*(12), 69–76.

Kellough, J. E. (2005). *Understanding affirmative action: Politics, discrimination, and the search for justice* .Washington, DC: Georgetown University Press

Kingdon, G. G. (2007). The progress of school education in India. *Oxford Review of Economic Policy, 23*(2), 168–195.

Kingdon, G. G. (2010). The impact of the right to education act in India. *Economic and Political Weekly, 45*(43), 40–45.

Kumar, P., Kumar, A., & Sinha, N. (2021). Parental education and its impact on children's educational attainment in India. *Educational Studies.*

Kumar, R., & Rao, P. (2022). Educational disparities among social groups in India: A comprehensive analysis. *Social Science Research Journal.*

Kundu, T. (2023). Inequality of opportunity in elementary level school education: Evidence from India. *Indian Journal of Human Development, 17*(2), 253–270. https://doi.org/10.1177/09737030231194848

Lefranc, A., & Kundu, S. (2020). Machine learning approaches to inequality of opportunity measurement: A comparative study. *Applied Economics, 52*(16), 1723–1741.
Mehta, B. S., & Dhote, S. (2022). Inequality of opportunity in India: Concept and measurement. *IASSI Quarterly, 41*(1 and 2), 165–183.
Mehta, B. S., Dhote, S., & Srivastava, R. (2023). Decomposition of inequality of opportunity in India: An application of data-driven machine learning approach. *The Indian Journal of Labour Economics, 66*(2), 439–469. https://doi.org/10.1007/s41027-023-00446-5
Mohan, P., & Kumar, R. (2021). Socioeconomic factors influencing educational outcomes in India. *Journal of Development Economics.*
Muralidharan, K., & Prakash, N. (2017). Cycling to school: Increasing secondary school enrollment for girls in India. *American Economic Journal: Applied Economics, 9*(3), 321–350. https://doi.org/10.1257/app.20160004
Oakes, J., Gamoran, A., & Page, R. N. (1992). Curriculum differentiation: Opportunities, outcomes, and meanings. In *Handbook of research on curriculum* (pp. 570–608).
Patel, S., & Sharma, R. (2020). The role of parental occupation in determining educational outcomes in India. *Indian Journal of Educational Research.*
Ramos, X., & Van de Gaer, D. (2016). Approaches to inequality of opportunity: Principles, measures and evidence. *Journal of Economic Surveys, 30*(5), 855–883.
Rawls, J. (1971). *A theory of justice: Original Edition.* Harvard University Press. https://doi.org/10.2307/j.ctvjf9z6v
Rawls, J. (1999). *Collected papers.* Harvard University Press.
Reddy, A., & Sinha, R. (2018). Impact of parental occupation on children's educational attainment in rural India. *Economic and Political Weekly.*
Resh, N., & Sabbagh, C. (2016). Justice and education. In C. Sabbagh & M. Schmitt (Eds.), *Handbook of social justice theory and research* (pp. 349–367). Springer. https://doi.org/10.1007/978-1-4939-3216-0_19
Sabbagh, C., & Schmitt, M. (Eds.). (2016). *Handbook of social justice theory and research.* Springer. https://doi.org/10.1007/978-1-4939-3216-0
Salas-Rojo, P., & Rodríguez, J. G. (2022). Inheritances and wealth inequality: A machine learning approach. *The Journal of Economic Inequality, 20*(1), 27–51.
Sharma, S., & Gupta, A. (2021). Regional variations in educational attainment in India: A data-driven study. *Regional Development Studies.*
Singh, V., & Gupta, A. (2019). Educational attainment and economic disparities in India: A review. *South Asian Journal of Education.*
Tilak, J. B. G. (2002). Determinants of household expenditure on education in rural India. National Council of Applied Economic Research.
Tilak, J. B. G. (2007). Post-elementary education, poverty, and development in India. *International Journal of Educational Development, 27*(4), 435–445.
UNESCO. (2012). *Education for all global monitoring report: youth and skills—putting education to work.* UNESCO.
Yadav, S., & Sharma, M. (2022). Parental education and its effect on students' academic performance in India. *International Journal of Educational Development.*

Chapter 6
Inequality of Opportunity in Healthcare Services

Keywords Health Inequality · Health Care Opportunity · Maternal Health · Child Health · Inequal Distribution of Health Care

6.1 Introduction

Ensuring healthy lives and promoting well-being for all ages is a significant global challenge, as emphasized by SDG Goal 3 of the United Nations Sustainable Development Agenda for 2030. This goal specifically targets child and maternal health, aiming to reduce the maternal mortality ratio (MMR) to 70 per 100,000 live births and to end preventable deaths of newborns and children under 5 years of age. The target is to reduce neonatal mortality to as low as 12 per 1000 live births and under-5 mortality to as low as 25 per 1000 live births (UN, 2015). Between 2000 and 2020, the MMR fell by 34%, yet it remains alarmingly high, with 287,000 women dying during childbirth in 2020. A staggering 95% of these deaths occurred in low and middle-income countries (LMICs) (WHO, 2024). Sub-Saharan Africa and South Asia accounted for 87% (253,000) of these maternal deaths, with 70% of the deaths in Sub-Saharan Africa and 17% in South Asia (WHO, 2024). These high maternal mortality rates reflect significant disparities in access to quality health services. For

---

Disclaimer: The presentation of material and details in maps used in this chapter does not imply the expression of any opinion whatsoever on the part of the Publisher or Author concerning the legal status of any country, area or territory or of its authorities, or concerning the delimitation of its borders. The depiction and use of boundaries, geographic names and related data shown on maps and included in lists, tables, documents, and databases in this chapter are not warranted to be error free nor do they necessarily imply official endorsement or acceptance by the Publisher or Author.

B. S. Mehta et al., *Predicting Inequality of Opportunity and Poverty in India Using Machine Learning*, India Studies in Business and Economics,
https://doi.org/10.1007/978-981-96-2544-4_6

instance, in 2020, the MMR in low-income countries was 430 per 100,000 live births, compared to just 13 per 100,000 live births in high-income countries (WHO, 2024).

Similarly, the annual number of under-five deaths has decreased from 12.8 million in 2000 to 4.9 million in 2022. Despite this reduction, millions of children still die before reaching the age of five, with the majority of these deaths concentrated in sub-Saharan Africa and South Asia (UNICEF, 2023). The global decline in child mortality masks the inequalities among vulnerable populations. A child born in sub-Saharan Africa is 18 times more likely to die before turning five than a child born in Australia or New Zealand. Additionally, the risk of a child dying before the age of five in a high-mortality country is 80 times greater than in a low-mortality country (UNICEF, 2023). In this context, the focus of Goal 3 on all ages is crucial. An equitable development process should provide equal opportunities to individuals at all stages of life, especially children who often face unequal access to basic opportunities due to circumstances beyond their control (Barros et al., 2009). This lack of access prevents children from getting a fair start in life, which underscores the need for social and economic policies that level the playing field and reduce the correlation between circumstances and unequal access to opportunities. Therefore, focusing on reducing inequality of opportunity serves as a valuable policy guidepost. A critical first step is to have an adequate measure of this inequality (Barros et al., 2009).

6.2 Relevance of the Study

Developing countries like India face significant health disparities that impact its population's overall well-being. Addressing health inequality and health inequality of opportunity is crucial for several reasons. India has made progress in reducing maternal and child mortality rates, but the numbers remain high compared to global standards. In 2020, India's MMR was 103 per 100,000 live births, significantly higher than the target set by the United Nations (WHO, 2024). Similarly, the under-5 mortality rate in India is 34 per 1000 live births, which is still above the global average (UNICEF, 2023). There are stark regional disparities in health outcomes within India. States like Kerala and Tamil Nadu have significantly better health indicators compared to states like Uttar Pradesh and Bihar. These disparities highlight the need for targeted interventions to address the specific needs of different regions. Health outcomes in India are closely linked to socio-economic status. Poorer communities have less access to quality healthcare services, leading to higher mortality and morbidity rates. Addressing these inequities is essential to ensure that all individuals, regardless of their socio-economic background, have access to necessary health services. Women in India face significant health disparities, particularly in rural areas. Maternal health services are often inadequate, leading to high maternal mortality rates. Additionally, cultural factors and gender discrimination can prevent women from accessing healthcare services. This health inequality can hinder economic development. A healthy population is more productive and can contribute more effectively to the economy. Reducing health disparities can lead to a more equitable and prosperous society.

There are only few studies highlights the health IOp especially in the Indian context. Globally, studies have emphasized the persistent nature of health inequalities despite economic progress. For example, Wagstaff et al. (2016) analysed health inequality in low- and middle-income countries (LMICs) and found that economic growth alone does not suffice to reduce health disparities. Factors such as education, regional differences, and household economic status significantly contribute to inequality in health opportunities. Similarly, studies by Victora et al. (2017) highlight that inequality in child health outcomes, including immunization and nutrition, remains high in many LMICs. These studies emphasize the importance of targeted interventions that address the underlying determinants of health inequality, including socioeconomic and regional factors.

Singh (2011) uses the IOp Index (Dissimilarity Index or D-Index) and the Human Opportunity Index (HOI) to measure changes in IOp among Indian children regarding access to immunization and minimum nutrition between 1992–1993 and 2005–2006. This study diverged from traditional methods such as the rich-poor ratio, concentration curves, and concentration indices, which have been commonly used to measure inequality in access to various maternal and child health services. Singh's findings revealed that despite India's high economic growth, IOp in terms of access to immunization and nutrition remained high and showed minimal improvement over the 13-year period. Furthermore, significant inter-regional disparities were evident, with the central region performing the worst in terms of immunization IOp and the eastern region performing the worst in terms of nutrition. The HOI scores also showed little change, remaining low between 1992–1993 and 2005–2006. However, regional differences were noted, with the southern region showing improvements in HOI, whereas the eastern and central regions maintained low HOI scores across both time periods.

Similarly, Pal (2015) employed the D-Index and HOI to measure IOp in immunization access between 2002–2004 and 2007–2008 using district-level health survey data. Pal's study found that the IOp in immunization decreased in India from 2002–2004 to 2007–2008. However, regional variations persisted, and some states lagged behind others even in 2007–2008. The decomposition exercise in Pal's study identified region, parents' education, and the economic background of households as the most significant contributors to IOp (Pal, 2015). These studies underscore the need for policies that address the root causes of health inequality. Both studies highlight the significant impact of parental education and economic status on children's health opportunities. Furthermore, the regional disparities revealed in these studies suggest that health policies should be tailored to address the specific needs of different regions within the country. This approach can help ensure more equitable access to health services and improve overall health outcomes.

This brief literature on health IOp highlights the persistent and multifaceted nature of health disparities. Both global and Indian studies emphasize the need for comprehensive policies that address socioeconomic and regional factors to reduce health inequality. However, there is a lack of comprehensive studies that explore the determinants of health IOp in India, both at the national and regional levels. It is urgently necessary to identify these determinants so policymakers can focus on the factors that contribute to creating a fairer and more equitable health system where everyone has the opportunity to lead a healthy life.

In this context, addressing health inequality and health inequality of opportunity is essential for ensuring equitable development and improving overall well-being. The disparities in maternal and child health outcomes highlight the need for targeted interventions, particularly in low and middle-income countries and regions such as South Asia, including India. Addressing these health issues is crucial in India for reducing regional and socio-economic disparities and promoting gender equality. Focusing on reducing health inequality can help create a fairer and more just society where everyone has the opportunity to lead a healthy life. This is especially important for children, who often have unequal access to basic opportunities due to circumstances beyond their control (Barros et al., 2009). Therefore, reducing inequality of opportunity in health becomes a valuable policy guidepost. A critical first step is to have an adequate measure to reduce inequality in society (Barros et al., 2009).

6.3 Study Framework

6.3.1 Human Opportunity Index (HOI)

The Human Opportunity Index (HOI) is a measure designed to assess both the level of coverage of basic opportunities and the extent to which the distribution of these opportunities depends on circumstances beyond an individual's control (Barros et al., 2009). Essentially, the HOI combines the overall coverage of opportunities and the IOp (measured by the Dissimilarity Index or D-Index) into a single metric (Vani & Madheswaran, 2018). This is particularly useful for evaluating access to health services. For instance, in the context of health services, the HOI reflects both the overall access rate to health services and how equitably this access is distributed across different socio-economic groups. By adjusting for the inequality in distribution, the HOI provides a more nuanced understanding of health opportunities in a society (Sanoussi, 2017). It shows not only how many people have access to health services but also whether this access is fairly distributed.

Estimating HOI Using the Random Forest Classification ML Model: To estimate the HOI, this chapter employs the Random Forest (RF) Classification model. This model is used to specify a functional relationship between an individual's circumstances and outcome such as their access to healthcare services. In this model, access to a healthcare service is denoted by 1, and lack of access is denoted by 0. The RF classification model helps to estimate the predicted probability of access to a particular service such as healthcare service for each individual. The overall probability of access to health care ($\overline{p}$) is then estimated using individual probabilities and the D-Index. The equation is as follows:

$$\overline{p} = \sum_{i=1}^{n} w_i p_i \text{ where: } w_i = \frac{1}{n} \text{and } n \text{ is the sample size}$$

$$D = \frac{1}{2\overline{p}} \sum_{i=1}^{n} w_i |p - \overline{p}|$$

After calculating the overall probability of access to health care and the D-index, the HOI is calculated using the following formula:

$$\text{HOI} = \overline{p}(1 - D)$$

Random Forest Classification ML Model: Random Forest (RF) classification model is chosen over logistic regression due to its sophisticated modelling capabilities. Logistic regression requires calculating the marginal contribution of each circumstance variable by executing models on all possible permutations of the remaining variables, which can be computationally time-consuming. Each permutation's predicted probabilities and D-Index must be calculated, leading to substantial computational time. In contrast, the Random Forest classifier has an inbuilt variable importance function, allowing for decomposition without needing to drop and re-evaluate each variable's contribution. This efficiency makes the RF classifier particularly suitable for predicting individual probabilities and creating the D-Index and HOI.

The HOI along with advanced Random Forest Classification ML model, offers a deeper understanding of health IOp. The HOI not only measures overall access to health services but also assesses the fairness of their distribution, providing a comprehensive view of health opportunities within a population. This approach supports the principle of equality of opportunity and aids in developing policies that foster a more equitable health system, ensuring everyone has the chance to lead a healthy life (Barros et al., 2009; Sanoussi, 2017).

Hierarchical Clustering for Regional Analysis: Apart from supervised ML method (RF classification), hierarchical clustering, an unsupervised learning method, is also used to perform regional clustering analysis by building a hierarchy of clusters. This method groups data points based on their differences or similarities. There are two types of hierarchical clustering: agglomerative and divisive (James et al., 2023). Agglomerative clustering constructs the hierarchy from the bottom up by merging the closest or most similar data points into a desired number of clusters. In contrast, divisive clustering creates a hierarchy from the top down, splitting the most dissimilar data points until each one forms its own cluster. To link data points and create clusters, hierarchical clustering employs the following linkage criteria, including:

- Single Linkage: Defines the distance between two clusters as the minimum distance between any pair of points in the two clusters.
- Complete Linkage: Defines the distance between two clusters as the maximum distance between any pair of points in the two clusters.
- Average Linkage: Defines the distance between two clusters as the average of all pairwise distances between points in the two clusters.
- Ward Linkage: Measures the distance between two clusters based on the increase in total variance within clusters after merging.

In this chapter, the agglomerative approach is used to perform hierarchical clustering of districts in India, specifically focusing on access to maternal and child healthcare services. The Ward linkage criterion is chosen because it minimizes the variance within clusters, leading to more homogeneous clusters with similar data points (or districts, in this case).

6.3.2 Variables and Data Sources

This study analyses health IOp with a focus on maternal and child healthcare services in India. It uses two measures: the D-Index and the Health Opportunity Index (HOI). The study also evaluates access to five key healthcare indicators: (i) place of delivery (whether a child was born in a public or private institution), (ii) immunization (whether the child received vaccinations), (iii) prenatal care (whether important health checks and tests were performed during pregnancy), (iv) prenatal care by trained professionals (whether the care was provided by a qualified doctor or health worker), and (v) antenatal care (whether the mother had at least four prenatal visits). Additionally, the study creates a composite index called 'adequate care', which includes all these factors to determine if a child and mother received comprehensive health care. The hierarchical clustering is also based on five key variables as discussed above that assess access to maternal and child healthcare services. Using these variables, the analysis aims to identify clusters of districts with similar levels of access to maternal and child healthcare services, providing valuable insights into regional disparities and areas needing improvement.

Data for this analysis was sourced from the National Family and Health Survey (NFHS-5) (2019–2021), conducted by the International Institute for Population Sciences (IIPS), Mumbai, and the Ministry of Health and Welfare, Government of India. The NFHS sample includes 190,355 children for whom parental information is available. The circumstance variables, such as parental education and occupation, are calculated using the children's data file, men's data file, and household member file from NFHS-5. The seven circumstance variables include: (i) Gender of the child (male or female); (ii) Sector, indicating the child's place of residence or birth (rural or urban area); (iii) Social group (Scheduled Caste (SC), Scheduled Tribe (ST), Other

Backward Class (OBC), General Category (GC)); (v) Income quintile or classes ranging from Q1 to Q5, where Q1 represents the poorest and Q5 the wealthiest; (vi) Region, indicating the geographical area the child belongs to (north, south, east, west, central, or northeast); (vi) Mother's education level (no education, primary education, secondary education, or higher education); (vii) Father's education level (no education, primary education, secondary education, or higher education); This comprehensive dataset helps to understand the different factors contributing to inequality in access to healthcare services in India.

6.3.3 *Measurement of Health IOp*

The HOI and D-Index are tools for measuring health IOp in maternal and child healthcare services in India. The D-Index shows how access to basic health services varies among children based on their circumstances, with a range from 0 to 100%, where 0 indicates perfect equality. It calculates both the average access rate and the share of services needed to ensure equal access (Barros et al., 2009; Sanoussi, 2017). The HOI evaluates two aspects: the overall coverage of basic health services and the fairness of their distribution. It combines these two factors to give a single measure of how health opportunities are shared across a population (Barros et al., 2009). The HOI reflects both the level of access to health services and the inequality in that access. The RF Classification model predicts the likelihood of individuals accessing a health service based on their circumstances. It uses a functional relationship to estimate this probability as mentioned above, where access is coded as 1 and no access as 0. The model helps estimate the overall probability of access to health services in the population.

6.4 Results and Discussions

6.4.1 *Sample Profile*

This analysis presents a comprehensive overview of the demographic and socio-economic characteristics of the sample population, highlighting the distribution across gender, sector (rural/urban), social group, economic quintiles, regions, and parental education levels. This detailed breakdown is important for understanding the disparities in access to maternal and child healthcare services in India (Table 6.1). The sample includes 190,355 children, with a nearly equal number of boys and girls. Most of these children live in rural areas, with a smaller portion in urban regions. Socially, the largest group of children belongs to Other Backward Classes (OBC), followed by Scheduled Tribes (ST), the general caste group, and Scheduled Castes (SC). Economically, the children come from households with different income levels, with highest concentration in the poorest households or Q1 (26%) and the lowest concentration in richest households or Q5 (14%). Geographically, the children are spread across different parts of India, with the highest concentration in central India and the lowest in the western region. In terms of parental education, a significant proportion of mothers have secondary education, while less have higher or no education. Similarly, most fathers have secondary education, with relatively less having higher or no education. This data shows the diverse backgrounds of the children, highlighting the complexity of the social and economic setting in India.

6.4.2 Access to Healthcare Services

In the sample, more than half (56%) of the children had received at least one vaccination, while mothers of less than half (45%) of the children had more than four antenatal care visits (Table 6.2). The majority of mothers (86%) had institutional deliveries, and a significant portion of mothers (66%) had access to important tests during prenatal care. Nearly all mothers (88%) received prenatal care from a trained professional. However, when considering the overall access to all the selected maternal and child healthcare services, only a small portion of children or their mothers (26%) had comprehensive access to these essential services, highlighting gaps in the provision and utilization of maternal and child healthcare services in India.

6.4.3 Health IOp

(i) **Average Coverage Rate (*p*) and D-Index**: As discussed earlier the average coverage rate (*p*) represents the proportion of the population with access to specific health services. The dissimilarly index quantifies the proportion of opportunities that need redistribution to achieve equality, which also highlights the extent of inequality in accessing health services (Table 6.3).

Place of Delivery: The coverage rate for delivery in private or public health centres is high at 86.5% (Nair & Sadanandan, 2017). This high rate reflects increased efforts in improving institutional deliveries through programs like Janani Suraksha Yojana (JSY), which incentivizes deliveries in health facilities (Jain & Gupta, 2016). The dissimilarly index for the place of delivery is 6.4% (Srivastava & Mishra, 2020). This indicates a moderate level of dissimilarly index, suggesting that redistribution efforts could enhance access to institutional deliveries, particularly in marginalized communities (Ghosh, 2021).

Prenatal Care by Skilled Staff: Access to prenatal care by skilled staff is also high at 88.8% (Gupta et al., 2019). This high rate indicates effective outreach and availability of skilled professionals, though regional disparities persist (Balarajan et al., 2011). The dissimilarly index for prenatal care by skilled staff is 5.2% (Nair &

Table 6.1 Basic sample profile

		%
Gender	Male	48.4
	Female	51.6
	All	100.0
Sector	Rural	78.5
	Urban	21.5
	All	100.0
Social group	Gen	21.5
	OBC	37.1
	SC	20.2
	ST	21.2
	All	100.0
Income quintile	Q1 (poorest)	26.2
	Q2	22.9
	Q3	19.4
	Q4	17.3
	Q5 (highest)	14.1
	All	100.0
Region	Central	26.9
	East	17.2
	North	17.9
	North East	15.8
	South	12.5
	West	9.7
	All	100.0
Mother's education	Higher	13.4
	No Edu	21.5
	Primary	13.0
	Secondary	52.1
	All	100.0
Father's education	Higher	16.2
	No Edu	12.9
	Primary	14.2
	Secondary	56.7
	All	100.0

Source Authors calculation from, NFHS, 2019–2021

Table 6.2 Access to maternal and child health services

Health services	No	Yes	Total
Vaccination	44.35	55.65	100.00
Antenatal care	55.03	44.97	100.00
Place of delivery	13.47	86.53	100.00
Access to prenatal care	34.18	65.82	100.00
Access to prenatal care by trained staff	12.15	87.85	100.00
Adequate care	73.69	26.31	100.00

Source Authors calculation from NFHS, 2019–2021

Table 6.3 Health IOp: access to maternal and child health services

Healthcare access indicator	Average coverage rate or prevalence (*p*)	Inequality of opportunity (D-Index)	(1-D)	HOI
Place of birth	0.8650	0.0636	0.9364	0.8100
Immunization	0.5560	0.0600	0.9400	0.5226
Prenatal care	0.6586	0.0873	0.9127	0.6012
Prenatal care given by skilled staff	0.8778	0.0524	0.9476	0.8318
Atleast four antenatal visits	0.4502	0.1515	0.8485	0.3820
Adequate care	0.2630	0.1928	0.8072	0.2123

Source Authors Calculation from NFHS, 2019–2021

Sadanandan, 2017). This lower dissimilarly index reflects relatively better equity in access compared to other services, though disparities remain in certain regions (Mukherjee & Sikdar, 2019).

General Prenatal Care: The general coverage rate for prenatal care is 65.8% (Singh & Kumar, 2018). Despite significant improvements, some areas still struggle with inadequate prenatal care access due to infrastructural and socio-economic barriers (Kumar et al., 2019). The dissimilarly index for general prenatal care is 8.7% (Gupta et al., 2019). This relatively higher dissimilarly index indicates presence of inequality, with some gaps in access between different socio-economic groups and regions (Roy & Gupta, 2020).

Immunization Services: Immunization services have a lower coverage rate of 55.6% (Pathak & Singh, 2021). This lower rate is attributed to issues such as vaccine supply disruptions and logistical challenges in reaching remote areas (Mishra & Sharma, 2017). Despite the lower coverage rate, the dissimilarly index for immunization services is 6% (Pathak & Singh, 2021). This suggests that even though immunization services are less accessible, the distribution of these services could be improved to reduce disparities (Kumar et al., 2019).

At Least Four Antenatal Visits: Access to at least four antenatal visits is even lower, at 45% (Desai & Sinha, 2021). This is indicative of gaps in routine check-ups and follow-ups, particularly in rural and underserved regions (Pandey & Ladusingh, 2019). The dissimilarly index for access to at least four antenatal visits is 15% (Desai & Sinha, 2021). This higher IOp reflects presence of inequality, indicating that effort is needed to ensure all women receive the recommended number of visits (Jain & Gupta, 2016).

Overall Adequate Health Care: Overall adequate health care, encompassing all necessary maternal and child health services, has the lowest coverage rate at 26% (Patel & Chatterjee, 2020). This reflects significant gaps in comprehensive care delivery, influenced by various socio-economic and regional factors (Srinivasan & Patel, 2015). The dissimilarly index for overall adequate care is the highest at 19% (Patel & Chatterjee, 2020). This higher DI figure highlights the extensive redistribution required to ensure equitable access to comprehensive maternal and child health services (Singh & Kumar, 2018).

Overall, the high coverage rates were observed for institutional deliveries and prenatal care by skilled staff. Prenatal care coverage, immunization, and at least four antenatal visits had relatively lower coverage. Only around one-fourth of children and their mothers had comprehensive access to all selected health services, reflecting gaps in antenatal care and immunization. The IOp for place of delivery, prenatal care by trained staff, immunization stands at low, while four antenatal visits stand at relatively high, which need redistribution for equal access. Overall inequality in healthcare services is at 19%, which is higher than any single service.

(ii) **Human Opportunity Index (HOI)**: The HOI integrates the average coverage in distribution of equitably health services as given in Table 6.3.

Place of Delivery: The HOI for the place of delivery is 0.81, indicating that 81% of the existing opportunities are equitably distributed (Srivastava & Mishra, 2020). This relatively high HOI reflects the effectiveness of interventions aimed at increasing institutional deliveries but also highlights room for improvement (Jain & Gupta, 2016).

Prenatal Care by Skilled Staff: The HOI for prenatal care is 0.83 reflecting that 83% of the prenatal care covered by skilled staff (Nair & Sadanandan, 2017). This high value also suggests that access to skilled prenatal care is relatively well-distributed, although disparities in some regions remain (Gupta & Sinha, 2019).

General Prenatal Care: The HOI for general prenatal care is 0.60, indicating that 40% of did not have access to general prenatal care (Srivastava & Mishra, 2020). This lower HOI indicates significant inequality in access to prenatal care services, with substantial disparities based on socio-economic and regional factors (Kumar et al., 2019).

Immunization Services: The HOI for immunization services is 0.52, indicating that around 48% did not have immunization services (Pathak & Singh, 2021). This reflects moderate distribution, with considerable room for improvement in ensuring equal access across different population groups ((Mishra & Sharma, 2017).

At Least Four Antenatal Visits: The HOI for access to at least four antenatal visits is 0.38, which reflect 68% did not have at least four antenatal visits (Desai & Sinha, 2021). This lower HOI indicates significant inequalities, suggesting that much more needs to be done to achieve equitable access to routine antenatal care (Jain & Gupta, 2016).

Overall Adequate Care: The HOI for overall adequate care services is 0.21, which shows that about 79% did not have adequate access to maternal and child care health services (Patel & Chatterjee, 2020). This very high inequity in access to adequate maternal and child health services, underscoring the poor healthcare services in the country (Singh & Kumar, 2018).

The HOI scores show that high inequality in access to prenatal care, immunization and at least four antenatal visits healthcare services, while the most mothers have access to institutional deliveries, and prenatal care services by skilled staff.

6.4.4 Variable Importance in Access to Healthcare Services

Understanding the factors that influence access to health services is important for creating effective policies and interventions. The variable importance metric helps to identify which factors play significant roles in determining access to various health services (Table 6.4).

Table 6.4 Variable importance

Health service	Place of birth	Immunization	Prenatal care	Prenatal care by trained staff	Antenatal care	Adequate care
Child gender	0.038	0.101	0.051	0.048	0.055	0.074
Fathers education	0.121	0.125	0.129	0.123	0.119	0.129
Mothers education	0.184	0.109	0.175	0.161	0.162	0.177
Region	0.241	0.212	0.211	0.231	0.247	0.214
Sector	0.039	0.070	0.054	0.046	0.055	0.059
Social group	0.147	0.178	0.166	0.152	0.150	0.156
Wealth index	0.231	0.205	0.213	0.239	0.213	0.193

Source Authors Calculation from NFHS, 2019–2021

Place of Delivery: For the place of delivery, region is the most important variable, accounting for 24.1% of the variation in access to public or private healthcare facilities for delivery. This is because regional disparities often reflect differences in healthcare infrastructure, availability of skilled professionals, and accessibility of medical facilities. Studies in India have shown that urban regions tend to have better healthcare facilities compared to rural areas, leading to higher institutional delivery rates in urban regions (Ghosh, 2021). The quintile group (wealth index) contributes 23%, indicating that wealthier families have better access to quality healthcare facilities for delivery. Wealth enables families to afford transportation to hospitals, pay for medical expenses, and access private health care, which is often perceived as better than public health care (Mukherjee & Sikdar, 2019). Mother's education, accounting for 18.4%, plays a critical role as educated mothers are more likely to be aware of the benefits of institutional deliveries and are better equipped to navigate the healthcare system (Singh et al. 2021). Social group and father's education also play significant roles, contributing 14.7% and 12.1%, respectively. Social group often reflects caste-based disparities in access to health care, with marginalized communities having less access to institutional deliveries (Balarajan et al., 2011). Father's education often influences household decisions regarding health expenditures and healthcare-seeking behaviour (Srivastava & Mishra, 2020). In contrast, the child's gender and sector (whether rural or urban) contribute minimally to access, with 3.8% and 3.9%, respectively. Gender biases in access to delivery care are minimal compared to other health services, and sector differences are already captured by the region variable (Mishra & Sharma, 2017).

Immunization: Access to immunization services is also heavily influenced by region, which accounts for 21.2% of the variation. The quintile group follows closely with a 20.5% contribution. Regional disparities in healthcare infrastructure and outreach programs significantly impact immunization rates. Urban areas with better healthcare facilities and outreach programs tend to have higher immunization rates (Banerjee et al., 2004). The quintile group indicates that wealthier families are more likely to access immunization services due to better awareness, affordability, and access to healthcare facilities (Shrivastava & Shrivastava, 2020). Social group is next at 17.8%, reflecting caste-based disparities where marginalized groups have lower immunization rates due to historical neglect and discrimination in health care (Subramanian & Smith, 2006). Father's education (12.5%) and mother's education (10.9%) also play significant roles. Educated parents are more likely to understand the importance of immunization and ensure their children receive the necessary vaccines (Pathak & Singh, 2021). The child's gender and sector again play minimal roles, contributing 10.1% and 7%, respectively, indicating that gender biases are less pronounced in immunization and that urban–rural differences are already accounted for by the region variable (Kumar et al., 2019).

Prenatal Care: In the case of prenatal care, the quintile group and region are the most critical factors, each contributing 21.1% to access. Mother's education follows with a 17.5% contribution, social group at 16.6%, and father's education at 12.9%. Wealth enables access to quality prenatal care services, and regional disparities reflect differences in healthcare infrastructure (Gupta et al., 2019). Mother's education significantly influences access to prenatal care, as educated mothers are more likely to seek regular check-ups and understand the importance of prenatal care (Roy & Gupta, 2020). Social group disparities highlight the impact of caste-based discrimination in accessing prenatal care services (Acharya, 2023). The child's gender and sector have marginal impacts, contributing 5.1% and 5.4%, respectively, indicating minimal gender biases in prenatal care access and that urban–rural differences are already captured by the region variable (Desai & Sinha, 2021).

Prenatal Care by Trained Staff: Access to prenatal care provided by trained staff is primarily determined by the quintile group (wealth index) at 23.9% and region at 23.1%. Mother's education contributes 16.1%, social group 15.2%, and father's education 12.3%. Wealth enables families to afford care from trained professionals, and regional disparities reflect differences in the availability of trained staff (Nair & Sadanandan, 2017). Mother's education influences the likelihood of seeking care from trained staff, as educated mothers are more aware of the benefits (Paul & Singh, 2019). Social group disparities again highlight caste-based discrimination (Ravindran & Misra, 2020). The sector and child's gender contribute the least, at 4.6% and 4.8%, respectively, indicating minimal impact from gender biases and that urban–rural differences are already accounted for by the region variable.

Antenatal Care: For antenatal care, region plays a major role, accounting for 24.7% of the variation in access. The quintile group contributes 21.3%, mother's education 16.2%, social group 15%, and father's education 11.9%. Regional disparities in healthcare infrastructure and outreach programs significantly impact antenatal care access (Pandey & Ladusingh, 2019). Mother's education influences access to antenatal care, as educated mothers are more likely to seek regular check-ups (Rao & Singh, 2020). Social group disparities reflect caste-based discrimination in accessing antenatal care services (Jain & Gupta, 2016). Sector and child's gender again have minimal impact, with contributions of 5.5% and 5.5%, respectively, indicating minimal gender biases in antenatal care access and that urban–rural differences are already accounted for by the region variable.

Overall Adequate Care: Overall access to adequate care is heavily influenced by region, which contributes 21.4%. This is followed by the quintile group at 19.3%, mother's education at 17.7%, social group at 15.6%, and father's education at 12.9%. Regional disparities in healthcare infrastructure and outreach programs significantly impact access to adequate care (Singh & Kumar, 2018). Mother's education significantly influences access to adequate care, as educated mothers are more likely to seek regular check-ups and understand the importance of adequate care (Kumar et al., 2019). Social group disparities highlight the impact of caste-based discrimination in accessing adequate care services (Srinivasan & Patel, 2015). Sector and child's gender play minor roles, contributing 5.9% and 7.4%, respectively, indicating minimal gender biases in access to adequate care and that urban–rural differences are already captured by the region variable (Patel & Chatterjee, 2020).

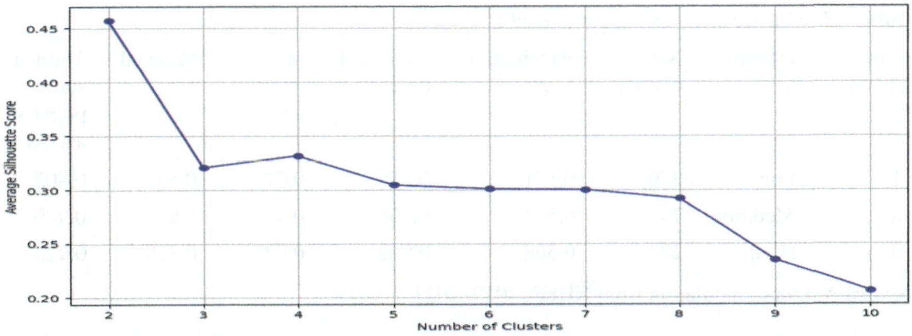

Fig. 6.1 Average Silhouette scores. *Source* Authors Calculation from NFHS, 2019–2021

The analysis highlights the critical role of socio-economic factors, especially region and wealth index (quintile group), in determining access to health services. Parents' education, particularly the mother's education and social group, play significantly role in access to health service, while the sector (rural or urban) and child's gender have minimal influence.

6.4.5 *Regional Health IOp*

The average silhouette score has been used to determine the optimal number of distinct clusters for the regional analysis. This score indicates that the minimum and maximum suitable number of clusters ranges from 2 to 10, which helps in creating geographical clusters in India to understand regional differences in accessing healthcare service inequality (Fig. 6.1). However, using only two clusters does not adequately capture India's regional diversity. Therefore, for a more detailed regional analysis, three clusters have been formed to categorize districts into those with poor access, moderate access, and better access to healthcare services.

The three clusters have been formed out of 706 districts in India. Cluster 1 includes 239 districts, cluster 2 has 193 districts, and cluster 3 comprises 274 districts (Table 6.5). The average access to vaccination was roughly the same across all the districts in the three clusters (around 55–57%), However, districts in cluster 1, when compared to districts in cluster 2 and 3, had lower acess to services such as antenatal care (29%), institutional delivery (78%), prenatal care (55%), and prenatal care by trained staff (81%). Compared to districts in cluster 1, the districts in cluster 3 had higher access to these services, but were lower compared to the districts in cluster 2 (Table 6.5). Therefore based on access to maternal and child healthcare services the cluster are classified in low (Cluster 1), medium (Cluster 3), and high (Cluster 2).

Map 6.1 maps the spatial distribution of these clusters, showing where districts with low, medium, and high access to maternal and child health services are concentrated (Appendix Table 6.6). The districts with low access to these health services

Table 6.5 Cluster analysis: access to health services

Cluster number	Health access	No. of districts	Vaccination access	Antenatal access	Inst delivery access	Prenatal care access	Trained staff prenatal access
1	Low	239	0.551	0.289	0.776	0.551	0.807
2	Medium	193	0.572	0.705	0.970	0.816	0.970
3	High	274	0.568	0.502	0.927	0.718	0.923

Source Authors Calculation from NHFS, 2019–2021

(Cluster 1) are primarily found in the eastern and central parts of India, including Uttar Pradesh (UP), Bihar, Jharkhand, northern Chhattisgarh, and the northeastern region of Madhya Pradesh. Conversely, the districts with high access (Cluster 2) are mostly located in southern India, particularly in states like Kerala, Tamil Nadu, and southern Karnataka. Additionally, western and eastern Maharashtra have districts with high access to health services, whereas central and northern Maharashtra have a mix of medium and low access districts. Central Odisha and West Bengal also feature districts with high access to maternal and child care services. This distribution highlights the regional disparities in healthcare access across India.

Better Access to Healthcare Services in Low Performing Cluster: In states like Uttar Pradesh (UP), Jharkhand, and Madhya Pradesh (MP), there are specific districts that perform well in terms of access to health services (Appendix Table 6.7). In UP,

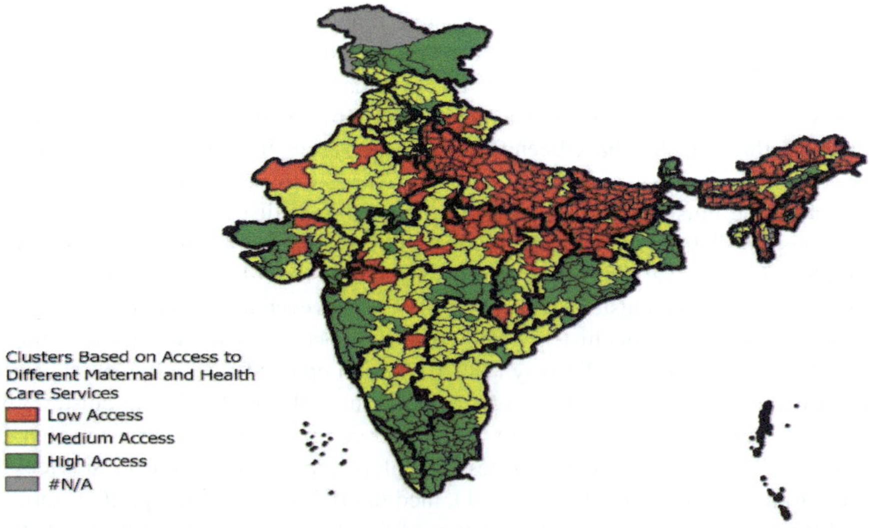

Map 6.1 Distribution of Districts across Clusters. *Source* Authors Calculation from NFHS, 2019–2021

districts such as Lucknow, Ghaziabad, and Kanpur fall into Cluster 2, indicating a medium level of access to health services. Similarly, in Jharkhand, districts like Purbi Singhbhum, Kodarma, and Saraikela-Kharsawan show better access compared to other districts in the state. In Chhattisgarh, around 14 districts have medium access to healthcare services, including Raipur and Sukma. Additionally, districts like Uttar Bastar Kanker, Durg, Balod, and Rajnandgaon in Chhattisgarh exhibit high access, outperforming the northern parts of the state. In Madhya Pradesh, which generally has medium and low access districts, Indore and Agra stand out with high access. In Rajasthan, where most districts have medium access, Kota, Chittaurgarh, and Jhalawar are notable for their high access to health services. This highlights that even within states with generally low or medium access, there are pockets of districts that achieve better healthcare access.

Poor Access to Healthcare Services in High Performing Cluster: Though low-access districts are primarily found in Uttar Pradesh (UP), Bihar, and Jharkhand, there are also districts with low access to maternal and child health services in states that generally have medium access (see Table 6.6). In Punjab, Fazilka district struggles with low access to these health services. In Uttarakhand, the districts of Almora, Garhwal, Hardwar, Tehri Garhwal, and Chamoli face similar challenges. In Haryana, Palwal and Mewat have low access to maternal and child health services. Rajasthan has several districts with low access, including Jaisalmer, Churu, Bharatpur, Alwar, Dhaulpur, Sawai Madhopur, and Karauli. In Gujarat, Banas Kantha and Surendranagar districts have low access. In Maharashtra, several northern districts such as Parbhani, Dhule, Nandurbar, and Jalgaon have low access. Lastly, in Karnataka, the northern districts of Gulbarga and Koppal also face low access to maternal and child health services. This shows that while some states may generally have better healthcare access, there are still specific areas within these states that need significant improvements.

6.5 Summary and Conclusion

The analysis reveals differences in accessing maternal and child healthcare services across India. Over half of the children have received at least one vaccination, and a significant proportion of mothers had institutional deliveries and access to prenatal care by trained professionals. However, comprehensive access to all selected maternal and child health services remains low at only 26%. There are significant gaps in antenatal care and immunization, with access to at least four antenatal visits being particularly low. The Health Inequality of Opportunity (IOp) indicates a moderate to high level of inequality, with significant disparities in access to general prenatal care, immunization services, and overall adequate care, suggesting that improvements are needed in both the distribution and quality of healthcare services.

There are several key factors impact how people access healthcare services, including geographical region: where people live can greatly affect their access to health care, rural or remote areas often have fewer healthcare facilities, wealth or income classes: families with higher incomes usually have better access to healthcare services. In contrast, those with lower incomes may struggle to afford or reach necessary care; parental education: the education level of the mother significantly influences how well she can access healthcare services. More educated mothers are more likely to seek and receive appropriate care. Immunization rates are also affected by where people live and their income levels. Areas with better healthcare infrastructure and services generally have higher vaccination rates. However, less developed regions often face challenges in providing sufficient immunization coverage. There are significant inequalities in accessing healthcare services, especially for prenatal care and immunizations. This problem is severe not only in economically less developed states like Uttar Pradesh, Bihar, Jharkhand, and Madhya Pradesh but also in some districts of more developed states like Gujarat, Maharashtra, and Karnataka.

This suggests that there is need to focus on implementing and improvements at the local or district-level policies to better address local needs and disparities in healthcare access. Enhancing healthcare facilities in rural and remote areas will make essential services more accessible, while educating communities and families (parents) about maternal and child health will improve overall health outcomes. It is also important to work on reducing inequalities related to socio-economic status and caste to ensure fair access to health care. By continuously striving to distribute resources equitably, all families, regardless of their income or location, can access quality maternal and child healthcare services. Through these efforts, India can reduce health inequalities, particularly in maternal and child health care, and ensure more equitable access to healthcare services across the country.

Appendices

See Tables 6.6, 6.7, and 6.8.

Table 6.6 State-wise districts in each cluster

State name	Cluster 1 (low access)	Cluster 2 (high access)	Cluster 3 (medium access)
Jammu & Kashmir	0	13	7
Himachal Pradesh	0	2	10
Punjab	1	4	17
Chandigarh	0	1	0
Uttarakhand	5	1	7
Haryana	2	3	16
Delhi	1	6	4
Rajasthan	7	3	23
Uttar Pradesh	63	0	12
Bihar	38	0	0
Sikkim	0	3	1
Arunachal Pradesh	18	0	2
Nagaland	11	0	0
Manipur	5	4	0
Mizoram	4	0	4
Tripura	1	1	6
Meghalaya	11	0	0
Assam	16	7	10
West Bengal	0	14	6
Jharkhand	21	0	3
Odisha	0	21	9
Chhattisgarh	9	4	14
Madhya Pradesh	18	2	31
Gujarat	2	11	20
Daman Diu and Dadra Nagar Havelli	0	2	1
Maharashtra	4	19	13
Andhra Pradesh	0	2	11
Karnataka	2	16	12
Goa	0	2	0
Lakshadweep	0	2	0
Kerala	0	11	2
Tamil Nadu	0	30	2
Puducherry	0	3	1
Andaman and Nicobar Islands	0	2	1

(continued)

Table 6.6 (continued)

State name	Cluster 1 (low access)	Cluster 2 (high access)	Cluster 3 (medium access)
Telangana	0	2	29
Ladakh	0	2	0

Source Authors Calculation from NFHS, 2019–2021

Table 6.7 Better healthcare access districts in low performing clusters

District name	State	Cluster three	Access
Saraikela-Kharsawan	Jharkhand	3	Medium
Purbi Singhbhum	Jharkhand	3	Medium
Kodarma	Jharkhand	3	Medium
Lucknow	Uttar Pradesh	3	Medium
Kanpur Nagar	Uttar Pradesh	3	Medium
Auraiya	Uttar Pradesh	3	Medium
Sant Kabir Nagar	Uttar Pradesh	3	Medium
Jalaun	Uttar Pradesh	3	Medium
Varanasi	Uttar Pradesh	3	Medium
Hamirpur	Uttar Pradesh	3	Medium
Mahoba	Uttar Pradesh	3	Medium
Mahrajganj	Uttar Pradesh	3	Medium
Deoria	Uttar Pradesh	3	Medium
Mau	Uttar Pradesh	3	Medium
Ghaziabad	Uttar Pradesh	3	Medium
Bemetra	Chhattisgarh	3	Medium
Mungeli	Chhattisgarh	3	Medium
Gariaband	Chhattisgarh	3	Medium
Kabeerdham	Chhattisgarh	3	Medium
Sukma	Chhattisgarh	3	Medium
Uttar Bastar Kanker	Chhattisgarh	2	High
Dakshin Bastar Dantewada	Chhattisgarh	3	Medium
Kondagaon	Chhattisgarh	3	Medium
Narayanpur	Chhattisgarh	3	Medium
Durg	Chhattisgarh	2	High
Raipur	Chhattisgarh	3	Medium
Balod	Chhattisgarh	2	High
Koriya	Chhattisgarh	3	Medium
Dhamtari	Chhattisgarh	3	Medium
Raigarh	Chhattisgarh	3	Medium
Mahasamund	Chhattisgarh	3	Medium
Janjgir-Champa	Chhattisgarh	3	Medium
Rajnandgaon	Chhattisgarh	2	High
Indore	Madhya Pradesh	2	High
Agar	Madhya Pradesh	2	High
Kota	Rajasthan	2	High

(continued)

Table 6.7 (continued)

District name	State	Cluster three	Access
Chittaurgarh	Rajasthan	2	High
Jhalawar	Rajasthan	2	High

Source Authors Calculation from NFHS, 2019–2021

Table 6.8 Low healthcare access districts in better performing cluster

District	State	Cluster three
Fazilka	Punjab	1.0
Almora	Uttarakhand	1.0
Garhwal	Uttarakhand	1.0
Hardwar	Uttarakhand	1.0
Tehri Garhwal	Uttarakhand	1.0
Chamoli	Uttarakhand	1.0
Palwal	Haryana	1.0
Mewat	Haryana	1.0
North	Delhi	1.0
Jaisalmer	Rajasthan	1.0
Churu	Rajasthan	1.0
Bharatpur	Rajasthan	1.0
Alwar	Rajasthan	1.0
Dhaulpur	Rajasthan	1.0
Sawai Madhopur	Rajasthan	1.0
Karauli	Rajasthan	1.0
Banas Kantha	Gujarat	1.0
Surendranagar	Gujarat	1.0
Parbhani	Maharashtra	1.0
Dhule	Maharashtra	1.0
Nandurbar	Maharashtra	1.0
Jalgaon	Maharashtra	1.0
Gulbarga	Karantaka	1.0
Koppal	Karantaka	1.0

Source Authors Calculation from NFHS, 2019–2021

References

Acharya, S. S. (2023). 4 differential access to maternal and child health across social groups. *Health and Nutrition of Women and Children in Empowered Action Group States of India: Status and Progress*, 57.

Balarajan, Y., Selvaraj, S., & Subramanian, S. V. (2011). Health care and equity in India. *The Lancet, 377*(9764), 505–515.

Banerjee, A. V., Deaton, A., & Duflo, E. (2004). Health Care Delivery in Rural Rajasthan. *Economic and Political Weekly, 39*(9), 944–949.

Barros, R. P. de, Ferreira, F., Vega, J., & Chanduvi, J. (2009). *Measuring inequality of opportunities in Latin America and the Caribbean.* World Bank Publications.

Desai, S., & Sinha, S. (2021). Antenatal care utilization and its determinants in India: Evidence from a national survey. *Journal of Public Health, 43*(3), 789–798.

Ghosh, S. (2021). Regional disparities in health infrastructure and health outcomes in India. *Social Science Spectrum, 7*(1), 1–14.

Gupta, R. K., Singh, V. K., & Bhushan, P. (2019). Determinants of maternal health care utilization in India: Evidence from a recent round of a national survey. *Journal of Health Management, 21*(2), 123–134.

Gupta, S., & Sinha, S. (2019). The role of maternal education in utilization of prenatal care in India. *Journal of Health Management, 21*(2), 123–134.

Jain, S., & Gupta, S. (2016). Caste discrimination in access to maternal health services: Perspectives from rural India. *Economic and Political Weekly, 51*(42), 66–75.

James, G., Witten, D., Hastie, T., & Tibshirani, R. (2023). *An introduction to statistical learning with applications in Python.* Springer. https://www.statlearning.com/

Kumar, S., Singh, A., & Singh, P. K. (2019). Socioeconomic disparities in utilization of maternal healthcare services in India, 1990–2006. *Journal of Public Health, 41*(3), 562–571.

Mishra, S., & Sharma, R. (2017). Immunization coverage and disparities in India. *Journal of Biosocial Science, 49*(4), 495–508.

Mukherjee, S., & Sikdar, S. (2019). Determinants of place of delivery in India. *Indian Journal of Community Medicine, 44*(1), 40–45.

Nair, H., & Sadanandan, R. (2017). Access to maternal and child health services in India. *Journal of Health Policy and Planning, 32*(4), 523–531.

Pal, R. (2015). *Decomposition of inequality of opportunity in access to immunization in India.*

Pandey, A., & Ladusingh, L. (2019). Antenatal care in India: Determinants and effect on health outcomes. *Journal of Health, Population and Nutrition, 38*(1), 14.

Patel, S., & Chatterjee, P. (2020). Socioeconomic disparities in health care access in India: Analysis of national family health survey data. *Journal of Health Management, 22*(4), 562–575.

Pathak, P. K., & Singh, A. (2021). Immunization inequalities in India: Evidence from a national survey. *Journal of Biosocial Science, 53*(2), 201–213.

Paul, P., & Singh, A. (2019). Mother's education and access to prenatal care: Evidence from India. *Journal of Public Health, 41*(2), 265–272.

Rao, M., & Singh, K. (2020). Maternal education and prenatal care utilization in India: A multi-level analysis. *Journal of Health Policy and Planning, 35*(3), 270–280.

Ravindran, T. S., & Misra, M. (2020). Caste and gender inequities in health: Evidence from India. *Economic and Political Weekly, 55*(18), 43–50.

Roy, P., & Gupta, S. (2020). Maternal education and prenatal care utilization in India: A multi-level analysis. *Journal of Health Policy and Planning, 35*(3), 270–280.

Sanoussi, Y. (2017). Measurement and analysis of inequality of opportunity in access of maternal and child health care in Togo. *BMC Health Services Research, 17*(2), 699. https://doi.org/10.1186/s12913-017-2647-8

Shrivastava, S. R., & Shrivastava, P. S. (2020). Immunization coverage in India: Progress and challenges. *Journal of Family Medicine and Primary Care, 9*(1), 3–6.

Singh, A. (2011). *Measuring inequality of opportunity in access to immunization and nutrition in India.*

Singh, B. P., Singh, T., & Chaurasia, A. R. (2021). Statistical study for utilization of institutional delivery: An evidences from NFHS data. *International Journal of Statistics and Applied Mathematics*, 6, 38–45.

Singh, A., & Kumar, S. (2018). Socioeconomic disparities in access to maternal health services in India. *Journal of Biosocial Science, 50*(1), 37–50.

Srinivasan, K., & Patel, V. (2015). Regional disparities in maternal health care utilization in India. *International Journal of Health Services, 45*(2), 301–318.

Srivastava, S., & Mishra, R. (2020). Influence of parents' education on children's health care utilization in India. *Journal of Family and Economic Issues, 41*(3), 429–439.

Subramanian, S. V., & Smith, G. D. (2006). The social determinants of immunization in India: Who gets vaccinated and why? *Social Science & Medicine, 62*(3), 563–576.

UNICEF. (2023). *Levels & trends in child mortality 2023.* United Nations Inter-Agency Group for Child Mortality Estimation (UN IGME). https://data.unicef.org/resources/levels-and-trends-in-child-mortality-2024/

United Nations. (2015). *Goal 3 | Department of Economic and Social Affairs.* https://sdgs.un.org/goals/goal3

Vani, B. P., & Madheswaran, S. (2018). Inequalities of human opportunities in India: A state-level analysis. *Indian Journal of Human Development, 12*(2), 248–264.

Victora, C. G., Barros, A. J., França, G. V., da Silva, I. C., Carvajal-Velez, L., & Amouzou, A. (2017). The contribution of poor and rural populations to national trends in reproductive, maternal, newborn, and child health coverage: Analyses of cross-sectional surveys from 64 countries. *The Lancet Global Health, 5*(4), e402–e407.

Wagstaff, A., Cotlear, D., Eozenou, P.H.-V., & Buisman, L. R. (2016). Measuring progress towards universal health coverage: With an application to 24 developing countries. *Oxford Review of Economic Policy, 32*(1), 147–189. https://doi.org/10.1093/oxrep/grv019

WHO. (2024). *Maternal mortality.* Retrieved August 2, 2024, from https://www.who.int/news-room/fact-sheets/detail/maternal-mortality

Chapter 7
Conclusion and Way Forward

This chapter synthesizes the key findings from the analyses presented in earlier chapters, highlighting the main challenges related to inequality of opportunity (IOp) and poverty. It also explores policy perspectives to address the emerging issues effectively and outlines a future research agenda.

7.1 Key Findings

Despite decent economic growth leading to a significant decline in poverty and overall inequality over the past two decades, inequality of opportunity has substantially increased during the same period, with notable regional differences in both IOp and poverty. This book delves into these two critical socio-economic aspects across five previous chapters of the book, covering consumption and income IOp, decomposition of labour income IOp, predicting poverty using machine learning and geospatial data, education IOp, and health IOp. The key findings and challenges associated with these topics are discussed below in detail.

7.1.1 Income Inequality of Opportunity

The study reveals that unequal circumstances significantly perpetuate income and consumption inequality. Specifically, these circumstances contribute approximately 26.2% to consumption inequality (MLD), 27.2% to labour income inequality, and 28.2% to wage income inequality. These statistics underscore how factors beyond an individual's control, such as parental background and geographic location, profoundly affect economic outcomes. Machine Learning models such as Conditional Inference Tree analysis supports these findings, indicating that about 24% of

B. S. Mehta et al., *Predicting Inequality of Opportunity and Poverty in India Using Machine Learning*, India Studies in Business and Economics,
https://doi.org/10.1007/978-981-96-2544-4_7

consumption and 28% of income inequality (MLD), can be attributed to unequal circumstances. The study also employs both ex-ante (circumstances) and ex-post (effort) approaches to estimate IOp. Ex-ante estimates (Gini), suggest that between 48% and 63% of income inequality is due to unequal circumstances. In contrast, ex-post estimates (Gini), show that approximately 34% of income inequality results from inequality within each group based on their circumstances also referred as within-tranche differences.

The relative IOp of consumption inequality, total labour income inequality, and wage income inequality has increased over time. This trend suggests that while economic outcomes have improved, disparities in opportunities have not diminished significantly and may have even widened. Notably, unequal opportunities in earnings for regular salaried has increased over the past two decades, whereas unequal opportunity in earnings for casual wage workers and self-employed has remained relatively stable. This pattern highlights the growing disparity in access to opportunities within the formal labour market, particularly in regular well-paid decent formal types of jobs in Indian labour market.

Key factors contributing to income IOp include:

- *Parental Education and Occupation*: Parental education and occupation are major contributors to income IOp, particularly for regular salaried workers. Children of parents with higher education and skilled occupations generally achieve regular employment with higher income levels. Conversely, children of parents with lower education and those involved in unskilled occupations face significant challenges with upward mobility due to limited access to educational and economic opportunities.
- *Sector and Geographic Location*: Significant disparities in income IOp exist between urban and rural areas. The urban–rural divide is influenced by better employment opportunities and higher wages in urban areas. Unequal opportunities across regions also persist, with individuals from eastern and central regions, such as Chhattisgarh and Jharkhand, exhibiting high-income IOp, while southern and northern states, such as Kerala and Himachal Pradesh, show lower income IOp. These regional disparities underscore the uneven opportunities, and distribution of resources and benefits, with individuals in rural areas of the northern, northeastern, and western regions experiencing highest income IOp. Regional disparities in income IOp are also pronounced in the self-employment category.
- *Gender and Social Groups*: Gender and social group disparities significantly contribute to unequal opportunities in earnings in self-employment and casual wage employment. Females, compared to males, and marginalized social groups such as Scheduled Castes (SC) and Scheduled Tribes (ST), face greater challenges and unequal opportunities in earnings in self-employment and casual wage work. This reflects the persistence of historical social and economic inequalities, which continue to hinder the progress of these groups.

7.1.2 *Predicting Poverty Using Machine Learning Models and Geospatial Data*

India has experienced a remarkable reduction in poverty, with rates falling from 37% in 2004–05 to 17% in 2021–22, based on the international poverty line for LMICs. Similarly, multidimensional poverty decreased from 55.1% in 2005–06 to 16.4% in 2019–21. While this significant decline is a positive indicator, it raises questions, particularly during periods of economic slowdown and the COVID-19 pandemic, about the accuracy of these figures. This has sparked debate on the measurement issues of poverty. Traditional surveys often lack timely and frequent data on income, consumption and other socio-economic indicators, making it difficult to capture the true extent of poverty. The integration of machine learning models with geospatial data offers the potential to enhance the accuracy of poverty predictions, providing more timely and granular estimates.

The Random Forest machine learning algorithm, utilizing variables such as nightlight intensity, point of interest density, and land surface temperatures, has shown particularly high effectiveness. It demonstrated a strong predictive accuracy, with an R-square value of 0.91 for poverty headcount and 0.85 for multidimensional poverty. The algorithm also achieved high accuracy levels in district-level poverty predictions. The results further indicate that nightlight intensity (NTL) and point of interest (POI) are negatively and highly correlated with poverty rates, while higher land surface temperatures are positively correlated with poverty rates. The NTL and POI have strong predictive power in predicting poverty, which reflect access to economic activities and essential facilities are crucial for alleviating poverty. These proxies for economic activity and access to services highlight geographical isolation from key amenities, such as markets, health care, education, banks, and drinking water, as a major barrier to accessing economic opportunities.

Although significant declines in poverty rates have been observed over the last two decades, regional disparities persist, with high poverty rates concentrated in eastern states such as Bihar, Jharkhand, Odisha, and Uttar Pradesh. This uneven poverty reduction highlights the concentration of poverty in underdeveloped regions and among marginalized social groups, affecting access to education, healthcare services, and employment opportunities.

7.1.3 *Educational Inequality of Opportunity*

Educational attainment in India has significantly improved over time, as evidenced by the low educational inequality, with the Gini coefficient now at 0.22. However, this figure is still considerably high when considering the entire population. Despite the overall progress, IOp in education remains a pressing issue, with 35% of educational inequality attributable to unequal opportunities. This means that more than one-third of the disparities in education are rooted in circumstance rather than individual effort or choice. A stark disparity persists between educational opportunities in urban and rural areas, with rural regions facing significant disadvantages.

Urban areas exhibit higher educational IOp compared to rural areas due to better educational facilities. Disparities based on gender, social group, and region are evident, with marginalized social groups, scheduled tribes and scheduled castes achieving lower educational attainment compared to other backward classes and general category.

Programs such as Sarva Shiksha Abhiyan (SSA) and the Right to Education, which mandate free compulsory education, have positively impacted elementary education and indirectly improved post-elementary education continuation. However, significant differences in enrolment and completion rates across states remain. States like Bihar and Rajasthan experience high educational inequality, while Kerala shows lower levels of inequality. Parental education is a crucial factor contributing to unequal opportunities in educational, followed by geographical region, parent's occupation, sector, social group, and gender. Disadvantaged individuals include those with less educated parents, engaged in low-skilled jobs, and residing outside southern regions. Contrarily, the children of parents with higher education and skilled occupations tend to achieve better educational outcomes. Gender biases and social norms also often limit educational opportunities especially for girls, and particularly those residing in rural areas.

7.1.4 Health Inequality of Opportunity

Access to healthcare services, particularly maternal and child health care, varies significantly, with considerable gaps in antenatal care, prenatal care, and childhood vaccinations. While most mothers access institutional deliveries and prenatal care services by skilled staff, the overall coverage of adequate health care—including all necessary maternal and child health services—is only 26%. The Human Opportunity Index for overall healthcare services reveals that 79% of the mothers and children faces unequal access to comprehensive maternal and child healthcare services. This high level of inequality is primarily due to disparities in access to four antenatal visits, immunization, and prenatal care services.

Factors such as family income, geographic location, mother's education, social group, and father's education contribute significantly to inequality in accessing maternal and child healthcare services. Low-income families face more significant challenges due to their limited capacity to pay for healthcare services. Regional disparities in the effectiveness of maternal and child healthcare services are evident, with better health indicators in more economically developed states compared to less developed ones. However, some districts in developed states also show poor access to healthcare services. Health disparities also exist among different social groups, with marginalized communities experiencing poorer health services and outcomes due to limited access to healthcare resources.

The findings across chapters highlight significant income inequality and poverty, exacerbated by social categories (Scheduled Tribes, Scheduled Castes, Other Backward Classes, and General) and regional disparities. Urban areas generally exhibit higher income levels due to better employment opportunities and higher wages compared to rural regions. Children from higher income families, with parents who have higher education and skilled occupations, access better educational and health opportunities, whereas those from lower income families face challenges in upward mobility due to limited access to opportunities. Despite improvements in overall economic outcomes, disparities in opportunities have persisted, with higher IOp in income, education, and health due to differences in parental background and regional disparities. Although poverty has significantly declined over the years, the reduction in inequality has been marginal. The substantial role of circumstances beyond individual control in overall inequality underscores the need for targeted interventions to address the uneven distribution of resources and benefits and to improve access to education, health, and economic opportunities across all segments of society.

7.2 Policy Perspectives

There are various initiatives have been introduced by both central and state governments to tackle poverty and inequality in India. However, there remains a lack of detailed and reliable information needed to effectively formulate suitable policies, implement and monitor these initiatives over time and space. Based on the above findings, the following are the key policy suggestions to enhance efforts to poverty and inequality and achieve the targets set by the Sustainable Development Goals.

Establish a Comprehensive Social Protection Floors: Establish a comprehensive social protection floor, grounded in a right-based approach, which is essential for achieving inclusive growth and reducing poverty and unequal opportunities. This includes ensuring the multifaceted dimensions of basic social security guarantees—health care, income security, employment, food security, and housing to all individuals, regardless of their socio-economic status throughout their life cycle (ILO, 2012, Srivastava, 2013, 2021). As discussed in detail with proper implementation roadmaps below.

- *Universal Healthcare Access*: Ensure that everyone has access to health care by expanding health insurance schemes to cover outpatient expenses as well as inpatient care. Specifically, the Ayushman Bharat Yojana, which serves over 100 million poor and vulnerable families, should also include primary healthcare services to reduce the heavy out-of-pocket expenses that burden households. Expand the maternal and childcare schemes that cover all essential maternal and childcare health services, to ensure everyone has access to necessary medical care. Conduct educational campaigns to inform the public about these schemes.
- *Children's Access to Essential Services*: Guarantee access to nutrition, education, care, and other essential services for all children. Expanding initiatives like the

Integrated Child Development Services (ICDS), Right to Education Act, and the Right to Food Act, with proper implementation are crucial in securing these rights.

- *Income Security for Workers*: Ensure income security for working-age individuals who cannot earn sufficient income due to unemployment, sickness, maternity, or disability. Programs like MGNREGA should be strengthened and expanded to provide timely and adequate availability of non-farm employment opportunities.
- *Support for Vulnerable Groups*: Expand coverage and increase benefits under social pension schemes for the elderly, widows, and other vulnerable groups. The National Social Assistance Programme should be properly implemented and expanded with adequate benefits to ensure income security for the elderly.
- *Implementation of National Food Security Bill*: Ensure the proper implementation of the National Food Security Bill to provide subsidized food grains to the needy section of the rural and urban population, with a focus on the most vulnerable households. Programs like the Antyodaya Anna Yojana (AAY) should ensure higher entitlements for these groups.
- *Adequate Housing for All*: Strengthen rural and urban housing policies to align with the right to adequate housing. Expand affordable housing options for the urban poor and enhance rural housing programs to ensure everyone has a safe and decent place to live.

Expand Existing Targeted Welfare Programs: Expanding existing targeted welfare through direct cash or kind transfer to the most vulnerable populations especially in regions with high poverty and inequality, which can significantly improve their economic stability. By focusing on these regions can reduce consumption inequality of the poor and ensure that everyone has access to basic necessities. This immediate support can prevent families from falling into poverty trap.

Increase Educational Subsidies: Increase funding for education and provide scholarships and educational subsidies for children from low-income families, particularly in high inequality regions. This can bridge the educational gap created by disparities in parental education and occupation. In particular, the educational subsidies at higher education make it more affordable for low-income families. This can increase enrolment rates in colleges and universities, leading to a more educated or skilled workforce. With higher education, individuals can access better job opportunities and higher wages, which can reduce income inequality in the long run.

Improve Rural Education Infrastructure and Quality of Education: Invest in educational infrastructure especially in rural areas, which is important for providing equal opportunities for students in both urban and rural settings. This includes building better school facilities, providing access to modern digital technologies, and ensuring that rural schools have well-trained teachers. Enhanced facilities and teacher training can address disparities in educational quality, ensuring that all students receive a high-quality education. With these improvements, rural students can compete on an equal footing with their urban counterparts.

Promote Gender-Sensitive Policies: Designing policies to address gender disparities in education and employment is essential for promoting gender equality. This includes offering scholarships, vocational training, and mentorship programs tailored to women's needs. Additionally, the suitable work environment with provision of child care, flexibility, safety and security can encourage more women to participate in the workforce, which can have positive ripple effects on families and communities, improving overall social and economic outcomes.

Proper Implementation of Affirmative Action for Marginalized Groups: Proper implementation of affirmative action policies and financial assistance is crucial for improving opportunities for children and youth from marginalized people, such as those belong to scheduled tribes, scheduled castes, other backward classes, low-income families, and others such as disabled, and others. Focusing on education, employment, and economic resources can help these groups overcome historical disadvantages and achieve social mobility.

Use Machine Learning Algorithms and Geospatial Data to Monitor Socio-Economic Progress: Use of machine learning algorithm and geospatial data can provide accurate, timely, and granular estimates of socio-economic indicators. This technology can help create detailed and accurate poverty maps and track progress in other socio-economic areas. With accurate information, policymakers can design targeted interventions and allocate resources effectively. For example, geospatial data can identify regions or district in a state of India with high poverty, allowing for focused efforts to alleviate poverty in those areas. This can help in real-time monitoring of socio-economic indicators, which enables governments and other stakeholders to quickly respond to emerging challenges and adjust strategies as needed. Real-time data can also enhance transparency and accountability in policy implementation.

Predictive Analysis for Resource Allocation: Use of predictive analysis to forecast poverty and inequality trends in income, education, and health can help allocate resources more effectively. By understanding future trends, policymakers can proactively address the concentration of poverty and inequality in underdeveloped regions. Predictive analysis provides data-driven insights to make informed decision-making. This approach ensures that resources are allocated based on evidence and anticipated needs rather than reactive measures. For instance, if predictive models indicate rising poverty in a specific region, targeted interventions can be implemented to mitigate the issue before it escalates. This can lead to better outcomes in reduction of poverty and inequality.

Regular Update and Integration of Data: Timely updates of survey data on income, consumption, education, and health are crucial for accurately monitoring socio-economic progress. Regular data collection and updates provide a clear picture of current conditions and trends, allowing for informed policy decisions. Integrating data from multiple sources, including surveys, administrative records, and geospatial data, using machine learning models, can provide a holistic view of socio-economic trends. This comprehensive approach ensures that all relevant factors are considered in analysis and policy formulation.

Foster Cross-Sector Collaboration: Foster collaboration between governmental and non-governmental organizations to enhance data collection and poverty and inequality assessment efforts. By pooling resources and expertise, organizations can achieve more comprehensive and accurate assessments of socio-economic conditions. Cross-sector collaboration ensures that various stakeholders work towards shared goals of poverty reduction and inequality alleviation. This approach can lead to more coordinated and effective interventions, avoiding duplication of efforts and maximizing impact. Collaboration between different stakeholders can improve the quality and reliability of data.

Develop Localized Strategies and Decentralized Decision-Making for Proper Implementation of Various Development Programs: Develop and implement localized (State/District Level) strategies and specific programs to address poverty and inequality in different regions. This includes programs for infrastructure development, education, health care, and employment generation. By focusing on regions with high inequality and poverty rates, such as districts in Bihar, Jharkhand, Odisha, and Uttar Pradesh, targeted interventions can be more effective. Localized strategies should involve local government, communities in the planning and implementation process. This decentralized approach ensures that local needs are addressed more effectively and development programs are more successful. Community involvement also fosters a sense of ownership and responsibility, leading to more sustainable outcomes. These targeted efforts can reduce regional inequalities and promote equitable society.

7.3 Future Research Agenda

Expanding Analysis with Following Non-conventional Data Sources

- *Incorporating Big Data*: Utilize data from social media, mobile phone usage, and online transactions to gain real-time insights into economic activities and consumer behaviour. This can help in understanding the socio-economic conditions of different populations.
- *Satellite Imagery and Remote Sensing*: Enhance spatial resolution by incorporating high-resolution satellite imagery to monitor changes in land use, infrastructure development, and environmental conditions. This can provide a more detailed understanding of regional disparities.
- *Crowdsourced Data*: Leverage data from crowdsourcing platforms to gather information on local economic conditions, employment opportunities, and access to services. This can help in filling gaps where traditional surveys are limited or outdated.
- *Administrative Data Integration*: Integrate data from government administrative sources, such as tax records, social security databases, and health records, to obtain a comprehensive view of income distribution and health inequality.

Expand Analysis Using Enhanced Spatial Resolution Maps

- *High-Resolution Poverty Mapping*: Develop high-resolution poverty maps that can capture variations within smaller geographic units, such as villages. This can help in identifying micro-level pockets of poverty and targeting interventions more precisely.

- *Dynamic Spatial Analysis*: Implement dynamic spatial analysis techniques that can track changes in poverty and inequality over time. This can provide insights into the effectiveness of policies and programs and guide future interventions.
- *Geospatial Data Integration*: Combine geospatial data with traditional survey data to enhance the spatial resolution of poverty estimates. This can help in understanding the geographic dimensions of poverty and inequality.

Use Machine Learning Models for Poverty and Inequality Estimates

- *Cost-Effective Insights*: Machine learning techniques provide cost-effective and timely insights into poverty and inequality trends and dynamics. These methods can analyse vast amounts of data quickly, offering real-time information that traditional surveys may not capture.
- *Improved Accuracy of Poverty and Inequality Estimates*: Integrating machine learning with geospatial and survey data can enhance the accuracy of poverty estimates. This allows for more precise identification of vulnerable populations and regions in need of assistance.
- *Targeted Interventions*: With improved data accuracy, policymakers can design better-targeted interventions that address the specific needs of different communities. This can lead to more effective poverty alleviation programs and reduced inequality.
- *Predictive Analytics for Policy Planning*: Machine learning models can be used to predict future poverty trends and assess the potential impact of various policy interventions. This can help policymakers plan more effectively and allocate resources where they are needed most.
- *Data-Driven Decision-Making*: The integration of advanced data analytics into policy formulation can support data-driven decision-making processes. This ensures that policies are based on robust evidence and can adapt to changing socio-economic conditions.

Integrate Geospatial and Survey Data for Improved Analysis, Policy Design and Monitoring and Evaluation

- *Comprehensive Data Integration*: Combining geospatial data with traditional survey data provides a comprehensive understanding of poverty and inequality. This integration can reveal patterns and correlations that may not be evident from survey data alone.
- *Enhanced Policy Design*: Policymakers can use integrated data to design policies that address both spatial and socio-economic dimensions of poverty. For example, infrastructure development projects can be planned in areas with high poverty rates to improve access to services and economic opportunities.
- *Monitoring and Evaluation*: Integrated data can be used to monitor and evaluate the effectiveness of poverty alleviation programs. This allows for continuous improvement of policies based on real-time feedback and outcomes.

- *Inclusive Development*: By using high-resolution data, policies can be tailored to ensure inclusive development. This means addressing the needs of marginalized groups and ensuring that all regions benefit from economic growth.

Validate and Investigate Prediction and Stability of Relationship

- *Validate Prediction with Ground Truth Data to Enhance the Accuracy*: Regularly validate predictions with ground-truth data from household surveys to ensure that models accurately reflect the real-world distribution of poverty and inequality, particularly in regions where the relationship between non-conventional data with poverty and inequality is complex.
- *Investigate Stability of Relationships*: Conduct a long-term study to examine whether the relationships observed between nightlight intensity, point of interest and other non-conventional data with poverty and inequality remain stable over time, particularly as economic conditions change. This will help ensure the robustness of results.

7.4 In Conclusion

There are some limitations for using geospatial data to predict poverty. For nightlight data, issues like saturation in bright areas can make it hard to capture differences, low spatial resolution can blur distinctions between rural and urban, and weather conditions can affect the intensity of the light captured. For Point of Interest (POI) data, challenges include incomplete coverage, errors in location, the difficulty of keeping data up-to-date information, urban biasness where detailed data is mostly available for cities, and underrepresentation of rural and remote areas. Privacy concerns also arise when dealing with sensitive locations. In some cases, the limitations of sample survey data also make it difficult to accurately estimate poverty, inequality, and IOp in income, education, and health at granular levels, such as state and district levels. Specifically, there is often a lack of an adequate sample with information about individuals and their parents to perform these estimates.

Despite the challenges and limitations inherent in using geospatial data and sample estimates, the findings presented in this book are invaluable for deepening our understanding of poverty and inequality in India. These insights go beyond mere statistics; they offer a nuanced view of how socio-economic disparities are distributed across different regions. For policymakers, governments, and stakeholders, this book serves as a crucial resource for understanding where interventions are most needed and how they can be most effective. The spatial analysis of poverty and inequality presented in the book lays the groundwork for targeted, evidence-based strategies that can drive real change. Moreover, this work is not just a conclusion but a call to action. It underscores the importance of continuing to refine the tools and methods used in the book to better capture the complexities of socio-economic issues. The insights gained from the analysis in the book should inspire further research and innovation, pushing the boundaries of how we understand and address poverty and inequality.

In closing, while the journey to fully grasp and combat poverty and inequality is ongoing, the contributions of this book represent a significant step forward. It highlights the potential for data-driven approaches to inform policy and create a more equitable society. Let this be the beginning of even more rigorous and insightful work in the years to come, with the hope that together, we can build a future where no one is left behind.

References

International Labour Organization. (2012). Recommendation R202—Social Protection Floors Recommendation, 2012 (No. 202). Retrieved from https://normlex.ilo.org/dyn/normlex/en/f?p=NORMLEXPUB:12100:0::NO::P12100_INSTRUMENT_ID:3065524

Srivastava, R. S. (2013). *A social protection floor for India.* International Labour Office, Subregional Office for South Asia.

Srivastava, R. (2021). Interrogating a framework for universal social protection in India. Retrieved from https://hdl.handle.net/10539/33903

9789819625437